ROME AND HER ENEMIES

An Empire Created and Destroyed by War

ROME AND HER ENEMIES

An Empire Created and Destroyed by War

Editor
Jane Penrose

First published in Great Britain in 2005 by Osprey Publishing Ltd.
This edition published 2008 by Osprey Publishing Ltd,
Midland House, West Way, Botley, Oxford OX2 0PH, UK
443 Park Avenue South, New York, NY 10016, USA
Email: info@ospreypublishing.com

Material previously published in Campaign 36: *Cannae 216 BC*, Campaign 84: *Adrianople AD 378*, Essential Histories 16: *The Punic Wars 264–146 BC*, Essential Histories 21: *Rome at War AD293–696*, Essential Histories 42: *Caesar's Civil War 49–44 BC*, Essential Histories 43: *Caesar's Gallic Wars 58–50 BC*, Elite 50: *The Praetorian Guard*, Elite 110: *Sassanian Elite Cavalry AD 226–642*, Elite 120: *Mounted Archers of the Steppe 600 BC–AD 1300*, Elite 121: *Ancient Siege Warfare: Persians, Greeks, Carthaginians and Romans 546–146 BC*, Elite 126: *Siege Warfare in the Roman World 146 BC–AD 378*, Men-at-Arms 46: *The Roman Army from Caesar to Trajan*, Men-at-Arms 93: *The Roman Army from Hadrian to Constantine*, Men-at-Arms 121: *Armies of the Carthaginian Wars 265–146 BC*, Men-at-Arms 129: *Rome's Enemies (1) Germanics and Dacians*, Men-at-Arms 137: *The Scythians 700–300 BC*, Men-at-Arms 158: *Rome's Enemies (2) Gallic and British Celts*, Men-at-Arms 175: *Rome's Enemies (3) Parthians and Sassanid Persians*, Men-at-Arms 180: *Rome's Enemies (4) Spanish Armies*, Men-at-Arms 243: *Rome's Enemies (5) The Desert Frontier*, Men-at-Arms 283: *Early Roman Armies*, Men-at-Arms 291: *Republican Roman Army 200–104 BC*, Men-at-Arms 360: *The Thracians 700 BC–AD 46*, Men-at-Arms 373: *The Sarmatians 600 BC–AD 450*, Men-at-Arms 374: *Roman Military Clothing (1) 100 BC–AD 200*, Men-at-Arms 390: *Roman Military Clothing (2) AD 200–400*, Warrior 9: *Late Roman Infantryman AD 236–565*, Warrior 15: *Late Roman Cavalryman AD 236–565*, Warrior 17: *Germanic Warrior AD 236–568*, Warrior 30: *Celtic Warrior 300 BC–AD 100*, Warrior 39: *Gladiators 100 BC–AD 200*, Warrior 50: *Pictish Warrior AD 297–841*, Warrior 71: *Roman Legionary 58 BC–AD 69*, Warrior 72: *Imperial Roman Legionary AD 161–284*, Fortress 2: *Hadrian's Wall AD 122–410*, New Vanguard 78: *Greek and Roman Siege Machinery 399 BC–AD 363*, New Vanguard 89: *Greek and Roman Artillery 399 BC–AD 363*.

FRONT COVER IMAGE: Corbis

A CIP catalogue record for this book is available from the British Library

ISBN 978 1 84603 336 0

Page layout by Ken Vail Graphic Design, Cambridge, UK
Index by David Worthington
Maps by The Map Studio Ltd
Originated by PPS Grasmere Ltd, Leeds, UK
Printed and bound in China through World Print Ltd

08 09 10 11 12 10 9 8 7 6 5 4 3 2 1

CONTENTS

INTRODUCTION
by Tom Holland

Rome was the supreme carnivore of the ancient world. Predatory and intimidating, the Romans' civilisation was both eerily like our own, and utterly, astoundingly strange. It is this tension, between what is familiar and what is not, that best explains the fascination that Rome still holds for us to this very day. What theme is there, after all, to compare for drama with that of the Roman Empire? The famous words that Gibbon applied to its ruin might equally well describe the entire parabola of its thousand-year rise and fall. 'The greatest, perhaps, and most awful scene, in the history of mankind.'

Lying at its heart is a mystery as profound as any in the records of human civilisation. How on earth did the Romans do it? How did a single city, one that began as a small community of cattle-rustlers, camped out among marshes and hills, end up ruling an empire that stretched from the moors of Scotland to the deserts of Iraq? So solidly planted within our imaginations are the brute facts of this rise to superpower status that we have become, perhaps, de-sensitised to the full astonishing scale of the Roman adventure. Virgil, the great laureate of his people's achievement, saw in it the fulfilment of a mission entrusted to them by the gods. 'Your task, O Roman,' he wrote in celebrated lines, 'is to rule and bring to men the arts of government, to impose upon them the arts of peace, to spare those who submit, to subdue the arrogant.' Rome's enemies, unsurprisingly, were inclined to interpret her motives a little differently. 'Warmongers against every nation, people and monarch under the sun,' spat Mithridates, an Asiatic king of the first century BC who devoted his life to resisting the encroachments of Roman imperialism. 'They have only one abiding motive – greed, deep-seated, for empire and riches.' So it has ever been, of course: one man's peacekeeper will invariably appear another's brutal aggressor. Yet both Virgil and Mithridates, profoundly though they may have disagreed as to the character of Rome's dominion, had not the slightest doubt as to what had made it possible. Rome's truest talent was for conquest. There were other peoples, perhaps, who excelled the Romans in the arts, or in philosophy, or in the study of the heavens, but there were none who could match the legions on the battlefield. Rome's greatness was won and maintained, above all, by her genius for war.

A destiny manifest in her very origins. The city was founded, after all, by a man who had drunk in savagery from a she-wolf's teat. The story of Romulus' suckling was one that always caused the Romans much embarrassment – for it was the habit of their enemies, shocked by the legions' savagery, to condemn Rome as 'the city of the wolf'. The image of the Romans as a killer breed, sniffing the wind for prey, feasting on raw meat, is a powerful illustration of the impact that this alarming people could have on their neighbours, and of the terror that they inspired. Not for nothing did the Romans regard red as the colour of war: red, the colour of viscera; red, the colour of blood.

Yet evident although the strain of violence in Roman militarism always was, such murderousness would have been nothing without a parallel reserve of self-control. There could be no place in Rome's legions for ill-disciplined vainglory. When a soldier fought, he did so not for himself, but for the army as a whole. Duty and cohesion of the line were all. True, for a century after the expulsion of the last king in 509BC, and the establishment of a republic, the Romans had struggled to put these principles into practice. Racked by social convulsions, they failed to turn their predatory instincts upon their neighbours. All that changed in the year 390BC, when the Republic suffered a salutary and shocking humiliation. An invading horde of Gauls, having wiped out an entire Roman army, swept into Rome itself, and pillaged the city mercilessly. This was the episode, more than any other, which served to put steel into the Roman soul, and transform Rome into the world's deadliest military power. The Republic, from that moment on, was resolved never again to tolerate defeat, dishonour or disrespect.

For their neighbours, slow to wake up to the character of the mutant state in their midst, the consequences were devastating. A century and a half after the Gallic occupation, Rome had emerged as the dominant power of the western Mediterranean. It was not in victory, however, that she best demonstrated the unique quality of her militarism, but in catastrophe, disastrous and seemingly total catastrophe. On 2nd August, 216BC, the largest army that the Roman Republic had ever put into the field was effectively wiped out. More soldiers, it has been estimated, were slaughtered in that single day's fighting than were killed on the first day of the battle of the Somme – the scene of carnage, it is said, 'was shocking even to the enemy'. The battle of Cannae, the greatest victory of Rome's greatest enemy, Hannibal Barca, wiped out perhaps a fifth of her available manpower, and the universal presumption among the victors was that Rome was now bound to surrender. But she did not. Against all the conventions of warfare at the time, implacably and barely believably, the Romans fought on, even going to the shocking extreme of human sacrifice in an attempt to appease the angry gods. And in the long run, completing one of the most sensational comebacks in military history, they emerged triumphant – first against Hannibal, and then against anything that any power anywhere could throw against them. By the first century BC, the Romans were the undisputed masters of the Mediterranean.

The legions conclusively established themselves as the world's most menacing instrument of war. The blend of discipline and flexibility that they brought to a battlefield had proven itself triumphantly adaptable to any circumstance, whether the headlong rush of a barbarian warband or the measured bristling of a Hellenistic phalanx. The Romans themselves took this supremacy entirely for granted. Not for them the delusory glamour of charismatic would-be Alexanders. The spoils of war were owed rather to the Roman people as a whole – for what was a legion, after all, but an expression of the Republic itself in arms? So it was, an intriguing and suggestive fact, that none of the generals who fought against Hannibal, not even Scipio Africanus, his ultimate conqueror, could ever compare for fame with the great Carthaginian himself. Why, there were even statues of Hannibal placed in the very streets of Rome. Scipio himself, by contrast, when his fellow citizens began to worry that he was getting above himself, had been brutally put in his place: menaced with prosecution, he had been forced into retirement from public life. While there was certainly nothing that could rival the addiction of the Roman people to glory, that same addiction in a general, if it turned selfish and pathological, could only be regarded with suspicion. Hence, in example after example, the posthumous celebrity of Rome's enemies, and the comparative oblivion of her own generals is evident. In 71BC, the richest man in the Republic, Marcus Crassus, was so desperate to advertise his crushing of a servile revolt that he nailed captives to crosses all along the Appian Way, billboards grotesque even by the standards of Roman self-promotion – yet it was Spartacus, the slave he had defeated, who would end up being played by Kirk Douglas, and having a film named after him. Glamour, among the Romans, was rarely regarded as a virtue.

All of which explains why Julius Caesar, the most celebrated military genius in his city's history, should also, in many ways, have been the least typical. Not that he was uniquely aberrant. In truth, he was only one of a number of warlords who found, in the growing reach of the Republic's armies during the first century BC, unprecedented opportunities for self-aggrandisement. The further-flung that Roman campaigns became, and the longer they lasted, so the more distant the traditions of the Forum might start to seem to those who fought in them. Legionaries, with that instinctive craving for comradeship that was the mark of all Romans, might easily find themselves attaching their fortunes to those of their commander, and locating their identity in the reflected glory of his name. As a result, what had previously been citizen militias began increasingly to take on the characteristics of private armies, a trend only encouraged by a second momentous development: the creeping professionalisation of the legions. Traditionally, only those citizens who could afford to equip themselves for war had been eligible for military service; but in 107BC a fateful reform had opened the army up to every Roman, regardless of whether he owned property or not, with weapons and armour starting to be supplied by the state. On one level, this restructuring of the army had reaped spectacular dividends: by 50BC, Roman eagles had been planted in the wilds of Armenia, and on the northernmost coast of Gaul. Yet it ultimately served to menace Rome herself with implosion – for in the second half of the first century BC, the greatest battles waged by the legions were not against barbarians, but amongst themselves. A series of terrible civil wars were fought, out of which first Julius Caesar, and then his nephew, Octavian, emerged as the undisputed masters of the Roman world. The Republic, having lived by the sword, had duly perished by the sword. The only alternative to anarchy and the total breakdown of Roman power, it appeared, was military dictatorship – and that, in a sense, is precisely what Octavian provided.

Yet his genius was to hide it. 'What is happiness?' asked Horace, in the aftermath of the horrendous civil wars. 'Not a soldier, his blood pumping to the sound of a fierce trumpet.' The Romans, weary of the militarism that had brought them their greatness, now found themselves preferring the comforts of slavery and order to the turmoil of liberty and chaos. Octavian, awarded the splendid honorific of 'the August One' – 'Augustus' – banished the legions from Italy. The umbilical link between military service and the civic institutions of the ruined Republic was forever broken. Henceforward the legions would stay far distant from Rome, recruited increasingly from among non-Italians, stationed on frontiers where their loyalty to the emperor could be represented to civilians back in the capital as a stewardship of peace. So it was that the traditional Roman genius for war became the underpinning of the Pax Romana, and there were few regrets, even among the senatorial aristocracy who would once have hoped to captain the legions on spectacular foreign adventures, for the old days of the Republic. Barring one savage flare-up of civil war in AD68/69, the peace established by Augustus held for almost two centuries. In that period, although occasional conquests were made – Britain, Dacia and, briefly, Mesopotamia were all constituted as new provinces – the duty of the legions was primarily to keep secure, rather than to expand, the limits of Roman dominion. As an example of a professional, centrally organised and predominantly peace-time military, it was unexampled in the ancient world.

And indeed, because legionaries could legitimately be subjected to a discipline that even the SAS might find insupportable, the result was troops both more honed and more brutalised than any to be found in the armies of the modern world. The oath sworn by a recruit when he first joined the legions, the *sacramentum*, was of a rare ferocity: vowing duty to Caesar, to his officers, and to the eagles, he consecrated his own life and possessions as the stake of his loyalty. Passing into the realm of Mars, he consciously forfeited the rights and privileges of his citizenship. He became subject, like a slave, to beatings – and his centurion, as the badge of rank, would carry a cane made of vine-wood, just to remind him as much. He would be obliged to carry, while marching at almost five miles per hour, a truly monstrous burden of armour and equipment – so that he would be jeered at by civilians, not even as a slave, but as a mule. The very pleasures and comforts of family life would be denied him: for private soldiers, from the time of Augustus onwards, were forbidden to marry. The military authorities did not want their men softened by women and sex. Marriage was only permitted to the eagles. Ferociously disciplined, super-fit, violently frustrated, legionaries were animated by a uniquely savage *ésprit de corps*.

Who could hope to stand against them? For centuries, there was no one. True, the occasional debacle, whether amid the bogs and forests of Germany, or the sand-dunes of Mesopotamia, might periodically engulf an expedition, to the fleeting panic of everyone back in the distant capital; but equilibrium would briskly be restored. Only Roman legions themselves could really threaten the security of the Empire; civil war, during the long years of the imperial peace, had come to seem an ever more distant memory. Maintenance of the chain of command, however, depended crucially upon the integrity of the centre: for the men of the Roman army were, in truth, given only a little slack, more than capable of destroying the very order that they were being employed to uphold.

This was to be brutally demonstrated during the third century AD, when legion after legion discovered that rewards potentially far richer than peacetime pay were to be had by promoting the interests of rival caesars. Simultaneously, as the Roman world collapsed into civil wars more internecine even than those that had destroyed the Republic, a fresh catastrophe loomed. In Persia, for the first time, an enemy emerged in the form of the Sassanid monarchy, capable of directly menacing Rome's dominions in the East. In 260, an emperor, the elderly Licinius Valerianus, was even taken prisoner. The wretched captive, still garbed in his imperial purple, was used for the rest of his life by the Persian king as a mounting block for climbing onto his horse. When Valerian, worn out by his humiliations, finally died, his corpse was flayed, and the empty skin filled with straw.

A potent symbol, perhaps, of an Empire in irrevocable decay? So it might have seemed – and yet the Roman order, resurrected from the grave, emerged during the fourth century upon a new and formidable footing. True, the Empire was one markedly different from that of three centuries before. Whereas Augustus, 'that subtle tyrant', had sought to veil the true foundations of his authority, emperors such as Constantine and his successors ruled nakedly as a military strongmen. Power, which had once resided far distant from the frontiers, now dwelt instead far distant from Rome, among the military strongholds that lined the Empire's outer limits. In a sense, the entire Roman world had been transformed into an armed camp, an autocracy of blood and steel. The security of the East, and parity with the Persians, had gradually been restored – but at an agonising cost. Spending on the military, it has been estimated, went up by some 40 per cent between the third and fourth centuries AD. Taxes, hardly surprisingly, shot through the roof. Rome's citizens were bled white. The entire machinery of government was subordinated to the requirements of the army. Once, in the early days of the Roman rise to greatness, only those with property had been permitted to serve in the legions. Now, in a bitter irony, the Empire itself was mortgaged to pay for its soldiers.

But what if those payments became impossible to make? In 378, at Adrianople, the Roman army of the East suffered a defeat at the hands of the Goths that contemporaries ranked as a disaster fit to compare with the slaughter at Cannae. In the war against Hannibal, of course, the Republic, tautening its sinews, mustering all its strength, had been able to summon fresh legions, and grimly, year by year, haul itself back from the brink. Five years after Adrianople, however, and even a seasoned imperial spin-doctor was obliged to confess that 'whole armies had vanished completely like a shadow'. The Empire was still far from finished, but Adrianople had given a foretaste of how it might indeed be brought to its knees. The Goths, by settling in what had formerly been Roman provinces, and plundering the Empire's very heartlands – even, in 410, to universal disbelief, the city of Rome itself – were steadily demolishing the foundations on which the imperial army had come to depend. Without wealth, there could be no taxes; without taxes, there could be no army; without the army there could be no wealth. Locked into this vicious cycle, the Roman Empire of the West, with startling and alarming speed, began suddenly to disintegrate. Between 395 and 420, it has been estimated, the army of the Rhine suffered the loss of almost two-thirds of its regiments. In 451, when the Roman army of the West won its last great victory, at the battle of Chalôns over Attila and his Huns, it had only been able to fight in alliance with Burgundians and Visigoths. Twenty-five years later, and the Empire itself, in the West at any rate, was over. With it had vanished forever the most successful fighting force in history. As it had been from the beginning, so at the very end: the story of the Roman army was the story of Rome herself.

EARLY REPUBLIC 753BC–150BC

The powerful Italian neighbours of Rome vied constantly for land, trade and the spoils of war.

Alliances were forged and broken as each city-state struggled for survival and dominance.

Rome's greatest allies could quickly become her most feared enemies...

BRITAIN
GERMANY
BELGICA
GAUL
DACIA
CISALPINE GAUL
ILLYRICUM
THRACE
ITALY
MACEDONIA
SPAIN
MEDITERRANEAN
SICILY
MAURETANIA
NUMIDIA
NORTH AFRICA
N
0
250 miles
0
500 km
The Roman Republic before the Punic Wars
Additional territory added to the Roman Republic by 150BC

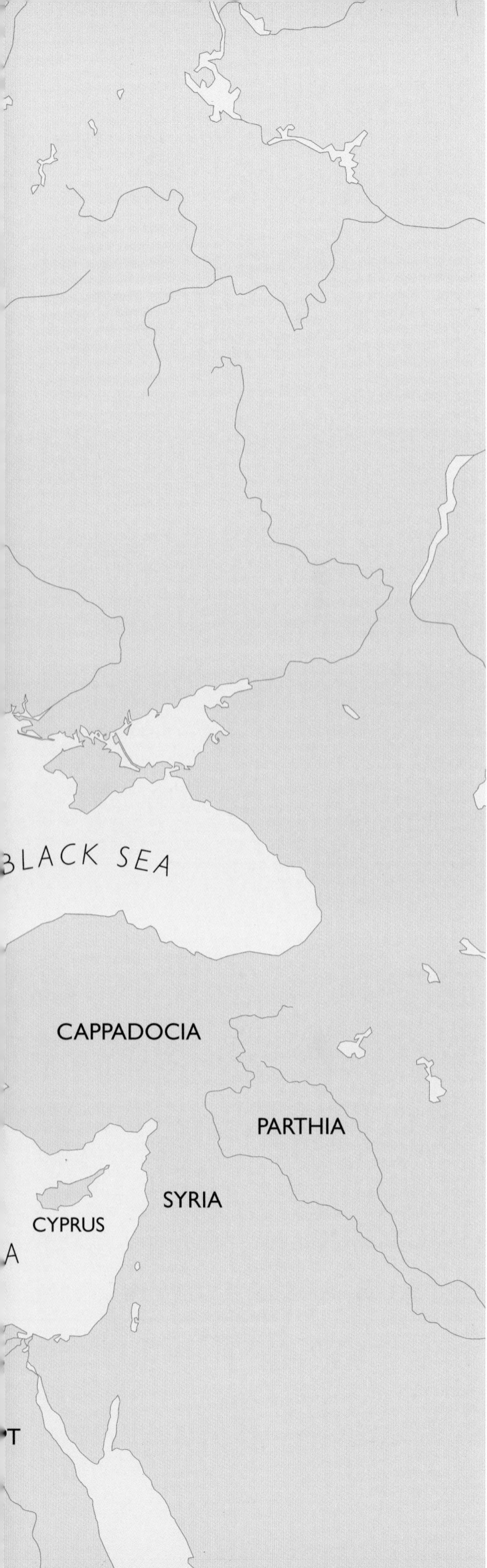

CHRONOLOGY

753 Romulus founds Rome and becomes its first king
715 Death of Romulus and accession of Numa Pompilius
673 Death of Numa Pompilius and accession of Tullus Hostilius
641 Death of Tullus Hostilius and accession of Ancus Marcius
616 Death of Ancus Marcius and accession of Tarquinius Priscus
579 Death of Tarquinius Priscus and accession of Servius Tullius
534 Death of Servius Tullius and accession of Tarquinius Superbus (Tarquin the Proud)
509 Tarquinius Superbus expelled from Rome, and the Republic is formed
508 Rome begins hostilities with neighbouring tribes
450 The Laws of the Twelve Tables published
390 Rome sacked by Gauls
343 Rome begins wars with the Samnites
290 Samnites defeated, and become allies of Rome
280 Rome begins war with Pyrrhus
275 Roman army defeats Pyrrhus at Beneventum
264 Start of First Punic War against the Carthaginians
241 Rome seizes Sicily, and ends First Punic War
218 Start of Second Punic War against Hannibal's army
214 Start of First Macedonian War between Rome and Philip V of Macedon
205 End of First Macedonian War
201 Rome seizes Spain, and ends Second Punic War
200 Start of Second Macedonian War
197 End of Second Macedonian War
171 Start of Third Macedonian War
168 End of Third Macedonian War
149 Start of Third Punic War against Carthaginians
148 Fourth Macedonian War
146 Roman soldiers destroy Carthage, and end Third Punic War
133 Start of Roman civil wars

The Rape of the Sabines was a popular image for artists of the Renaissance and beyond. Although not a proven event, it has become a key chapter in the story of the foundation of Rome. This version, by J L David in 1799, shows a later stage in the legend, when the Sabine men returned to Rome to try to reclaim their women. The Sabine wives, now fond of their Roman husbands and children, stood between the Roman and Sabine men to prevent them from fighting. (© Prisma/AAA Collection Ltd)

Chapter 1
THE ROMANS

Foundation, monarchy and republic

Background

The story of how Rome was born is steeped in violence. The legend of orphaned twins Romulus and Remus being suckled by a she-wolf and founding a city on the Palatine Hill in 753BC soon descends into fratricide, as Romulus kills his brother whilst jealously defending his new city. The method by which Romulus set about populating the city involved kidnap and rape, as the neighbouring Sabine women were abducted to become Rome's first mothers. Romulus himself eventually disappeared during a violent thunderstorm, believed to have

been taken up by his father, Mars, the god of War. Although the stuff of fables, these violent beginnings seem most appropriate for a city that grew into an empire by the strength of its sword and the ferocity and skill of its armies.

Earliest kings

Records of the organisation of Rome's military forces under the early monarchy are scarce, but the writings of Roman historians such as Livy and Dionysius can build a picture of the emphasis given to military organisation and war by Rome's first seven kings.

Romulus, the first king, was certainly military-minded, and built his power on his ability on the battlefield. This was considered a most appropriate kingly quality at a time when borders were constantly shifting, and the defence of one's own land, as well as the acquisition of others, was the means to success and survival. Romulus' successor, the Sabine Numa Pompilius (715–673BC), was a much more peaceful king, and concentrated on religious reform. Rome's third king, Tullus Hostilius (673–641BC) was very war-minded, and destroyed neighbouring Alba Longa, effectively doubling the population of Rome with Alban refugees. The successor to Hostilius, Ancus Martius (641–617BC), made shrewd military reforms in order to defend his city, and expanded Rome's frontiers and population through conquest. Although successful in war, the Roman army up to this time mainly consisted of groups of warriors fighting together under the command of wealthy nobles. This had some proven efficacy, but would have to adapt and become a more homogenous unit to be able to survive the battles ahead.

Etruscan rule and reform

The fifth king of Rome was the first Etruscan to hold the position. According to Livy, Lucius Tarquinius Priscus (616–579BC) waged war with the neighbouring Latins in order to garner favour in his new kingdom. Certainly, the period of Etruscan rule in Rome saw

In Roman legend, the three Horatii brothers from Rome had a symbolic fight with the Curatii triplets from Alba, as a way of settling a dispute between the two states. This took place during the reign of Tullus Hostilius, the third king of Rome. This is a 19th-century engraving of the event. (© R Sheridan/AAA Collection Ltd)

its most significant military reforms of the early period, due to the introduction of the Etruscan form of phalanx warfare and Greek-style hoplite tactics in the Roman army around this time. Much of the conversion to hoplite tactics is associated with the sixth king of Rome, who was the second Etruscan in this role. Servius Tullius (579–534BC) was said to have introduced a sweeping reform, replacing the order of citizenship based on race by one based on residence, thus increasing the pool of military manpower. These newly defined citizens were divided into one of five classes, determined by their wealth. From these classes, groups of troops called centuries were drawn, providing the basis for an army where the wealthy were bound to serve and to provide their own military equipment. The class system also controlled who could vote at assemblies, which meant political and military life were unavoidably, and indeed deliberately, interwoven.

Fall of monarchy and rise of republic

The reign of Tarquinius Superbus (534–509BC), or 'Tarquin the Proud', is marked by cruelty and violence, but his success as a warmonger ensured the continued, and rapid, rise of Rome as an early superpower. It was, however, the cruel streak of Tarquinius and his family that resulted in the final toppling of the monarchy in Rome, and the establishment of the early Republic. Lucius Junius Brutus, the nephew of Tarquinius, led his fellow citizens in an uprising against the corrupt and violent monarchy, and thus became the founder of the Roman Republic in 509BC. The new regime established in the new Republic was to be based on patriotism and courage. However, it was the strength of its armies, and the military resolve of its leaders, that would dictate the success or failure of the Republic.

The Republic was ruled by a senate and two consuls – chief magistrates or judges – the consuls being elected annually. The dominant power of the aristocratic class, or patricians, in the senate was a matter for protest, and was increasingly challenged by the common people, or plebeians, until by 300BC the plebeians had obtained the right to hold any office. More offices were added to the political organisation, including *tribunes* (who were originally to protect the plebeians' rights against the patricians, but later became military officers), *quaestors* (prosecutors or judges, later becoming paymasters or treasurers), *aediles* (magistrates responsible for supervising public building and games, the police, and the corn supply), *censors* (responsible for taking the census of citizens and regulating taxes) and *praetors* (magistrates junior to the consuls).

Rome gradually extended her power to neighbouring peoples, and by the start of the fifth century BC, Rome was the most important city in Latium. The threat to the region from a number of Apennine hill tribes resulted in a common defensive alliance, aimed at presenting a united front against the enemy tribes. Much of the fifth century BC saw Rome at war alongside the Latins, defending Latium against the Sabines, Volsci and Aequi who were eager to settle in more fertile territory. In 396BC, Rome effectively doubled the territory under the control of the Republic, following a six-year-long siege of the important Etruscan city of Veii, about 20km north of Rome. However, a run of success and dominance was about to come to an end, when Gallic Celts, who had been fighting their way south from northern Italy, came to within a few miles of Rome. A Roman army met them, but the Celts were far more numerous, ferocious and skilled in battle than the Romans had expected, and the Roman army fled after severe losses.

The victorious Celts proceeded to overrun the city of Rome, burning and demolishing temples and killing innocent citizens. A small number of soldiers would not leave a garrison in the city, and remained trapped there for seven months under their leader, Marcus Manlius. News that their homelands were being sacked in their absence eventually convinced the Celtic leader, Brennus, that their might was needed elsewhere, and the Celts finally left Rome to be rebuilt by her surviving citizens, returning from where they had fled across the Tiber.

Rome's next major wars were undertaken against the Latin towns of Tibur and Praeneste, and after a number of victories over others of the Latins, Rome had no serious challenger in Latium, and possessed a secure northern border with Etruria. It was Rome's next entanglements that were to draw her into new theatres.

Expansion

War with the Samnites in 343BC took the Romans into the southern highlands of Italy, and after suppressing a rebellion from the Volsci in 338BC, the Romans fundamentally reformed their relationship with the Latins and their other allies. Many communities lost their independence and became *municipia* with Roman citizenship; others negotiated new treaties with Rome. Roman expansionist policies continued to anger the Samnites, and a final Third Samnite War saw a grand alliance of Samnites, Etruscans, Celts and Umbrians defeated piecemeal by the Roman army, so that by the middle of the third century BC Rome's dominance seemed beyond challenge. As Rome had extended her hegemony, she had come into conflict with Greek cities scattered around the peninsula's southern coastlines. One of these cities, Tarentum (Taranto), had appealed to Pyrrhus, king of Epirus for help. Crossing the Adriatic in 280BC, Pyrrhus defeated the Romans in a hard-fought contest, prompting him to exclaim: 'Another such victory and we are undone', giving rise to the immortal expression, a 'Pyrrhic victory'.

Punic and Macedonian Wars

Responding to an appeal from the Greek city of Syracuse, Pyrrhus crossed over to Sicily in 278BC and was soon in possession of most of the island, driving the Carthaginians into its western extremity. His high-handedness, however, eventually lost him the support of the Greek cities he had come to assist and he was forced to withdraw. As he set sail he looked back and prophetically observed 'what a field we are leaving to the Romans and Carthaginians to exercise their arms.' True enough, from 264BC until 146BC, the arms of both the Romans and Carthaginians would be exercised to exhaustion in the Punic Wars. Eventual Roman victory was achieved at massive cost.

During the period of the second Punic War, Rome was also engaged in a number of conflicts with the Macedonians. Philip V of Macedonia signed a treaty with Hannibal after his defeat at Cannae in 216BC, then pursued expansionist policies from Illyria northwards. The Romans struck a deal with the Aetolians of Greece, long-standing enemies of the

Macedonians, to help halt Philip's advance, but Philip's violent presence in Aetolian lands caused them to drop their Roman allegiance. Once Hannibal had been forced out of Italy, back to Carthage in 205BC, Scipio could finally deal with the Macedonian threat, and he assembled an army to fight the Macedonians. However, peace terms were agreed between Scipio and Philip, allowing Philip to keep most of his land gains in return for no further expansion. A primary concern for the Romans was probably to keep Philip from aiding Hannibal, so the peace terms were suitably generous and seemed to please both sides.

Against the terms of his agreement with Scipio, Philip promptly went on to gain more territory in Greece, through force. Roman ambassadors sent to demand his withdrawal from the lands of their allies were unsuccessful, and war was declared. Titus Quinctius Flaminius took Roman command in 198BC, and pursued a more aggressive policy against Philip. In 197BC the two sides met at the battle of Kynoskephalai. By now the Roman army had adopted a more flexible way of fighting than the phalanx, and their increased manoeuvrability helped them to defeat the Macedonian phalanx. Philip had to give up all his lands in the Roman allied territory of Greece, and all Greek cities came under the direct control of Rome. Due to the limited resources left to Rome after the recent Second Punic War, there were not enough Roman soldiers to garrison Greece, so Flaminius granted Greece her freedom from either a Roman or Macedonian military presence. This was a shrewd move, as it served to make the Greeks even firmer allies of the Romans, without any need to draw on Roman manpower reserves.

Scipio was renowned as a merciful leader, as the many portrayals of his continence show. This 17th-century tapestry shows Scipio Africanus the Elder pardoning supplicants. (© C Hellier/AAA Collection Ltd)

RELIGION IN EARLY REPUBLICAN ROME

As the Romans extended their conquests, so they absorbed the religion and culture of the races they had subjected, and in the process, modified their own earlier animistic worship. It was the influence of the Greek cities in southern Italy and later in Sicily that made the greatest impact. By the third century BC the Romans had assimilated the Greek gods and goddesses. Greek names were Romanised: Demeter became Ceres; Poseidon and Ares became Neptune and Mars; and Aphrodite and Hestia became Venus and Vesta, though this renaming did not change their fickle natures and wanton ways.

There was no established church as we know it, with a hierarchy, creed and moral code. Nor was there a single all-powerful god, but rather a multiplicity of deities interfering with and squabbling over their different interests and moral protégés. To the majority of Romans the mythology that we regard as little more than a collection of fables was, in varying degrees, a portrayal of immortals to whom established rites were due and who had to be propitiated. The fulfilment of these obligations would ensure the safe return of mariners by Neptune or victory in battle by Mars, while Ceres would provide an abundant harvest and Jupiter, rain. Neglect, on the other hand, would lead to abandonment, if not the purposeful infliction of disaster. Nevertheless, there were a few hardy souls like the consul Appius Claudius Pulcher who, before the battle of Drepana off Sicily, lost patience when the sacred chickens would not eat and so provide a favourable omen. He flung the birds overboard with the short-tempered advice: 'If you won't eat, then try drinking instead'. Whether his subsequent disastrous defeat can be ascribed to his irreverence is a matter for conjecture, though the gods cannot have been too enraged since he managed to escape with his life.

As there was no church, when Rome became a republic the responsibility for official religious ceremonies became a function of the state, the chief officials being the College of Pontiffs, headed by the Pontifex Maximus (Chief Priest), who were the judges and arbiters of divine and human affairs and the interpreters of portents, augurs and omens. Their role was of great significance since the gods could only make their wishes known through coded messages. Divination, however, was not confined to these officials; so long as he could afford to do so, no citizen entered into an undertaking of any importance without offering a sacrifice and reading for himself the signs in the victim's entrails.

Beliefs varied considerably, and religion and its role in determining the course of men's lives was as varied as it is now. Even so, after allowing for this individuality, there can be little doubt that religion influenced military decisions. Major ventures were frequently not undertaken through lack of favourable portents, causing delay and hesitancy. Among soldiers too, individual interpretations inevitably had some bearing on the way they faced an impending battle. A favourable omen could raise morale, but an unfavourable one could cause anxiety.

Shortly before the Third Punic War, Scipio Nasica, the grandson of the military genius of the Second Punic War, Scipio Africanus, warned the Senate that though Rome's position as a dominant power should be preserved, Carthage should not be destroyed as a rival. Were this to occur, there would be no check to Rome's arrogant disregard for the legitimate interests and concerns of smaller states. Moreover, in the absence of any external threat, the Roman Confederation would be in danger of disintegrating as fractious political and social groups pursued their own self-interested ends. Events proved Scipio's prediction to be remarkably perspicacious.

Who were Rome's soldiers?

Citizen soldiers

During her early history, Rome depended entirely upon a citizen militia to protect herself and to conquer the local tribes. This levy, or *legio* – which gave the legion its name – was called up only in times of emergency and was discharged as soon as that emergency ended. The men were primarily farmers and traders, and served for a few weeks or a month or two per year at most. They provided their own arms, armour and equipment, though the state did pay them a small allowance to compensate for loss of earnings, and they fought because, as citizens, they had a vested interest in the security and expansion of Rome. As Rome grew in size, however, the need to defend it required a more extensive, and centrally organised force.

The reforms of Servius Tullius in the sixth century BC extended the pool of resources from which the Roman army could draw. The role of soldier was no longer solely dependent on the financial ability to buy the most expensive armour and weapons. Citizens with average incomes could afford to arm themselves as light infantry, and play an equally important part in the army as their richer neighbours. The division of Rome into five classes neatly pigeon-holed each man of fighting age into the area of service most appropriate for his income. It also meant that the centuries provided by each class were all fighting in a similar manner, with the same sorts of arms. This made military planning far more scientific and predictable.

By the time of the First Punic War, a new type of levy based on the tribe – there were four urban tribes and 16 rural tribes of Rome at this time – had been introduced in an attempt to ease the burden on the wealthier classes of Rome, and to ensure a more equal distribution of the load amongst those citizens who had obtained their citizenship in more recent times. At the beginning of each year the two consuls were elected, and their first task was to appoint 24 military tribunes, six for each of the four legions of Rome. On specially appointed days, all male citizens between the ages of 17 and 46 and who owned property above the value of 11,000 *asses* had to assemble on Capitoline Hill, where they were arranged by height and age group. The men were then brought forward four at a time for selection by the tribunes of each legion, the legions taking it in turn to have first choice in order to ensure that the experienced men and those of the best physical condition were evenly distributed among the legions. One recruit then swore an oath of obedience, and all the others said *'Idem in me'* ('the same for me'). They were given a date and place of assembly, and then dismissed. Men between the ages of 47 and 60 were also enrolled in times of need to serve as garrison troops. Those citizens who fell below the minimum wealth level, called *proletarii*, were under no obligation to serve in the army, although they were sometimes levied during the Punic Wars.

The men in each legion were divided into four classes according to age and experience: the *triarii*, consisting of the oldest men and therefore the most experienced or veteran troops (for Rome was continually at war), who provided a reserve and a steadying influence; the *principes* and *hastati*, men in the prime of life who had been in service before, mature, tough and experienced – the main strength of any legion; and finally the *velites*, light troops or skirmishers, consisting of the poorest and youngest citizens who had little or no experience in warfare.

Although, theoretically, the legionaries were still expected to provide their own arms and armour, by the time of the Punic Wars these were normally purchased from the state,

This reconstruction shows what an early Roman warrior band may have looked like in the seventh century BC. The armed figure on the left is a warrior, and the figure on the right a priest. (Painting by Richard Hook © Osprey Publishing Ltd)

giving a uniformity of armour and weapons which was now essential because of the introduction of the manipular formation, which required that all men within the *hastati* and *principes* classes be armed and armoured in a similar fashion. As a result of the state supplying the men's armour, the citizen militia was stripped of its class character, and from then onwards the legionaries were armed and armoured very much alike, the only real distinction remaining between the heavy infantry, armed in the hoplite fashion, and the unarmoured light troops.

By around 215BC, the property qualification for army service was lowered drastically from 11,000 *asses* to 4,000. This meant a substantial number of the *proletarii* were suddenly available for service in the legions, possibly as many as between 75,000 and 100,000 men. The *proletarii* had been levied for service in the past, mainly to provide rowers for the navy, but occasionally to serve in the army in times of grave danger. On these occasions they were armed at public expense and served in non-regular units quite separate from the legionary order of battle. It is even possible that the *proletarii* were levied prior to Cannae, when six new legions were raised, for the senate is hardly likely to have resorted to recruiting slaves, criminals and youths of 16 and younger when many thousands of adult *proletarii* citizens were still available.

Colonial and allied contingents

Though Roman garrisons were established at strategic points in allied lands and Roman colonies, after the fourth century BC the land belonging to the allied states was seldom encroached upon. The allies were, however, expected to provide troops organised on Roman lines and grouped alongside a Roman legion to form a consular army. The allies did not have to pay for their soldiers' food and weapons, and when called upon to provide troops in excess of their treaty obligations, they received special payments from Rome. In this way Rome was able to field a substantially greater number of men than her limited manpower would have allowed.

After Rome's victory over the Latins in 338BC, a new type of Roman citizenship was introduced. This was the *civitas sine suffragio* (citizenship without the vote), a status whereby the holder was liable for taxation and military service but could not participate in Roman political affairs or hold office. These grants hugely increased available manpower, but Rome pursued another policy that must also have had the same effect. This was the appropriation of some of the land of a number of defeated opponents. Land confiscation allowed the settlement of Roman citizens – citizens who may previously have been too poor to be liable for Roman service under the Servian system. But now, with their new land, they would become sufficiently wealthy to qualify for military service.

When legionaries were recruited at the beginning of each year, recruiting officers were also despatched to the Latin colonies and allied cities of Italy to ensure that their contingents were up to strength. In 218BC the 30 Latin colonies, ranging from Placentia (Piacenza) and Cremona in the north to Brundisium in the south, could supply 80,000 infantry and 5,000 cavalry. The Italian allies, all other states in the Italian peninsula under

The Romans made their mark on their colonies through construction and engineering. This road was built by Roman soldiers in Santiponce, Andalucia, in Spain in 206BC. (© Prisma/AAA Collection Ltd)

Roman control, could provide another 250,000 infantry and 26,000 cavalry. This gave a total manpower of over 600,000 men.

The actual proportion of Roman citizens to allies varied from campaign to campaign, but during the Second Punic War it was never less than 1:1, and sometimes a greater proportion of allies was provided. It is also probable that during that war Rome relied more heavily on the Latin colonies than on her Latin allies: not one of these colonies went over to the Carthaginians – not even after Cannae, when many of the Italian allies changed sides – and this provided Rome with a series of reliable strongholds running the length and breadth of Italy throughout the war.

It is difficult to tell how the contingents from the colonies and allies were organised and armed. The various contingents were commanded by their own officers, and each 'legion' was under the overall command of three Roman officers called *praefecti*, who were nominated by the consuls. It is reasonably certain that the men were organised and armed very much in the Roman fashion, for it was normal practice to have Roman and allied legions arrayed side by side, which would have made the army difficult to control, and rendered the Roman legions' method of fighting much less effective, if the legions were organised and armed differently. This is particularly true of the battles of Zama in 202BC and Great Plains in 193BC, where the interaction of the three lines would have been totally ineffective, if not impossible, if the various contingents had not been organised and armed in a similar manner.

Mercenaries

Mercenaries were employed by the Roman army, as ways of building up manpower, and for their particular military skills. After the disastrous Roman defeat at Trebia in 218BC, the preparations for the next campaign included an appeal for help to King Hiero of Syracuse, who sent '1,000 archers and slingers, a force well adapted to cope with Moors and Baliares and other tribes which fought with missiles'. The battle of Lake Trasimene in June 217BC therefore may have seen the debut of the archer in the Roman army.

After the fall of Cartagena in 209BC the Romans gradually recruited more and more mercenaries – Celts, Spanish cavalry and infantry and, of course, the famous Balearic slingers. For the battle of Zama in 202BC the Romans also obtained many Numidian allies, both infantry and cavalry.

Roman military reform

Individual warriors

The first Roman army was probably made up of bands of warriors, each under the command of a nobleman, or a particularly skilled and brave warrior, defending the city from the tribes that surrounded it, as well as pushing back the borders by fighting neighbouring peoples for control of their land. These warriors would have fought as individuals, and although their successes were often to the benefit of the larger group, personal gain and glory must have motivated many of them. Just a few centuries later, the Roman army was involved in battles being fought with tens of thousands of troops on both sides, and complex strategies that required a detailed knowledge of set pieces. So how did a band of warriors become one of the most highly organised and well-trained fighting forces in history? The answer is, by constant reform.

The hoplite phalanx

The earliest possible reliable information concerning the size and organization of the earliest Roman army describes how it was recruited from three 'tribes'. This is because Roman society was at some early stage divided into three tribes and 30 *curiae*. The word *curiae* comes from the Latin for 'assembly of armed men'. Each tribe appears to have contributed 1,000 men. There were horsemen in this early army, but true cavalry probably did not exist at this time. The first really major change to this army must have been the adoption of hoplite tactics in the sixth century. The original hoplites were Greek, from the seventh century, and were armed spearmen who fought as a group in tightly packed lines, usually about eight ranks deep – a phalanx. Hoplite tactics soon spread to Etruria, where their use is confirmed in a wide variety of contemporary artwork. From Etruria, this new

This Greek carving from 400BC shows hoplite warriors grouped together in the traditional phalanx. The strength of the unit is clearly overcoming the enemy, who are crushed beneath the shields and spears. (© R Sheridan/AAA Collection Ltd)

form of warfare spread to Rome and the other Latins. The phalanx system worked by columns of men standing in tight formation, with overlapping shields, armed with long spears and swords. The resulting dense body of men was difficult to penetrate and operated almost like one vast weapon.

The introduction of hoplite tactics to Rome is associated in Roman historical tradition with Servius Tullius, as part of his major changes in the organisation of Rome, in which he divided society into five classes, divided by wealth. Each of the five newly created classes had to contribute centuries of men to fight. The centuries who fought using hoplite tactics were drawn from the wealthiest class. The cavalry were drawn from this wealthy class too, due to the high cost of horses – however, the number of cavalry remained very small, and it is unlikely that Rome possessed any true force of cavalry before the last decades of the fifth century BC. The middling classes were more lightly armed, and the poorest class were exempt due to the cost of arming themselves. The hoplite army of Servius Tullius had a strength of 4,000 and was later augmented to 6,000 at the end of the fifth century BC.

Manipular warfare

Whilst hoplite warfare remained dominant from the middle of the sixth century BC down through the fourth in Latium and many areas of Italy, at some point during the fourth century BC the Roman hoplite phalanx was completely abandoned, and replaced by the much more flexible 'manipular' formation. Essentially, the manipular formation consisted of a number of lines of infantry, each line made up of blocks of troops or maniples (which translates literally as 'handfuls') with wide spaces separating the maniples, enabling them

This romanticised epic portrayal of a battle during the Second Punic War shows vast numbers of Carthaginian troops, including infantry, cavalry and elephants. (© Prisma/AAA Collection Ltd)

to advance or withdraw independently of the movement of the battle-line as a whole. In addition to this flexibility of manoeuvre, each line of maniples could be armed differently. Some historians think this reform was as a result of the massive crushing defeat experienced by Rome at the hands of the Gallic Celts.

Dionysius, writing in the first century BC, and Plutarch, writing in the first century AD, certainly believed that some form of tactical change was employed by the Romans when the Gauls next returned. Dionysius tells how the Roman soldiers ducked down under the blows of the Gallic swords and took them on the shield, while striking at the enemies' groin with the sword. However, there is evidence to suggest that it was the wars with the Samnites that taught the Romans to abandon the phalanx. The rough terrain of central southern Italy, where the Samnite wars were mainly fought, rendered the phalanx much less effective than the more flexible formation used by the Samnites. The Samnites employed a large number of smaller and more manoeuvrable units of soldiers, equipped with heavy javelins and the *scutum*. By around 300BC the flexible formation of three separate lines divided into maniples was being used throughout the Roman army. The maniples were still based on the original centuries, but now reduced to between 70 and 80 men each.

Ancient sources record that after the massive Roman defeat at Cannae in 216BC there were drastic reforms in the army, the most notable of which was a complete re-organisation of the light troops. According to Polybius, writing in the second century BC, the proportion of light troops per legion was doubled – hardly the picture one usually has of the solid, sturdy, slow-moving Roman legion of predominantly heavy infantry. Another less dramatic change occurred when Scipio Africanus took Cartagena in 209BC. A considerable number of Spanish sword-smiths were captured, and set to work producing the excellent *gladius Hispaniensis*, for which they were famous. This weapon may possibly have been copied by the Romans at an earlier date, but they had never been able to achieve the extremely high-quality forging which was the main value of the weapon: now Scipio not only had Spanish smiths, but he forced them to teach his own smiths their secrets. Consequently, the Roman army which landed in Africa in 204BC was entirely equipped with the true *gladius Hispaniensis* and had been thoroughly trained and exercised by Scipio in its correct use. The new sword almost certainly contributed to Scipio's African victories, but prior to its widespread introduction to the Roman army around 200BC, Scipio's African legions would probably have been the only Roman troops using the true *gladius Hispaniensis*.

A snapshot of the Roman army at the time of the Punic Wars

Social background

The Romans of this period were predominantly a rural society. Their intellectual horizons had not been widened by close contact with others who possessed more questioning minds and more sophisticated standards, and the loosening of their strict, simplistic code of behaviour had hardly begun. The Roman *paterfamilias* ruled his family as an autocrat, instilling obedience, loyalty and integrity with a severity approaching the institutionalised training of the Spartan youth.

The result of this upbringing, upheld and fortified by the rigorous demands of public opinion, was that the Romans displayed high standards and set themselves an ideal of virtue based on willpower, self-restraint, a seriousness devoid of frivolity, perseverance and a binding sense of duty to the family, social group, or military unit, all established in the hierarchy of state authority. The importance of the individual was subordinated to his corporate responsibilities, and a willingness to sacrifice his own interests or even his life for the good of his group was accepted as the normal standard of personal conduct.

This gave rise to a pragmatic, dour and persistent breed of men, supported by obedient and respectful wives who occupied themselves with the running of their households and the rearing of children. Few would have held doubts about the rectitude of the state's policies and most were deeply conservative, probably not very imaginative, and profoundly superstitious. They were certainly parochial in outlook but bound together by a powerful moral code of reciprocal loyalty. They were hard working, brave through training, and hardened mentally and physically by the vicissitudes of nature and a life of laborious toil. They made hardy, courageous and disciplined soldiers, whose strength was tempered only by superstition and the usual measure of human failings.

Recruitment and service

The 'standing army' of Rome was four legions plus their cavalry – a total of 20,000 men at most – yet her adult male population has been estimated at 325,000 in 215BC, of whom

The Roman economy at this time was reliant upon agriculture, and most Roman men were peasant farmers. This Romano-German relief shows a Roman harvesting machine. The donkey pushes a scoop into the corn, knocking off the grains. (© R Sheridan/AAA Collection Ltd)

some 240,000 would have been available for military service. This does not include the *proletarii* who were below the minimum wealth required for service, and who were normally employed in the navy in time of war. Rome did indeed field considerably larger armies – a maximum of 25 legions after Cannae in 216BC, a total of at least 120,000 men – yet even this was only half her potential military strength.

Under normal conditions, all males between the ages of 18 and 46 who satisfied the proper criteria were eligible for military service and were recruited into the cavalry or infantry. Under the levy system, the legionaries were enrolled for the year, but would normally have been mustered for only one short campaign, after which they returned home. When the men were selected for service the next year they would have formed completely new legions, so the legions of this early period had no lasting identity as did those of Imperial times. However, during the Punic Wars, as the campaigns moved further and further from Rome, the length of service necessary rose accordingly, and it became increasingly difficult to recruit men and hold them in the ranks – being farmers and businessmen, reliant on these concerns for their main income, the men were not keen on extended periods of service and were forever agitating for their discharge.

By the Second Punic War, legions were being mobilised for an entire year at a time and it was necessary to introduce a rota system, with front-line troops being regularly replaced with men from home. The annual levy was then reduced to merely bringing the legions up to strength, and some kind of permanent legion did exist, though its content was constantly changing. The rota system was another reason why the total manpower of Rome was never utilised at any one time.

Military service was regarded as a mark of honour, without which public recognition and advancement were virtually impossible, especially since it was only after ten years' duty that a man could hold public office.

Organisation and deployment

A legion consisted of some 4,000 infantry, except in times of special danger when the number was increased to 5,000. The legion was divided into ten maniples of *hastati*, ten

The kneeling figure is a *triarius,* based on the earliest surviving sculptures showing legionaries: the Altar of Ahenobarbus. Polybius states that the *triarii* wore a single greave on their leading (left) leg. The middle figure is a *hastatus* or *princeps*. His mail shirt was backed by leather to maintain its shape and position, and would have weighed between 20 and 25 pounds. The figure on the right is the *veles* – supplied by the poor citizens this arm was completely unarmoured, with only agility and a light shield for defence. (Painting by Richard Hook © Osprey Publishing Ltd)

maniples of *principes*, and ten maniples of *triarii*. A maniple contained two centuries of between 70 and 80 men, giving a total of from 140 to 160 men. When deployed for battle, the legion formed three lines of *hastati, principes* and *triarii*. The *hastati* formed the front line, armed with two *pila* (see below), a large oval shield and a short sword, and wearing helmet, cuirass and possibly greaves. The *principes* formed the second line, armed and armoured in a similar fashion. The *triarii* made up the third line, kneeling, ready to move forward and fill any gaps in the lines ahead of them. The *velites* fought as skirmishers initially, but then normally returned to the rear rank and joined the reserve, providing the spearmen with missile back-up if necessary. In addition each legion also had 300 cavalry, or *equites*, attached to it, divided into ten *turmae* of 30 men, which in turn were divided into three groups of ten, each commanded by a *decurion* with an *optio* as second in command. The cavalry were deployed on the flanks.

There were about 100 metres between each of the lines of infantry. In a consular army the four legions might be deployed with the two Roman ones in the centre and the allies on the flanks, with the combined cavalry (in a maximum depth of eight ranks) on the extreme flanks, or Roman and allied legions might be alternated.

Each line of infantry was divided into its separate maniples, with a gap slightly wider than a maniple's frontage between each pair of maniples. The maniples of the *principes* covered the gaps in the line of *hastati*, and the *triarii* covered those in the line of *principes*, creating the so-called 'chequer-board' formation. It is most likely that the legionaries in each maniple were drawn up in open order, with a frontage of two metres per man, and that each successive rank covered the gaps in the rank in front. The number of ranks per maniple varied considerably, depending on the depth of the enemy's formation, and might range from six to 12, with a norm of eight or ten. Open order was necessary for the discharge of the *pila*, and for the men to be able to fight in their traditional manner as swordsmen once at close quarters. The men could change to close order by every other rank advancing into the gaps in the rank in front of it: this would have been necessary when on the defensive, receiving a missile attack, and possibly when receiving a charge. Open order in the sword-fighting phase would enable tired front-rank men to fall back as they killed their man, being replaced instantly by the man behind and to one side of their position. Sword fighting would have been restricted to stabbing motions from behind the shield when in close order, as there would have been insufficient room to swing the sword or to use the shield offensively.

Weapons

The main weapon, and therefore the most important, of the legions was the *pilum*, of which there were two distinct types: a light one with a socketed head, which had a maximum range of about 30 metres in the hands of an expert, and a heavier one with an overall length of three metres, of which half consisted of a barbed iron head on a long, thin iron shaft. The spear of the *triarii* was about four metres long. The *velites* used light, short javelins, and the cavalry had a Greek spear with a pointed iron ferrule, which could be used as a weapon if the spear was broken in combat. All infantry and cavalry carried the short iron sword, about 60cm long by 50mm wide, with double edge and an obtuse point. It was carried in a scabbard on the right side in the Greek fashion.

The *pila* were discharged at close range – the light one first, then the heavy one – during the advance to attack. In the confusion caused by this hail of missiles, which not only inflicted casualties in the enemy's line, but also rendered many opponents' shields useless because of

GLADIUS HISPANIENSIS

The Spanish sword was probably responsible for many victories during this period, since the side who favoured it often seemed to succeed in battle. The sword was made from exceptionally pure Spanish iron, and the manufacture process was a highly skilled job, and included cold hammering – this made it very strong and very sharp. An artillery manual written in around 250BC describes the Spanish sword blade thus;

> When they wish to test the excellence of these *[swords]* they grasp the hilt in their right hand and the end of the blade in the left: then, laying it horizontally on their heads, they pull down at each end until they touch their shoulders. Next they let go sharply, removing both hands. When released, it straightens itself out again and so resumes its original shape, without retaining a suspicion of a bend. Though they repeat this frequently, the swords remain straight.

During his campaigns in Spain, Hannibal noted the effect of these swords in the hands of his mercenaries, and adopted them for his own troops. In fact, the Carthaginian victory at Cannae is often attributed in part to the superiority of the Spanish sword over the short swords of Greek origin still being used by the Romans. Scipio the Elder noted the quality of the Spanish swords when he landed at Ampurias in 128BC; and Scipio Africanus, after he took Cartagena in 209BC, captured numerous Spanish sword-smiths there and forced them to manufacture weapons for his own troops. The Romans called this sword *gladius Hispaniensis* – sword of Spain – and it was widely in use in the Roman legions by 200BC, when it was used against the Macedonians.

the *pila* impaling them, the legionaries charged the final few yards and attacked with sword and shield. The *velites* would have withdrawn through the gaps in the lines of *hastati* before the discharge of the *pila*, either retiring to wait in reserve with the *triarii*, or, if necessary, moving outwards to the flanks between the lines of infantry, to reinforce the cavalry.

The Romans also made extensive use of siege and artillery weapons, which had been part of their arsenal since around 282BC. This arsenal included rams, ballistae and catapults: the ratio of heavy catapults and ballistae to light was about 1:6.

The Roman navy

The history of the Roman navy is strange indeed. Following the third treaty between Rome and Carthage, drawn up in 279BC at the time of Pyrrhus' campaign in Italy, Carthaginian naval supremacy had been recognised: they would aid the Romans by sea should the need arise. The Roman conquest of southern Italy had been achieved with just an army, and no attempt had been made to reduce the coastal cities using a combined land and sea assault, or even a blockade. Eventually, however, the Romans recognised their maritime deficiency and with their usual thoroughness set about putting things right. A Carthaginian

THE BRUTALITY OF THE ROMAN REPUBLICAN ARMY

One significant factor in the victories of Rome's Republican army must be the brutality of her soldiery. This feature might be explained as arising from the constant wars in which Rome became involved during this period, but these wars only served to exacerbate an already deeply rooted predisposition towards violence. The institutionalisation of violence, even in the gladiatorial pastimes of Roman society, fostered a thirst for violence in all forms of social activity, and more particularly a lust for war. Brutality and massacre were hallmarks of Roman methods of warfare, and the capture of a Greek city was normally followed by mass rape and massacre from which even the dogs were not spared.

The prospect of rape, violence and plunder in a foreign country has always been a potent weapon in the armoury of the recruiting sergeant. In the militarised society of Republican Rome the blandishments of sex and violence abroad helped greatly in diverting the attention of the poor from the appalling injustices of the Roman political system. Thus love of violence was not simply an unsavoury excrescence of the Roman social system, it was the gel which held it together. This brutality tended to paralyse the capacity of Rome's enemies to resist her effectively.

quinquereme which had run aground during a naval brush was dismantled and used as a model for the construction of an entire Roman fleet.

The recorded facts relate how 100 quinqueremes and 20 triremes were ordered to be ready in two months. While the workmen were busy building and fitting out the ships, the recruiting and training of the sailors proceeded apace. Skeleton ship frames were constructed along the shore and the rowers drilled under the command of their officers. It was a stupendous undertaking involving some 35,000 men, suggesting a considerable amount of pre-planning, with the crews being recruited, the timber felled and shaped, the skeleton frames constructed and the ships themselves all completed before the two months' training, including a period at sea, actually began. Even so, it is small wonder that in the first encounters with the Carthaginians, the Roman navy proved to be hopelessly inadequate.

To compensate for their lack of nautical expertise, however, the Romans introduced the *corvus* – a technical innovation that exploited their legionaries' aptitude for close-quarter fighting, and about which more will be explained in Chapter three.

Chapter 2
THE ETRUSCANS, APENNINE TRIBES AND LATINS

The Samnites were an ancient, warlike people, who occupied an area of the Sangro Valley region of the Abruzzo in Italy. There is evidence to suggest that Pontius Pilate was probably a Samnite. This statue of a Samnite warrior is Etruscan, from the sixth century BC. (© R Sheridan AAA Collection Ltd)

Warring neighbours

The origins of the Latin League

Italy in the early centuries BC was home to a number of different tribes and peoples, all occupying their own city-states, within distinct regions, ruled over by their own leaders and kings. Earliest records show that there were around 30 different *populi,* or independent states, but this number gradually decreased as neighbouring states either absorbed or destroyed each other. Friction between neighbouring states was inevitable, as power and land struggles caused the stronger tribes to expand their territories, and others to jealously guard theirs. Rome was by no means the first such city-state, although it turned out to be the most powerful and long-lived. It was also one of the best at absorbing and assimilating its neighbours, which may have been a key factor in its success. This ability to create allies and colonies, and increase Rome's own citizen-base served Rome well for many years, as it ensured a constant supply of manpower in the newly acquired lands of Europe and beyond.

Leagues between city-states in the same region were a logical step, such as happened with the Latium city-states in the early sixth century BC. This so-called Latin League united the Latium states in defence of their region against neighbouring regions. It also gave the member states certain rights of commercial trade (*commercium*), inter-marriage (*conubium*), and residency and citizenship between the communities. This league was an important defensive step, since Latium was a popular target for neighbouring tribes – the land was very fertile, and it had a coastline providing important trade links. The most ferocious neighbours of Latium were the Etruscans to the north, the Volscians in the south, and the Aequians to the east. These tribes were the ones who most frequently encroached on neighbouring land, looking for land, slaves, wealth and spoils. Small independent city-states were vulnerable and could easily be picked off by stronger states.

The Latin League agreed to present a united defence against the threat from these Apennine tribes, but how the alliance worked in practice is difficult to tell given the scarcity and unreliability of historical source material. All the Latin communities, including Rome, provided troops, but who commanded them? One literary fragment from the first century BC Roman antiquarian Cincius implies an annual command rotating between the various members of the alliance.

Conflict between Rome and the Latins, and the *foedus Cassianum*

Etruscan rule in Rome from 616BC to 510BC had already established Rome as a very powerful state in Latium, but it was the Latin League as a whole that eventually helped Rome defeat the Etruscan Lars Porsenna at Aricia in 504BC. Rome was left in a weakened position, but tried to assert independence. The other Latin states refused to accept Roman hegemony, seeing this as an opportunity to check the rising power of this city-state. Rome's allies in Latium turned against her, and the Latin League embarked on a war with Rome. This ended with a Roman victory at Lake Regillus in either 499BC or 496BC, the Romans later claming the mythological Castor and Pollux had aided them and secured triumph for Rome. A settlement was agreed between Rome and the Latin League, known as the *foedus Cassianum,* or the Cassian treaty. This was signed in 493BC and swore both parties to keep peace between each other, but also come to one another's military assistance in the event of attack. They were supposed to help protect one another by stopping the enemies of any of the states crossing their land, and to share any profit gained from military successes. It is notable that this treaty was between Rome and the rest of the league, which suggests that Rome already saw herself as a republic standing apart from the alliance of city-states.

The Apennine tribes

Latium at this time was increasingly threatened by a number of Apennine hill tribes. Eager to settle in more fertile lands, the Sabines, Volsci and Aequi regularly encroached on the borders of Rome and other Latin states, and they often proved formidable opponents.

The Sabines

Roman historians record that when the Sabine men went to rescue their women in early Rome, the women forced themselves between the fighting sides, and would not leave their new husbands and children in Rome. As a sign of peace, Romulus suggested that the Sabine king Titus Tatius stay in Rome, along with the rest of his people, and that Romulus and Titus could rule together. This seemed to work, since the following king of Rome was also Sabine – Numa Pompilius (715 BC–673) – and there were undoubtedly numerous Sabine mothers of first-generation Romans, if the kidnap of Sabine women by Romulus took place as recorded.

The Sabines were, however, a constant source of pressure on Rome's eastern borders. According to some histories they seized Rome in 460BC, but the city was back under Roman control by 449BC. Eventually, the Romans seemed to assimilate the Sabines into Roman citizenship, and important Sabine family names could be seen in positions of Roman

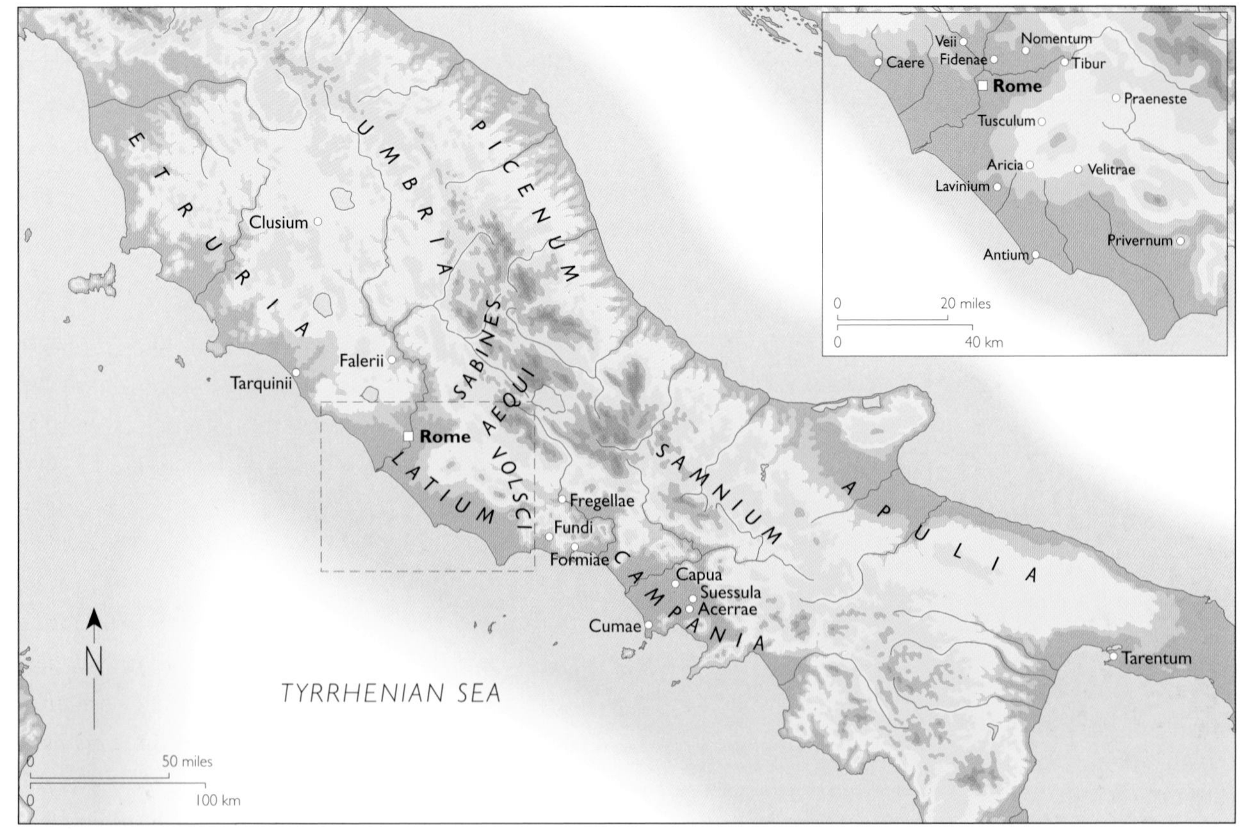

Early Rome and neighbouring lands.

government for years, particularly the Attus Clausus, who became the Gens Claudian, one of Rome's most elite and important families.

The Samnites were probably a strand of the Sabine people, and their military prowess was such that it caused Rome to reform her armies. The Samnites were some of Rome's fiercest enemies at this time, and caused one of Rome's most crushing and humiliating defeats at Caudine Forks in 321BC. Allies of the Carthaginians, the Samnites fought three wars with Rome in the 50 years between 340BC and 290BC. After seeing how the Samnite organisation of troops produced a swift and flexible force, the Romans abandoned the phalanx, and adopted the manipular formation, giving them greater manoeuvrability on the battlefield.

The Volsci and Aequi

The Volsci lived south of Rome, and the Aequi to the east, and the two fought almost annual battles against Rome and the Latins. In the early fifth century the Volsci conquered Antium – present-day Anzio – which threatened Rome's security. The Romans tried to drive the Volsci out of the city, but were unable to defeat them. Livy's history of this battle claims that one village, Corioli, was captured by the Romans under the command of Cnaeus Marcius, renamed (according to Livy) Coriolanus as a result of his small victory. This is the Coriolanus immortalised by Shakespeare. Coriolanus was not popular amongst the plebeians of Rome, and was eventually driven out of the city, whereupon he joined the Volscian army as a general. Coriolanus fought, and won, many battles against the Latins in the early fifth century BC. Livy and Dionysius list the city-states captured by Coriolanus, and Livy also notes that Coriolanus instructed his soldiers to spare the Roman rich, and only damage the property of the plebeians, one assumes as an act of revenge against his own state of exile.

The Volsci were said to have even reached the outskirts of Rome, and this may have been the event that changed the tide for the Romans, as they then embarked upon a period of reconquering lost lands, and finally defeated the Volsci in 431BC at the Algidus pass, under the command of Aulus Postumius Tubertus. Both the Volsci and the Aequi were forced back to the western highlands of Italy, and Rome and the Latins reclaimed lost lands. An attempted rebellion by the Latins in 341BC saw the Volscians actually join the Latins in their fight against Rome, but by 338BC the rebellion had been suppressed, and Rome was unarguably the victor.

The Etruscans

The rise of the Etruscans

An ancient Etruscan prophecy stated that the Etruscan people and nation would last for only nine centuries. This may have been self-fulfilling, as it was certainly accurate – the history of the Etruscan nation probably had its origins in the Villanovian culture around 900BC, and ended in the first century BC when it was effectively absorbed by Rome. At its zenith, the Etruscan nation was wealthy, cultured and deeply influential, but it could not hold back the tide of Roman expansion, although many Etruscan legacies lived on as assimilated elements of its conquering nation.

The name 'Etruscan' came from the Latin name for these people – the Etrusci, or Trusci. The Greeks knew them as the Tyrrhenoi (from which the Tyrrhenian Sea gets its name), but the Etruscans called themselves Rasenna. Historians are divided over where the Etruscans came from, but most recent research leans towards them being indigenous peoples, descendants of the Villanovans who lived in that region of Italy in the tenth and ninth centuries BC. The Etruscan nation encompassed Tuscany, Campania and a part of the Po Valley – rich in natural metal deposits; the land was a bountiful place to live, and very fertile, leading to a steady increase in the wealth and living standards of the Etruscans. Trade links were vital to Etruscan development, and as a result, they became excellent seamen, travelling by ship to trade their metal goods, pottery and wine around Europe, North Africa and the Mediterranean.

Etruscans made widespread use of slaves, and their society was based on a type of feudal structure, with slaves and servants working for wealthy nobles. Their slaves were drawn from the many lands they conquered and colonised, but their treatment of them was not always cruel – slaves were allowed to own their own houses. The use of slaves allowed Etruscans to farm on a scale that led to great wealth, and also left them the time to widen their search for goods to trade, and people to trade with.

The Etruscan economy relied on widespread use of slaves and servants to farm the land of wealthy nobles, leaving the nobles enough time to travel great distances establishing trade links. This Etruscan statue shows a typical plough, pulled by oxen. (© R Sheridan/AAA Collection Ltd)

The Etruscans were a cultured people, enjoying music, dance and art. An influx of Greek immigrants lead to impressive developments in art and technology, and surviving examples of Etruscan sculpture and painting reveal the nation's true appreciation of culture. The Etruscans had extraordinarily liberal views on the role and ability of their women – many examples of Etruscan art show women holding positions of similar superiority in a household to that of their husbands, and there is some evidence to suggest that Etruscan society ran along matrilineal lines.

Etruscans also seem to have had very liberal views on promiscuity and adultery, neither of which were considered to be undesirable or unacceptable. A forward nation in terms of literacy, the Etruscans had an alphabet, the roots of which can be seen in many subsequent alphabets.

The Etruscans followed a pagan religion, influenced by the gods of the Greek tradition. A belief in the afterlife was key to Etruscan religious ceremonies, and some of the most impressive surviving Etruscan paintings have been found in tombs, associated with funerary practices. The Etruscans also placed much faith in soothsayers and haruspices, who told the future by examining the entrails (particularly the livers) of sacrificed sheep. This unpleasant planning technique was something they passed on to the Romans.

Etruscan kings of Rome

The proximity of Etruscan lands to those of Rome made conflict inevitable between the two ambitious nations. For a while, however, Rome profited from Etruscan supremacy, as three

This hollow cinerary urn is known as the *Sarcophagus dei Sposi* and is a famous example of Etruscan art from 520 to 530BC. The married couple are reclining on a dining couch, in a tender pose, with the man's arm on his wife's shoulder. Both are smiling slightly. The Etruscans held women in high regard, and they were not portrayed as inferior to men in Etruscan art. (© AAA Collection Ltd)

of the first seven kings of Rome were Etruscan. Between them they initiated crucial reforms to Roman society and military. The first Etruscan king of Rome was Tarquinius Priscus (616BC–579), from the Etruscan city of Tarquinii. Under Tarquinius, Rome warred with neighbouring states, improving her local power. In fact, the first Roman games were established by Tarquinius as a way of celebrating his victory over the Latins and Sabines. The civic areas of the city were improved, too – Tarquinius installed drains in the city, founded a temple to the god Jupiter on the Capitoline Hill, and improved the buildings of the Forum. His successor, Servius Tullius (579–534BC) was responsible for some of the most important military reforms in the history of the Roman army (see Chapter one for more about these reforms). Servius Tullius also signed a treaty with the Latins, naming Rome as the leading city of Latium. Parts of the wall built by Servius Tullius after the attack on the city by Celts in 387BC, to protect Rome from further attack, still remain today.

The last Etruscan king of Rome was the last king of any nationality in Rome. Tarquinius Superbus (534–509BC) is recorded in history as a cruel leader – he warred with the Latins and so enraged his people that they rose up against him, thus founding the Republic of Rome. However, even he brought wealth and land to Rome from his war with the Volscians.

When the Etruscan kings were eventually driven from Rome they left behind them powerful legacies. Their military reforms were crucially important in the development of Rome's fighting techniques. The Etruscans fought using the Greek hoplite formation of a phalanx – this technique was introduced to the Roman army under Servius Tullius, and served it well for many years. Hoplites were citizen-soldiers who armed and armoured themselves out of their own pockets. Their motivation for fighting was the defence of their city-state, and shares in the spoils of battle.

The very symbols of power in the Roman government – the *toga praetexta* (a white toga with a purple border), the *curule* chair (a backless seat with heavy curved legs) and the *fasces* (an axe encased in a bundle of birch sticks) – were introduced by the Etruscans. Their construction of temples, drains and other public structures placed a very visible stamp on the city, and ensured their reigns were not forgotten, and their introduction of the public games is one of the enduring symbols of Rome today. Though their rule in Rome had come to an end, Etruscan military dominance prevailed elsewhere, and by around 500BC Etruscan power was at its height – many of the Umbrian cities were under Etruscan rule, along with much of Latium. Their prowess as sailors led to Etruscan colonies being established around the coastlines of Italy and Spain, including Corsica, Elba, Sardinia and the Balearic Islands. Trade links with their colonies and allies were well used and busy, and the wealth of some of the leading Etruscan nobles was dramatic.

The auletos, or double flute, was a popular instrument among the Etruscans. This depiction of an auletos player comes from the wall of the tomb of the Triclinium in Tarquinia. It was common for Etruscans to paint their tomb walls with lively, vibrant images, decorated with birds and plants. (© Mike Andrews/ AAA Collection Ltd)

Etruscan clashes with Rome

Lars Porsena marches on Rome

In around 508BC, unhappy with his ejection from Rome, Tarquinius called upon another Etruscan, Lars Porsena, to help him try to re-conquer the city. Porsena ruled over the Etruscan city-state of Clusium (near to modern-day Florence), and he put together an army and marched on Rome. What happened next is not agreed upon by historians or historical sources. The legendary course of events is that Porsena was so impressed at the bravery of Rome's defenders that he called off his attack and returned to Etruscan lands. This version of the story has been immortalised in poetry by Thomas Babington Macaulay, and in many artistic depictions of Horatius Cocles defending the bridge. It is said that, having quickly seized the Janiculum ridge in a sudden attack, the way lay open over the Tiber for Porsena to take the rest of the city. Livy records a story that Horatius Cocles rushed to the bridge, together with Spurius Larcius and Titus Herminius, and together the three held back the entire Etruscan army, while behind them work continued feverishly on the demolition of the bridge.

When scarcely anything was left of the bridge, Horatius sent back the two others and carried on the fight alone. With a crash and a deafening shout from the Romans the bridge finally fell. Horatius invoked Father Tiber, leaped into the river, and swam to the bank and safety. Other versions of this story have Horatius defending the bridge alone. This was not the only act that was supposed to have impressed the Etruscans – while they camped outside the walls of Rome, a Roman called Cauis Mucius crept into the camp in the dead

HORATIUS BY THOMAS BABINGTON MACAULAY, 1842

Sadly, space will not allow all 70 verses of this epic to be printed, but the abridged version below serves to give a good flavour of this poetic tribute to one of Rome's greatest heroes.

Horatius
A Lay Made About the Year Of The City CCCLX

I
Lars Porsena of Closium
By the Nine Gods he swore
That the great house of Tarquin
Should suffer wrong no more.
By the Nine Gods he swore it,
And named a trysting day,
And bade his messengers ride forth,
East and west and south and north,
To summon his array.

XI
And now hath every city
Sent up her tale of men;
The foot are fourscore thousand,
The horse are thousands ten.
Before the gates of Sutrium
Is met the great array.
A proud man was Lars Porsena
Upon the trysting day.

XII
For all the Etruscan armies
Were ranged beneath his eye,
And many a banished Roman,
And many a stout ally;
And with a mighty following
To join the muster came
The Tusculan Mamilius,
Prince of the Latian name.

XIII
But by the yellow Tiber
Was tumult and affright:
From all the spacious champaign
To Rome men took their flight.
A mile around the city,
The throng stopped up the ways;
A fearful sight it was to see
Through two long nights and days.

XVIII
I wis, in all the Senate, *[wis: know]*
There was no heart so bold,
But sore it ached, and fast it beat,
When that ill news was told.
Forthwith up rose the Consul,
Up rose the Fathers all;
In haste they girded up their gowns,
And hied them to the wall.

XIX
They held a council standing,
Before the River-Gate;
Short time was there, ye well may guess,
For musing or debate.
Out spake the Consul roundly:
'The bridge must straight go down;
For, since Janiculum is lost,
Nought else can save the town.'

XX
Just then a scout came flying,
All wild with haste and fear:
'To arms! to arms! Sir Consul:
Lars Porsena is here.'
On the low hills to westward
The Consul fixed his eye,
And saw the swarthy storm of dust
Rise fast along the sky.

XXVI
But the Consul's brow was sad,
And the Consul's speech was low,
And darkly looked he at the wall,
And darkly at the foe.
'Their van will be upon us
Before the bridge goes down;
And if they once may win the bridge,
What hope to save the town?'

XXVII
Then out spake brave Horatius,
The Captain of the Gate:
'To every man upon this earth
Death cometh soon or late.
And how can man die better
Than facing fearful odds,
For the ashes of his fathers,
And the temples of his gods,

XXIX
'Haul down the bridge, Sir Consul,
With all the speed ye may;
I, with two more to help me,
Will hold the foe in play.
In yon strait path a thousand
May well be stopped by three.
Now who will stand on either hand,
And keep the bridge with me?'

XXX
Then out spake Spurius Lartius;
A Ramnian proud was he:
'Lo, I will stand at thy right hand,
And keep the bridge with thee.'
And out spake strong Herminius;
Of Titian blood was he:
'I will abide on thy left side,
And keep the bridge with thee.'

XXXIV
Now while the Three were tightening

Their harness on their backs,
The Consul was the foremost man
To take in hand an axe:
And Fathers mixed with Commons
Seized hatchet, bar, and crow,
And smote upon the planks above,
And loosed the props below.

XXXVI

The Three stood calm and silent,
And looked upon the foes,
And a great shout of laughter
From all the vanguard rose:
And forth three chiefs came spurring
Before that deep array;
To earth they sprang, their swords they drew,
And lifted high their shields, and flew
To win the narrow way;

XLIX

But all Etruria's noblest
Felt their hearts sink to see
On the earth the bloody corpses,
In the path the dauntless Three:
And, from the ghastly entrance
Where those bold Romans stood,
All shrank, like boys who unaware,
Ranging the woods to start a hare,
Come to the mouth of the dark lair
Where, growling low, a fierce old bear
Lies amidst bones and blood.

LIII

But meanwhile axe and lever
Have manfully been plied;
And now the bridge hangs tottering
Above the boiling tide.
'Come back, come back, Horatius!'
Loud cried the Fathers all.
'Back, Lartius! back, Herminius!
Back, ere the ruin fall!'

LIV

Back darted Spurius Lartius;
Herminius darted back:
And, as they passed, beneath their feet
They felt the timbers crack.
But when they turned their faces,
And on the farther shore
Saw brave Horatius stand alone,
They would have crossed once more.

LV

But with a crash like thunder
Fell every loosened beam,
And, like a dam, the mighty wreck
Lay right athwart the stream:
And a long shout of triumph
Rose from the walls of Rome,
As to the highest turret-tops
Was splashed the yellow foam.

LVII

Alone stood brave Horatius,
But constant still in mind;
Thrice thirty thousand foes before,
And the broad flood behind.
'Down with him!' cried false Sextus,
With a smile on his pale face.
'Now yield thee,' cried Lars Porsena,
'Now yield thee to our grace.'

LVIX

'Oh, Tiber! Father Tiber!
To whom the Romans pray,
A Roman's life, a Roman's arms,
Take thou in charge this day!'
So he spake, and speaking sheathed
The good sword by his side,
And with his harness on his back,
Plunged headlong in the tide.

LXII

Never, I ween, did swimmer,
In such an evil case,
Struggle through such a raging flood
Safe to the landing place:
But his limbs were borne up bravely
By the brave heart within,
And our good Father Tiber
Bore bravely up his chin.

LXIV

And now he feels the bottom;
Now on dry earth he stands;
Now round him throng the Fathers;
To press his gory hands;
And now, with shouts and clapping,
And noise of weeping loud,
He enters through the River-Gate
Borne by the joyous crowd.

LXVII

And still his name sounds stirring
Unto the men of Rome,
As the trumpet-blast that cries to them
To charge the Volscian home;
And wives still pray to Juno
For boys with hearts as bold
As his who kept the bridge so well
In the brave days of old.

This Etruscan statue shows a bow typical of those used at this time. Tall, thin figures were a common style for Etruscan statues, and this bronze is from the eighth to sixth century BC. (© R Sheridan/AAA Collection Ltd)

of night, aiming to kill Porsena. Mucius was caught, and brought to Porsena, where Mucius addressed him with great confidence. To show his contempt of pain, Mucius plunged his right hand into a fire, and showed no pain as it burned to the bone. Porsena was so impressed by this act that he let Mucius go free, and from then on the hero was known as Scaevola ('left-handed'). The last act of bravery that allegedly convinced Porsena to abandon his siege of Rome was the gift of hostages made to him by the Romans, as a sign of good faith. The hostages were young children, and one of them was the consul Publicola's daughter, Valeria. The children escaped, and swam back to Rome, where they were promptly returned to Porsena by Publicola. Valeria escaped again, and Porsena was (once again) so impressed by the bravery of the children that he sent them all back, under the protection of his men. These events make good stories, but the evidence for them is only from Roman sources, none of them contemporary, and all of them have reason to paint Rome in a favourable light.

Other sources say that Porsena was successful in his invasion of the city, and that he left only after his triumph was acknowledged with the symbols of power – the *toga praetexta*, the *curule* chair and the *fasces* – and on the conditions that Rome give up their lands north of the Tiber, hand over their arms and not replace them. Porsena left Rome without attempting to install Tarquinius as king, which suggests his attack was for personal gain in the first place. Some historians view Porsena's attack on Rome as simply one siege on an Etruscan march southwards, looking for land in Latium and Campania (possibly due to the presence of Gallic Celts in northern Italy).

The fall of Veii

The Romans and Etruscans met again in around 483BC, when the Romans besieged the Etruscan city-state of Veii. Veii was the closest Etruscan city to the Roman borders, being situated only 12 miles north-east of Rome on the opposite bank of the Tiber. Rome was at war with Veii from 483BC to 474, during which time there occurred a famous Roman defeat at the battle of Cremara. The most important conflict with Veii, however, began in 406BC and lasted for ten years, at the end of which Veii was conquered by the Roman general Camillus. Veii was destroyed and her territory seized. This was the first time that Rome had destroyed and occupied an enemy state of comparable size, and it was a massive blow to Etruscan power.

Decline and fall

As the Etruscan city-states were effectively independent from each other, they were susceptible to attack, which is exactly what continued to happen after Veii. Etruscan colonies in Campania were soon taken by Samnites and other Latins, and trade routes were severely disrupted. Etruscan wealth suffered, and the nation became weaker. Constant battles with Rome throughout the fourth century depleted resources even more, and towards the end of this century the Etruscans even tried fighting together as one force to defeat the Romans, but they ended up fleeing in failure. A league of Etruscans, Samnites, Gauls and Umbrians did battle with Rome in the early third century BC but, once again, were defeated. Eventually the Etruscan city-states were absorbed one by one through Roman expansion, and by the end of the third century BC the Etruscans were fighting as allies of Rome, against the Carthaginians and Gallic Celts. An Etruscan slave uprising in Roman lands at the start of the second century was crushed with little difficulty, and the final blow to Etruscan nationality was delivered in 89BC, when the Etruscans were given Roman citizenship, and therefore effectively ceased to exist as Etruscans.

The Etruscan army

Recruitment

Etruscans were accustomed to using a census – resulting in the introduction of the census to Rome by one of its Etruscan kings, Servius Tullius. The Etruscan census determined recruitment of cavalry, hoplites (heavy infantry) and light infantry, as each was drawn from the appropriate class of wealth. Each city-state produced its own army, and the states very rarely fought together as one.

Although bronze examples of Etruscan armour are more likely to have survived than other materials, we know that the Etruscans also used wood and leather in making their armour. These bronze examples were found in Olympia, and show the typical round hoplite shield and cuirass as used by the Ancient Greeks. Etruscan armour would have looked much the same. (© R Sheridan/AAA Collection Ltd)

Although a Spartan rather than an Etruscan, this is a typical hoplite soldier of the sixth century BC, and is shown wearing armour of a type similar to that which the Etruscans would have worn – the greaves, cuirass. Etruscans also wore helmets with brush crests, like the one shown here. (© R Sheridan/AAA Collection Ltd)

Weaponry

Etruscan lands and colonies included those areas rich in ferrous metal mines, and as a result they could produce iron weapons, giving them a distinct advantage over their enemies. Swords were fairly rare, and highly prized, and the most common Etruscan weapons were the spear and battle axe (which was used for throwing as well as for striking). Etruscans were also skilled archers, and many bows and spears have been found in Etruscan tombs. Etruscans also used daggers and short blades for fighting.

Armour

The traditional image of the Etruscan hoplite shows much evidence of Greek influence. Examples of muscled cuirasses survive, although not all cuirasses would have been muscled. Cuirasses were often bronze, or fabric with metal studs for strength. They had shoulder flaps and often short skirts of armour. Etruscan helmets were usually bronze, and varied in shape, some with high crests, and others with round heads and nose guards. There were protective flaps to cover the cheeks, which could be raised on some helmets.

Hoplites wore bronze greaves, and carried a shield made from wood, bronze or leather. The most common image of the Etruscan shield shows it as being round, though rectangular shields were also used.

Organisation and deployment

As with most armies, the infantry was the key element of Etruscan forces, and the hoplites fought using the phalanx formation – a dense line of soldiers armed with spears and round shields, overlapping one another. As hoplites supplied their own arms, and there was no state uniformity, the phalanx may have contained many differently armed hoplites. However, its strength (and sometimes its weakness) lay in its cohesion as one unit.

The light infantry were armed with spears, but often wore no armour, and were used to attack from a distance, to provoke the enemy into weakness. There are few contemporary accounts of Etruscan battles, but their style of fighting was so influenced by the Greeks that we can use accounts of Greek hoplite warfare to give us an insight into the Etruscan way of battle. Xenophon in his *Anabasis* describes how a phalanx operated on the battlefield. On the advance the older, more experienced men in the rear ranks kept the line moving forward and made sure that nobody dropped out. There would be much shouting and calling by name as troops got too far ahead in some places and too far behind in others. Few hoplite armies were capable of advancing in line over any great distance without becoming disordered. Thucydides makes it clear that most armies had great difficulty advancing with their ranks in good order. Any unexpected obstacle could bring the phalanx to a complete halt or break its formation. As a result, generals selected plains on which to fight their battles, otherwise most hoplite armies would simply find it impossible to come to contact.

It was the job of the hoplites at the back to push forward those in front of them. Hoplites in the front ranks were physically unable to run away, since they could not push back through the rear ranks. Xenophon confirms that the charge would usually start when both sides were about 180m (600ft) apart. The hoplite line then broke into a run and roared out their battle-cry. In the final stages of this dash to contact, the hoplite would have adjusted the position of his weapons. His shield would have been swung forwards to cover as much of his body as possible. If the two sides did meet, then the two lines of shields clashed against each other, as each side tried physcially to push the other back. Experienced hoplites aimed their spears at undefended parts of the enemy's body above and below the shield, jabbing at them rapidly and repeatedly. The throat, groin and thighs were especially vulnerable.

When an army broke the results could be dramatic. Xenophon in his *Hellenica* describes how retreating hoplites were crushed, trodden under foot by one another, and suffocated. To escape more quickly, fleeing troops usually threw away their cumbersome weapons and shields. It was important for the victors to keep formation as they chased the enemy, who might have been victorious on the other wing.

The Etruscan cavalry were used for skirmishing, and for pursuing and routing the enemy armies. Chariots have been found in some large Etruscan tombs, but it is not known whether these were used simply as a means of transport to the field of battle, or if Etruscan soldiers fought whilst riding them. The Etruscans were also influenced by Greek military engineering, and were skilled in building siege engines and other defensive and offensive structures, as well as dismantling those of their enemies.

It is ironic that the methods by which the Etruscans were eventually subjugated by Roman military force were heavily influenced by the Etruscans in the first place. The Roman fighting techniques, their armour and their arms were all adopted and adapted from the Etruscans (who in turn had adapted them from the Greeks), and the Etruscan period of rule in Rome was a vital part of the development of the Roman army as the most effective fighting force in the world.

Chapter 3
THE CARTHAGINIANS

The Punic Wars tested Rome's armies and navy to the full. Three wars with Carthage between 264BC and 146BC saw the pendulum of power swing from victory to crushing defeat for both sides. A fearsome enemy, the strength of the Carthaginian army lay in its unrivalled mix of military skills, drawn from its vast empire, and outstanding leadership from a general whose methods are still studied in military science.

Carthaginian campaigns against Rome

Background

With hindsight, it is hard not to conclude that war between Carthage and Rome had a degree of inevitability, but at the time there seemed no reason why this should be so. Rome had established its hegemony over the whole of the Italian peninsula only relatively recently, and the Senate showed no inclination for further expansion. Carthage had no territorial designs beyond keeping her colonies and trading posts scattered around the Mediterranean seaboard. Although there may never be any way of determining exactly why Carthage and Rome went to war, there are two clearly identifiable factors which make such a war more probable. First, the Romans saw an opportunity to advantage themselves; secondly, they saw that the Carthaginians were unprepared militarily, and succumbed to this temptation. Sicily was the cause of this temptation. By the middle of the third century BC, Carthage had extended its commercial empire to the western half of Sicily. Whilst Sicily itself was not an important prize for either side in terms of wealth, its position made it valuable. The southern tip of the Roman Empire was too close to Sicily to ignore, and when a Carthaginian garrison appeared in Mamertine-controlled north-eastern Sicily, possession of the island seemed of more strategic importance than ever. Rome quickly answered the Mamertine call for support, recognising the opportunity to secure a foothold in Sicily.

The First Punic War (264–241BC)

In the First Punic War, naval victory was the key. After initial fighting in Sicily the war was taken to North Africa, and it was en route to Africa in 256BC that the largest naval victory was secured – only just – by the Roman fleet of 330 ships under their commander Marcus Atilius Regulus. One of the most important elements in their victory was the idge which could be hoisted up from a 12-foot required direction. At the end of the bridge was nich, when released, drove itself into the deck of ips together. Then the legionaries could storm ess crews, exploiting the Roman aptitude for ıl as the *corvus* was for enabling the Romans to e side effect of rendering the Roman warships ound 255BC.

mans advanced to within a day's march of t the hands of the newly organised Carthaginian outed by the Carthaginian elephants, the Roman cult land battle in Sicily, victory was once again omans emerged triumphant. Deserted, and with ıginian leader Hamilcar Barca was left to negotiate Catulus, the Roman commander. A treaty was ns would retain their arms but withdraw from mnity. After 24 years of fluctuating fortunes, with the war had ended, but it was not to bring peace

The Carthaginian Empire and its dependencies.

The Second Punic War (218–201BC)

In the spring of 218BC, Hannibal Barca, son of Hamilcar, set out from New Carthage on a campaign that was to last 17 years. His aim was not just to recapture Sicily, the loss of which to Rome 23 years previously could no longer be borne by the Carthaginians, but to arrest seemingly unconstrained expansion of the Roman Empire, which by then even occupied areas in the middle of Carthaginian territory. Hannibal's overall strategic objective, however, may have been more vast. From a treaty drawn up later between Hannibal and Philip V of Macedonia, we know that Hannibal aimed to break up the entire Roman Confederation and reduce it once more to a number of states. These could then be held in check by those whose independence had just been restored to them. The cohesive power of Rome lay in its army, so Hannibal's operational aim was clearly to inflict such defeats on the army that the subjugated states would be encouraged to rise in revolt. Polybius states that Hannibal's aims included the reduction of Roman manpower by stripping Rome of her allies, therefore forcing the Senate to the negotiating table.

In the years since the First Punic War, Carthage had expanded its empire to include much of Spain, and had put together an army that included large numbers of Spanish troops. By 218 the army was huge, which makes Hannibal's co-ordination of these troops in a march across the Alps even more impressive. His swift victories against the Romans in northern Italy were an unpleasant introduction to the sort of military genius that Rome was

Roman naval ability was crucial in the First Punic War. The Romans were not natural sailors, but recognised the need for naval superiority, and created many warships by copying examples of captured Carthaginian ships. This painting from 1930 by Albert Sebille shows a Roman warship. (© AAA Collection Ltd)

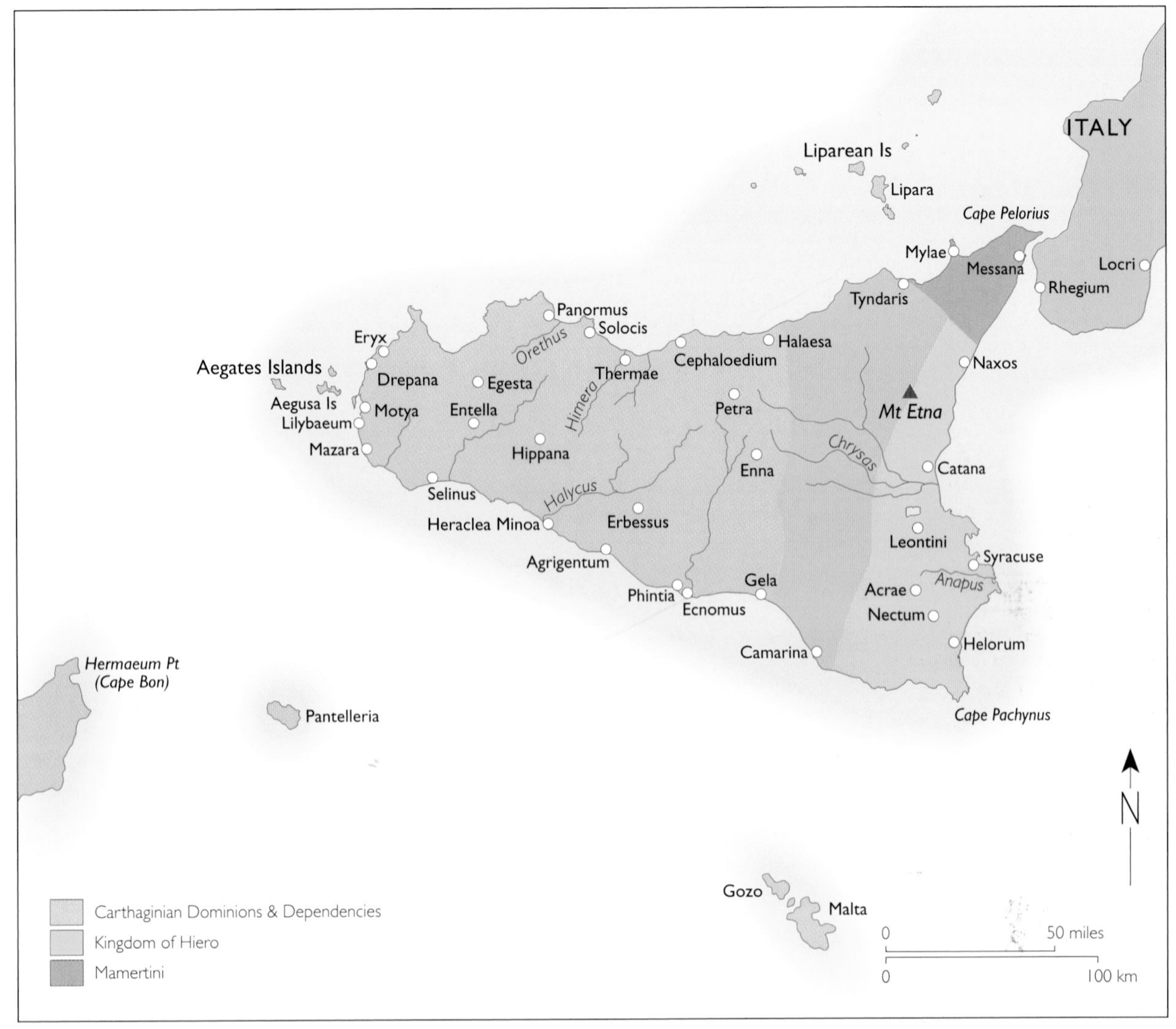

Sicily – the First Punic War.

up against. They also won Hannibal more recruits from Gaul – over 50,000 of them. Hannibal went on to defeat the Romans at Lake Trasimene, and then in 216BC Rome experienced her largest defeat ever when Hannibal's army destroyed the armies of Rome at Cannae.

In 210BC the Romans produced a 25-year-old military genius who they hoped would be at least a match for Hannibal. This was Publius Cornelius Scipio, who would later be known as Scipio Africanus. Knowing that Hannibal relied on Spain for most of his supplies, Scipio decided to cut Hannibal off logistically by taking Spain from him. Scipio began his assault on New Carthage almost immediately, from both land and sea. The city was soon secured, most of its citizens massacred, and an immense amount of booty taken. In 206BC Scipio finally defeated the Carthaginians at Ilipa, some ten miles north of modern Seville, to end the war in Spain. There were two main reasons for the Carthaginian defeat: first, their long enduring political dissension, reflecting the rivalry between those in Spain and Carthage; secondly, the

superior generalship of Scipio. Hitherto it had been the Carthaginians who had held the strategic initiative, but now it was the turn of the Romans, who would contain Hannibal in Italy while taking the offensive in Africa. After smashing their way across Carthaginian Africa, the Roman army proved too frightening a prospect for the political leaders of Carthage. In 202BC thirty members of the Carthaginian Council of Elders came to prostrate themselves before Scipio, and after cravenly blaming everything on Hannibal, sought his pardon. Scipio acted with commendable moderation in laying down his peace terms, which were accepted by the Carthaginians, and envoys were sent to Rome to seek ratification. Meanwhile, in the same year, Hannibal was brought to battle and his army destroyed at Zama, some 100 miles south-west of Carthage. Hannibal escaped, but as a defeated general rather than a victor. The war that had brought devastation to the whole of the Mediterranean during the previous 17 years had come to an end, leaving Rome as an imperial power of unmatched military might.

Hannibal was by no means the first military leader to employ elephants in warfare. Their use as a high point from which to fight, a heavy force with which to trample, and a way of gaining a huge psychological advantage over the enemy was also recognised by ancient Indian warriors, as this Macedonian ten-drachma coin from 325BC shows. Here, Alexander the Great attacks an Indian prince on an elephant. (© R Sheridan/ AAA Collection Ltd)

The Third Punic War (149–146BC)

The last Punic War was a much less honourable victory for Rome than the second had been, and a much more shocking waste of Carthaginian life. Concerned that the Carthaginians were once again becoming too powerful, Rome demanded that Carthage be abandoned, and the Carthaginians move to elsewhere in North Africa. Carthage's survival depended on its ability to trade via sea routes, so a move away from its seaboard was refused. War ensued. The adopted grandson of Scipio Africanus, Scipio Aemilianus, was given command in Africa, and he at once set to work constructing a huge mole which was to extend from the sandbar across Carthage's harbour mouth, bottling up the Carthaginian fleet, as well as sealing off any further supplies. Cut off from both land and sea, Carthage's fate was sealed. The Romans cleared the city of inhabitants, house by house, and after six days the Carthaginians offered to surrender, begging for their lives in return. After Scipio had accepted their request, some 50,000 terrified men, women and children, nearing the limits of exhaustion and starvation, filed out, later to be sold into slavery. The city was given over to plunder before the ruins were levelled to the ground.

After six centuries Carthage had been destroyed and the Carthaginians dispersed to suffer extinction, leaving no readily discernible religious, literary, political or social heritage. An eastern civilisation had been planted in the western Mediterranean, but after a period of luxuriant growth, it had been violently uprooted and exterminated.

Carthaginian troops

Carthage was primarily a trading nation seeking to extend its commercial connections, its sphere of influence, and its empire. A maritime nation supported by military force, Carthage was able to maintain her role and trading monopolies for three centuries, mainly through a superior navy. For home defence, expansion and ultimately the defence of her empire, Carthage came to rely almost entirely on soldiers levied from vassal states and allies, and on hired mercenaries. These soldiers seldom served in their own countries, except in Spain, and remained isolated from one another through differences of language and religion. They were largely dependent on the Carthaginian fleet for supplies, and discipline was enforced via a strict code, which included capital punishment.

The Numidians

The Numidians were nomadic tribesmen from modern Algeria: they and their land were so named by the Romans, Numidia meaning 'land of the nomads'. The camel had not yet been introduced into North Africa in the period of the Punic Wars, and these nomadic tribes relied exclusively on the horse as a means of transport – as a result their warriors were born horsemen, living on horseback from an early age. They used neither bit nor bridle, and rode bareback with only a neck strap of plaited rope for harness, using voice and a stick to guide their mount. The horses themselves were small but sturdy, accustomed to negotiating rough terrain, and were extremely agile and fast.

The tribesmen wore only their normal dress when in battle: a simple, short, sleeveless tunic, gathered at the waist by a belt, often of plaited rope. No doubt at night, and in the colder climate of northern Italy, the tunic was supplemented by a blanket or cloak of animal skin. Their only protection when fighting was a small, light, round shield and their own agility. This nimble, courageous and indefatigable cavalry were armed with spears and javelins; iron javelin heads and pointed iron butts have been found in a second-century BC prince's grave in Algeria. The Numidians do not seem to have had a second weapon, though no doubt they would have carried some form of knife or dagger in their belt. Excavations in Numantia in Spain have revealed slingshots of lead, baked clay and iron, some of them stamped and marked. Some of these are Roman, but others have been attributed to Numidian troops in the Roman army. The Numidians also fought dismounted, either in ambush or when overwhelming an enemy's cavalry by weight of numbers, and it seems likely they may have used the sling as a missile weapon in some circumstances – certainly their light javelins would have been of little use in a siege.

These lightly clad horsemen had superb fighting skills, both in the hills or on the plains, manoeuvring like flocks of starlings that wheel and change direction as if by instinct. Threatening and enticing, surprising with sudden and unexpected moves, there was no cavalry on the battlefield to match them. They would dart towards the enemy with great dash, hurl their javelins, then retreat before the enemy could strike back or make contact.

HANNIBAL

Born in 247BC, Hannibal Barca was only six years old when the First Punic War ended with his father's ignominious expulsion from Sicily. The event could hardly have affected him personally, had it not been for his father's enduring determination to seek revenge. Slowly, the enormity of the setback to Barcid pride and ambitions must have been conveyed to the boy, and then it was indelibly stamped upon his conscience during a religious ceremony. In 237BC, when Hannibal was ten years old and his father was preparing to take his army to Spain, while propitiating the gods with a sacrifice, he took the opportunity to make his son swear an oath on the sacrificial animal that when he grew up, he would never forget that Rome was the deadly enemy. Once in Spain, the mould of Hannibal's character and motivating force behind his life would have been forever cast. There could be no turning back, especially as Hannibal, like his father before him, was a warrior by nature.

Perhaps the highest tribute that can be paid to Hannibal's ability as a leader is to recognise the remarkable way in which he wielded such a disparate force of unpatriotic mercenaries into a cohesive fighting force, inspired with self confidence and audacity, ready to face severe hardships and near unbelievable risks.

That Hannibal understood fully the capabilities and limitations of those he commanded is shown in the way he deployed them on the battlefield. At Cannae, for example, it was the tough and reliable Libyans whom he placed in the two key flank positions where the encircling movement was to be hinged; his dashing and opportunistic Numidian cavalry were deployed on his open right flank.

Hannibal always led by example, whether swimming a river first in Spain, to encourage his men to follow, or, as Livy tells us, sharing their hardships and living like an ordinary soldier when campaigning, always sleeping on the ground wrapped only in his military coat.

Having praised Hannibal for his soldierly qualities, Livy proceeds to list, though without preliminary evidence, his shortcomings, depicting him as 'excessively cruel, with a total disregard for the truth, honour and religion, for the sanctity of an oath and all that other men held sacred'. The charge of cruelty might be a matter of mistaken identity: one of Hannibal's commanders is alleged to have advocated that his soldiers should be trained to eat human flesh, thus easing the army's logistics problem. It is possible that this ferocious individual, named Hannibal Monomarchus, committed acts of cruelty that were mistakenly attributed to Hannibal himself.

Admittedly, Hannibal must have shared many of the characteristics of a harsher age, but as a professional soldier he was undoubtedly a genius. His strategic vision threw the Romans on to the defensive and, for the first five years of the Second Punic War, permitted them to do little more than react to protect their homeland.

After the Second Punic War Hannibal was forced into exile, but wherever he sought refuge the Romans pursued him, accusing him of plotting against them – which he probably was – and demanded his extradition. Finally there was no way of escape. As Plutach wrote, Hannibal was cornered 'like a bird that had grown too old to fly', a state of affairs Hannibal himself must have recognised since he made no attempt to escape, contenting himself with saying 'Let us now put an end to the great anxiety of the Romans, who have thought it too lengthy and too heavy a task to wait for the death of a hated old man.' He took poison, and in 183BC, at the age of 64, the scourge of the Romans departed this life.

A profile of the popular image of Hannibal, from a 16th-century Italian coin. Hannibal's youth made him a popular hero figure both during his lifetime and beyond. There are some historians who now think that Hannibal could have been black, due to his ethnic origin as a Samnite from North Africa. (© R Sheridan/AAA Collection Ltd)

They were extremely adept at using cover, and time and time again lured their enemies into ambushes, or employed ruses in surprising their foes. They were superb in all these roles, or in pursuit, but were of little use as shock troops. At Cannae they were unable to break Rome's allied cavalry on their own, but once it had been broken by the Spanish and Celtic cavalry they were left to conduct the pursuit, which they did with the utmost effect.

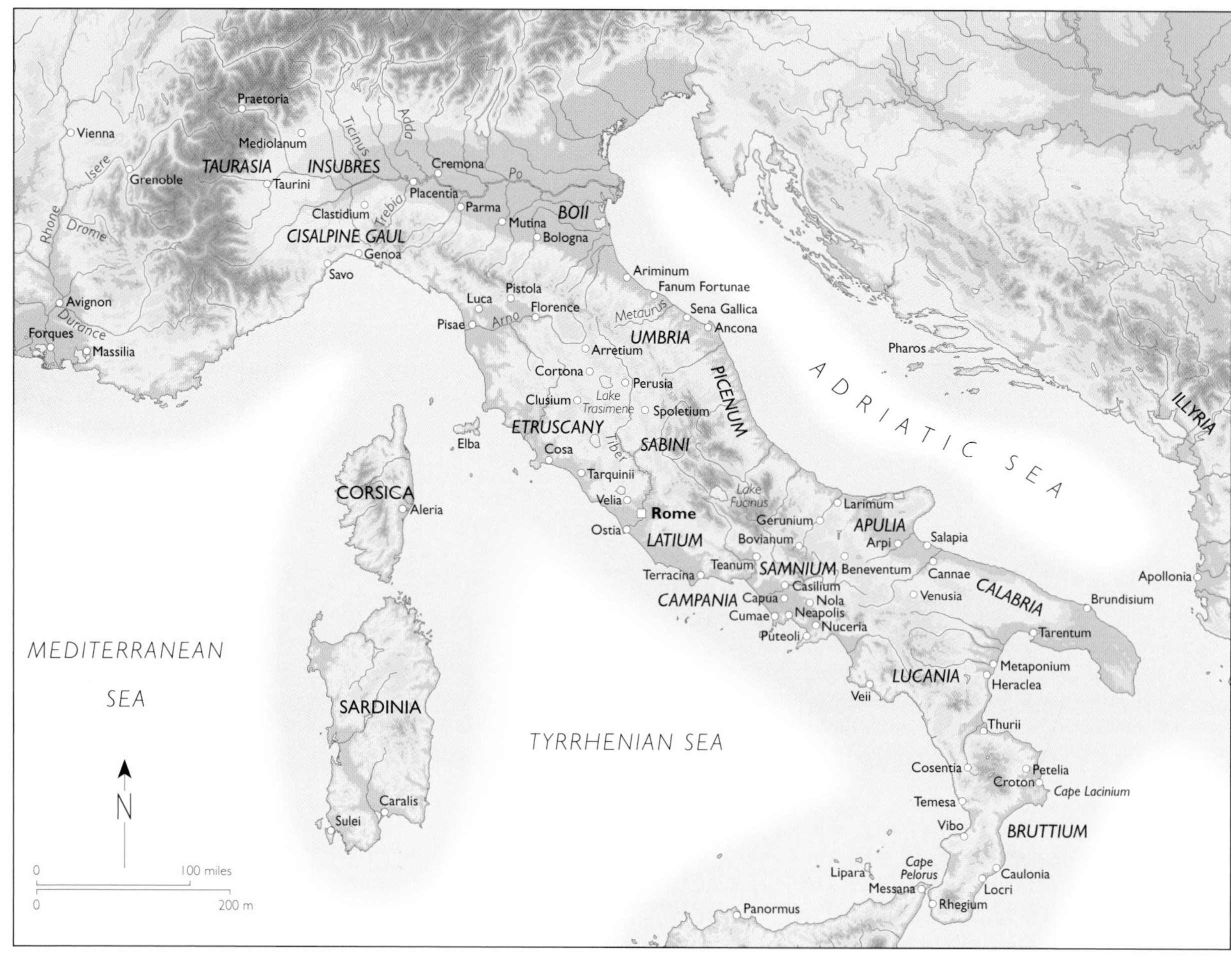

Italy – the Second Punic War.

Spanish troops

Though infantry soldiers were recruited from Spanish hill tribes, they were in perpetual conflict with one another, a national disharmony that had simplified the Carthaginian conquest of Spain. They were experts at guerrilla warfare but of temperamental disposition and doubtful loyalty, not best suited to set-piece battles. However, despite their shortcomings, the Spanish troops were a vital part of Carthaginian armies, and at Cannae Hannibal's army of 40,000 infantry and 10,000 cavalry included 2,000 Spanish cavalry, 6,000 swordsmen (heavy infantry) and 2,000 light troops. They were sorely missed after the battle of Ilipa (206BC) when many of Carthage's most powerful Spanish allies went over to the Romans.

Iberians

The original inhabitants of the Iberian peninsula were the Iberians, a people who were famed as warriors, and who served as mercenaries in many parts of the Mediterranean world. They had their own unique weapons and equipment, influenced by their experiences abroad. They served as mercenaries in the Carthaginian armies from at least 342BC.

The only source for the appearance of the Numidian warriors is Trajan's Column in Rome, erected some 150 years after the end of the Third Punic War. However, it would seem that the Numidian horseman portrayed on that column were no different from their predecessors – unarmoured and extremely mobile light cavalry, armed only with javelins and a small, light shield. The Numidian horseman is shown in combat with a Roman *eques*. (Painting by Richard Hook © Osprey Publishing Ltd)

Polybius says both infantry and cavalry wore a short white tunic with short sleeves, having a purple, or crimson, border at hem, neck and sleeves. It was gathered at the waist by a wide leather belt. Vase paintings of Iberian soldiers show them wearing the peasant's short tunic, probably of leather or wool. The Iberians did wear bronze helmets, but few have been found, and they seem to have been rare. It is probable that simple metal or leather helmets were worn by the ordinary soldier. Little is known of the body armour worn by the Iberians, if any. The limited evidence would suggest that only the chieftains wore mail armour. The cavalrymen wore long boots, which helped to protect their legs, with plain spurs attached. All heavy infantrymen were also protected by a large oblong shield. The light infantry used a distinctively Spanish shield, a light round buckler of leather or wood. This was used in conjunction with the sword, and the Spanish light infantry were

THE BATTLE OF CANNAE

The year 216BC marked the apogee of Hannibal's military career, with Cannae the foremost demonstration of his brilliance. In that year, the Roman Senate decided that Hannibal must be brought to battle, so four new legions were mobilised and ordered to join the four already shadowing Hannibal in Apulia; concentrated together they would then crush him, in accordance with traditional military thinking. Hannibal had occupied Cannae, giving his army an important opportunity to benefit from the excellent and much-needed food stores around the citadel. Ever mindful of the need to use every means in his power to force the enemy to fight, Hannibal had little doubt that the Romans would bring their army south to give battle.

So it was that the fatal day arrived, and it was Marcus Terentius Varro who exercised command at Cannae. At first light, he moved the Roman army across the river Aufidus on to the east bank. He positioned the cavalry on the right wing, resting on the river, with the legions next to them and the cavalry of the allies on the left wing. In front of the whole army were the light infantry. The deployment was conventional enough, but Varro shortened the frontages of the legions, and reduced the distances between the maniples within them. There was a reversion to the theory of sheer mass, so flexibility was renounced and the rigidity of the phalanx was reinstated. The Roman army numbered some 80,000 infantry and more than 6,000 cavalry. While the Romans were completing their deployment, Hannibal brought his army into line. His light infantry and Balearic slingers formed a screen behind which his main force matched the Roman deployment. On his left flank were the Spanish and Gallic cavalry, resting on the river, next to them his heavy infantry. The Gauls were thrown forward in an arc, facing and extending beyond the Roman front, with the Numidian cavalry on his right flank. Being thinly spread, Hannibal's 40,000 infantry retained the tactical flexibility to manoeuvre and slowly give ground before the massed Roman legions; the arc would be reversed to curve rearwards and as the Romans pressed forward, they would be enveloped. The risk was that the centre of the arc would be torn apart, in which case the battle would be lost, but Hannibal's cavalry were superior both in number – some 10,000 – and quality, so could be relied upon to defeat their Roman opponents and then complete the encirclement. That is exactly what happened. As the Romans pressed forward, the Carthaginian infantry overlapped their front and assaulted them on the flanks. Compressed together and unable to protect themselves, the casualties mounted and the forward momentum began to falter. Meanwhile, the Roman cavalry had been routed and the returning Numidians fell upon the Roman rear. Completely surrounded and still further compressed, the Romans were slaughtered where they stood. According to Polybius, only some 3,500 Romans managed to escape, while 10,000 were taken prisoner, and 70,000 left dead on the battlefield. Amongst those who escaped was the perpetrator of the disaster, Varro.

News of Cannae shook Rome to its very core. Even so, the Senate moved rapidly to assert social discipline and forbade public mourning or demonstrations of distress within the city. Taking the defeat as evidence of divine disfavour, a Celtic male and female and a Greek male and female were buried alive in the cattle market to placate the gods.

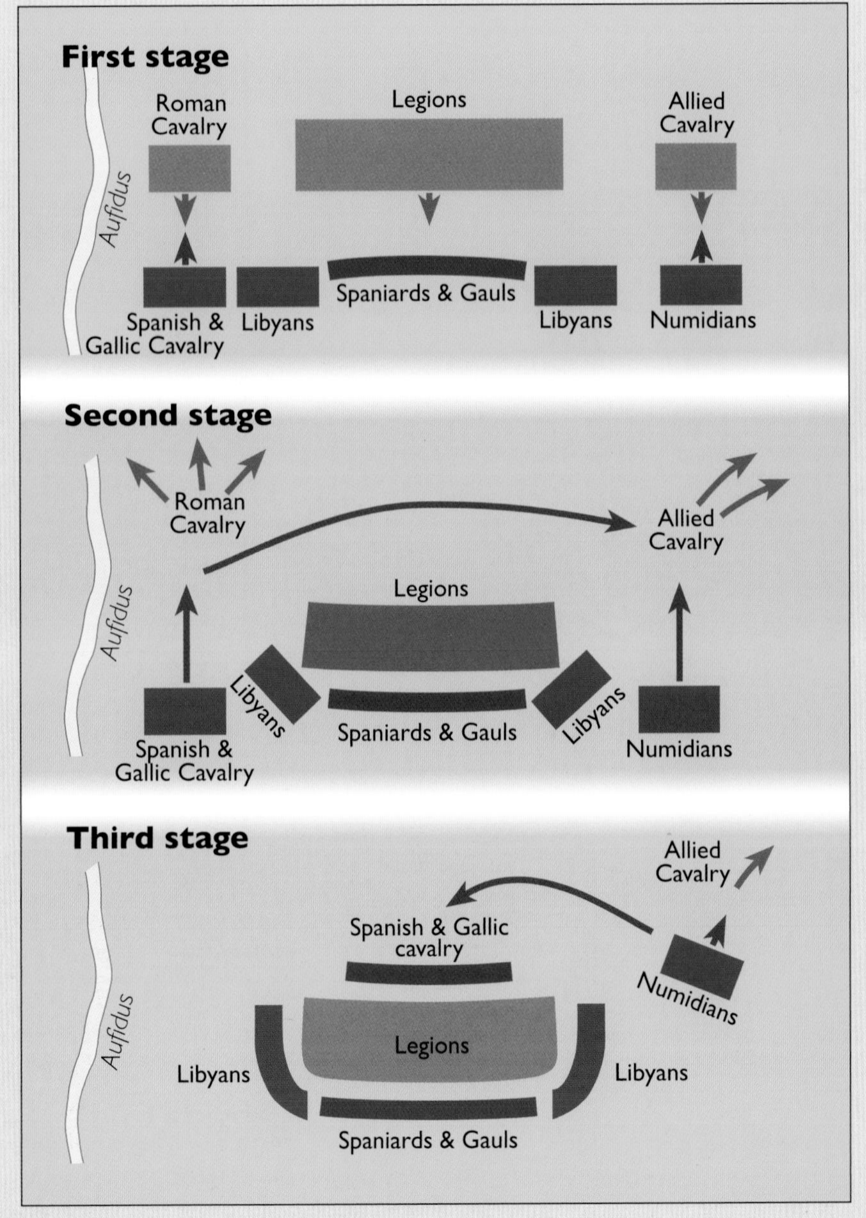

The battle of Cannae.

famous for their ability, speed and agility in this type of sword-and-buckler fighting. The sword was the main weapon of the Iberians. Single-edged for the first half of its length, the remainder of the blade was double edged and sharply pointed at the end. It was an excellent

The central figure is an Iberian horseman, based on contemporary sculptures, the rider on vase paintings, and his weapons on detail from coins and surviving examples. This type of horseman was essentially a light cavalryman (*jinete*). The figure on the left shows a Spanish heavy infantryman with definite Celtic influence on dress, arms and armour. The right-hand figure is an Iberian swordsman, armed with sword and buckler and completely unarmoured, as well described in ancient texts and represented in bronze figurines of warriors found in Iberian sanctuaries. (Painting by Richard Hook © Osprey Publishing Ltd)

weapon for cut and thrust work, and it was used thus by both the infantry and cavalry. In fact, the Carthaginian victory at Cannae is often attributed in part to the superiority of the Spanish sword over the short swords of Greek origin still being used by the Romans.

The Iberian heavy infantry of Hannibal's army seem to have been organised in small companies under their own chiefs – the troops using sword and buckler were included in this heavy infantry for, despite their lack of defensive equipment, their style of sword fighting verged on the acrobatic, and they were more than the equal of a Roman legionary in a straight sword fight. Another characteristically Iberian weapon was the slim javelin made entirely of iron, with a small leaf-shaped head, which was usually barbed. Pictorial sources show these javelins being used as a missile weapon, and according to Strabo it could penetrate helmet, shield and body armour. Another Iberian missile weapon was the *falárica*, described by Livy as a shaft of pine wood with a long iron head, around the end of which was a wrapping of tow and pitch, creating an incendiary weapon. Like so many other Spanish weapons, the *falárica* eventually entered the Roman arsenal as an artillery incendiary arrow. Iberian infantrymen also carried a dagger that was so broad at the base as to be almost triangular.

Spanish cavalry

The Iberian peninsula was famous for its horse breeding, and the Spanish horse was accustomed to difficult and mountainous terrain. Consequently, the Spanish cavalry, or *jinetes*, rivalled even the Numidian cavalry in swiftness and skill, though they seem always to have been deployed in the role of heavy cavalry on the battlefield.

Saddles do not appear to have been widely used, only a broad girth with a blanket, though a bridle and bit were used. The horse's head was often protected by some form of metal armour. The *jinetes* used the small, round buckler-style shields for defence, and their main offensive weapon was the lance. The cavalryman was also armed with a long, slightly curved sword, and often dismounted to fight alongside the infantry as necessary. Horsemen also sometimes carried other men on the back of their horse into battle, when the second man would dismount to fight on foot.

Balearic slingers

From the Balearic Islands came the formidable slingers. Balearic slingers were used in the Carthaginian armies from at least 337BC, and they formed an important part of the Carthaginian troops in the Punic Wars, giving them a decided advantage in skirmishes with javelin-armed light troops, for the sling had greater range and effectiveness. Balearic slingers were said to be superior in fire and accuracy to the best contemporary archers. They were generally organised into corps of 2,000 men who were armed with three types of slings, one for long-range engagements against a densely packed enemy, one for medium range fire, and the other for close-quarter, individual targets up to some 900 feet. Their delivery of stones or lead could penetrate a helmet or light protective armour. These were savage fighters who were often paid in women rather than gold or silver.

Balearic slingers wearing simple tunics and minimal equipment. They normally carried three slings, for different ranges. The knife is characteristic of finds in the Balearics and faintly similar to the *falcata* shape (see p121). (Painting by Angus McBride © Osprey Publishing Ltd)

The Libyans and Moors

The largest mercenary contingent in the Carthaginian army were the Libyans of Tunisia. Hardened by the harsh conditions of their own country, they were versatile fighters who served both as light infantry skirmishers and in the heavily concentrated infantry of the line. Polybius says they formed the nucleus of both the infantry and cavalry arms, but he does not give numbers. Moorish bowmen are mentioned at Zama in 202BC.

The Celts

Known to the Romans as Gauls, the Celts originated in southern Germania (Germany), but gradually spread across western Europe until, by the third century BC, they had overrun and settled in Belgica (Belgium), Noricum (Austria), Helvetia (Switzerland), northern Italia (Italy), Suebia (Bohemia), Hungaria (Hungary), Illyria, parts of Gaul, Hispania (Spain) and Britannica (Britain), and crossed into Asia to settle in Galatia (Turkey). The Celts had a long history of fighting the Romans, since they first attacked Rome in 390BC, sacking the city. Consequently, during the Punic Wars the Carthaginians found the Celts willing allies, and Hannibal's army arriving in Italy contained over 40 per cent Celts.

The upper and middle classes of the Celtic tribes were a warrior class – they lived only for war. Like most such warriors, they were fiercely proud and undisciplined: to a Celt, a battle consisted of simply charging straight for your enemy (preferably down a slope) and defeating him face to face, man to man, in a sword fight. They were excellent swordsmen, and when controlled by a general such as Hannibal proved to be valuable soldiers. In the Carthaginian armies the Celts were probably organised into small companies under their own chiefs.

The chieftains and richest warriors often wore armour, particularly after contact with the Greeks and Romans, whose armour they adopted. In earlier times, however, most Celtic warriors scorned the use of armour and preferred to fight without it, often stripped to the

The Celts carried large shields to protect the whole body – this was crucial considering that many Celts fought stripped to the waist, and their shield was their only form of armour. Some wealthy Celts wore helmets, but many preferred simply to stiffen their hair with limewash. This bronze shows a Gallic Celt. (© R. Sheridan/AAA Collection Ltd)

waist. Some Celtic tribes still fought without armour at the time of the Second Punic War. Strange to relate, therefore, that the Celts were manufacturing mail shirts from around 300BC: the high cost of manufacture was probably the main factor that restricted its use to the aristocracy. After the battles of Trebia (218BC) and Lake Trasimene (217BC) many of the Celts were probably equipped with mail shirts taken from the Roman dead, and this was almost certainly the case after the battle of Cannae (216BC). The Celtic shield was usually oval, made of oak planks, and reinforced with felt or hide. A wooden spindle-shaped boss covered a central hollow for a hand grip, and this boss was sometimes reinforced by a broad strip of iron nailed to the planking. The outer face was frequently painted with animal or geometric designs.

The Celtic warrior was essentially a heavy infantryman equipped with helmet, large shield and long sword. Even when totally unprotected except for a shield, he fought in the main body of the heavy infantry, not as a skirmisher, although some of the youngest and most inexperienced warriors were probably used as light troops, armed with javelins.

The Celt's sword was his prime weapon, between 75 and 80cm long, double edged, and with a somewhat rounded point. It was used as a slashing weapon, swinging from side to side, or by whirling it round the head and bringing it down like an axe. Its length and method of use required space, and the Celtic warrior fought independently as an individual, relying mainly on agility as a defence. It was this method of fighting which at first struck fear into the hearts of opponents; but the Romans soon came to realise that their disciplined ranks and the use of reserves could defeat the best Celtic warriors, and Hannibal seems to have used his Celts mainly as a softening-up force to break the Roman ranks before launching his prime troops – the African infantry. Despite heavy losses, the Celts accepted this role, for it gave them the position of honour. The Celts showed great dash in the attack, but they were sometimes unreliable, especially when hard-pressed.

The Carthaginians

There were also native Carthaginians in the army, but their number was never very great and they were mainly confined to a few hundred heavy infantry called the Sacred Band. From this force the long-term professional leadership was selected, thus ensuring that the generals who commanded the mercenary army came from amongst their own citizens. Prior to the First Punic War, the native Carthaginians are described as splendidly armed with iron breastplates and brazen helmets, bearing great white shields covering most of their bodies, and marching in a slow and orderly fashion. This suggests a phalanx formation. They were supported by four-horse chariots.

During the Second Punic War allies were recruited in Italy and Macedonia, and when the war moved to Africa and Carthage itself was threatened – in both the Second and Third Punic Wars – the citizens of Carthage also took the field. After the First Punic War Carthage was able to raise 10,000 citizen soldiers. No attempt was made to organise this heterogeneous mass of troops into a uniform army. Each native group fought in its own way and to its best advantage.

ELEPHANTS

The Carthaginians were introduced to the elephant by Pyrrhus, king of Epirus 295BC–272, and promptly abandoned their war chariots in favour of it. They first used the elephant against the Romans at Agrigentum in Sicily in 262BC. Initially the Carthaginians only used the African elephant found in the forests around Carthage, at the foot of the Atlas Mountains and along the coast of Morocco. This forest elephant was really too small to carry anything but an unsaddled warrior. There is a coin that shows a war elephant being ridden bareback by a cloaked driver, and it is almost certain that the elephant itself was the weapon. Later it seems probable that Hannibal obtained some of the larger Indian elephants from Egypt. Until tactics had been developed to counter them on the battlefield, elephants struck terror into men and horses alike, and their small numbers were disproportionately effective. When frightened, however, they sometimes wreaked devastation in their own ranks by turning and charging.

As early as 274BC, at the battle of Beneventum, the Romans had perfected tactics for dealing with elephants – light troops waving torches of burning straw. However, it seems each generation of soldiers had to encounter elephants at least once before being able to stand up to them successfully.

Despite two notable successes in the First Punic War, elephants were of little use in the second and third wars. Of the 34 which Hannibal tried to take to Italy, all but seven died during the crossing of the Alps, and only one survived the bitter winter that followed.

Hannibal obtained more elephants in 215BC, but seems to have used them primarily to frighten native tribes who had never seen elephants before, or against cavalry whose horses had not been trained to meet them.

Effectiveness of Carthaginian army

At the beginning of the First Punic War the Carthaginians were twice defeated by the Romans in Africa. We must assume they were still fighting in the phalanx formation. At about this time a Spartan adventurer called Xanthippus arrived at Carthage with a band of Greek mercenaries. His criticism of the Carthaginian army came to the ears of the Carthaginian leaders, and Xanthippus found himself appointed leader of that army! During the winter of 256–255BC, Xanthippus is said to have reorganised the army in the Greek style and to have drilled it to perfection. This would have meant a series of phalanxes, each of some 4,000 men in 256 files, each 16 men deep. Xanthippus also introduced successful new tactics to the Carthaginian army, as can be seen in their success in the battle of Tunes in 255BC. Placing 100 elephants in the front line to break up the legions, he positioned the cavalry and light troops on the flanks with the heavy infantry phalanxes extended across the whole battlefield. As the phalanxes were concealed by the cavalry and light troops, the Romans did not realise their own heavy infantry line was outflanked. Shattered by the elephants and outflanked on both wings, the Roman army was completely defeated, losing some 15,000 men out of 20,000.

The fact that Hannibal crossed the Alps with 34 elephants is well known. However, less well known is the fact that most of them died either on the journey, or in the harsh winter that followed. (© Prisma/AAA Collection Ltd)

The African infantry of Carthage continued to be armed and fight in this manner until after the battle of Lake Trasimene (217BC), when Hannibal re-armed his heavy infantry with Roman weapons and equipment and incorporated in their drill all the best features of Roman training and tactics.

The African infantry with Hannibal in Italy was gradually reduced in numbers and the losses were not made good. Hannibal received only one reinforcement from Africa during his 15 years in Italy – 4,000 Numidian cavalry and some elephants. The gaps in his ranks were instead filled with Celts and Italians, who were not of the same calibre.

Carthage's reliance on a mercenary army was probably caused by the shortage of manpower: there may have been just too few men to do any more than crew their extensive fleet of warships and numerous trading vessels without endangering their commercial activities. Historians differ in their views as to the effectiveness of the Carthaginian army. Some claim that the mercenaries were not united by any common or reciprocal interest and had no long-term concern for the well-being of those they served, who were, in turn, largely indifferent to the mercenaries anyway. Others point out that though there were incidents of desertion and cowardice, as well as bloody mutiny, such incidents were not exclusive to mercenaries. On balance, except for the long time it took to recruit, train and deploy a large mercenary army in an emergency, the defects and inadequacies of the system look exaggerated. To a large degree, the effectiveness of Carthaginian arms depended on the quality of the general and his ability to hold these forces together and use them in the most effective way. It was these abilities which made Hannibal such an outstanding commander: in all his 15 years of fighting in Italy there were only two occasions when he lost absolute control, and even then only small units deserted. Whatever the composition of Hannibal's army and however few Carthaginian officers he may have had in relation to his men, these were not factors of great significance; what mattered was the magnetism of his leadership.

The Carthaginian navy

The navy played a vital part in the Carthaginian war machine and, unlike the army, it was manned entirely by Carthaginians. There were three basic types of ships: large cargo vessels which were easily converted to troop transports; warships; and small, general-purpose vessels. There were two basic battle tactics. In both instances, the fleet was initially deployed in line ahead, but the subsequent action depended on the enemy's dispositions. If there was sufficient space, the Carthaginian ships would move alongside the enemy and by suddenly turning, ram them amidships. If there was not enough room for this manoeuvre then the Carthaginian vessels would break through gaps in the enemy line and turn about sharply to take them in the rear. The Carthaginians, then, had a potent navy, which assured them of sea supremacy at the outbreak of hostilities. With the versatile use of cargo ships as troop transports, they possessed a strategic mobility that offered a unique advantage over any opponent, so long as they had commanders capable of exploiting this superiority.

This 16th-century plate depicts Hannibal's cavalry defeating a large coalition of Spanish tribes on the banks of the Tagus river in 220BC. Hannibal subdued the Spanish tribes in preparation for his assault on Italy. Within two years he had subjugated the lands of Spain between the Tagus and Ebro rivers. (© R Sheridan/AAA Collection Ltd)

Chapter 4
THE HELLENISTIC EMPIRES

Macedonian campaigns against Rome

The Hellenistic power struggle

When Alexander the Great died in 323AD he left behind him three major Hellenistic kingdoms – the kingdom of Macedonia; the Ptolemaic kingdom of Egypt; and the Seleucid kingdom. The size and power of the Hellenistic empire under Alexander had far surpassed anything yet achieved by the Romans – Alexander had ruled over everything east of Rome. This expansionist policy did not die with Alexander, but went on to influence the strategic decisions and military activity of other Hellenistic rulers, and by around 200BC, the three main Hellenistic kingdoms effectively held control over the eastern Mediterranean.

Alexander the Great brought the Macedonian kingdom to great prominence before his death in 323BC. This mosaic from Pompeii depicts the battle of Issus, where the Persian king Darius III Codomannus was defeated by Alexander and his trusted general Parmenion. The fact that this scene should appear in a Roman house shows the esteem in which Alexander was held by the Romans, who wanted to associate themselves with his successes. (© Michelle Williams/AAA Collection Ltd)

The extent of Macedonia during this period.

The three kingdoms did not sustain an easy balance of power, and frequently fought with one another for territory and control over Hellenistic lands. Alliances were forged and broken between all three kingdoms, and appeals even made to Rome to intervene on the side of one or another of the powers. Rome, however, did not engage militarily with Greece until an alliance was forged which she could not ignore. Philip V became of serious importance as a threat to Rome when he allied himself with the recently triumphant Hannibal, just after the Second Punic War. It could well have been Hannibal who initiated

A coin showing Philip V of Macedonia, 238–179 BC. (© R Sheridan/AAA Collection Ltd)

this alliance, as he wanted assistance with his plan to capture Rome, and saw Philip V as a valuable ally. By making this agreement with Carthage, Philip V of Macedonia made the First Macedonian War unavoidable.

The First Macedonian War (214–205BC)

Although Rome probably never actually declared war on Macedonia in 214BC, the fact that Rome was at war with Carthage, and Carthage was allied with Macedonia (and, indeed, using Macedonian troops), meant that Rome was, by proxy or otherwise, also at war with Macedonia. The Roman praetor Marcus Valerius Levinus organised a fleet to watch out over the Adriatic from Apulia for any activity from Philip around the area of Illyria. Sure enough, in 214BC Philip was fighting in Illyria, so the Roman fleet crossed the Adriatic to engage with Philip's forces. Philip's only chance of escape was to burn his fleet of ships, which he did. It must have become apparent to Philip that his chances of effective campaigning by sea were slim, with Rome's navy watching from the coast opposite. However, Rome's land armies were severely depleted after their ongoing campaign with, and recent defeat at the hands of, Hannibal and the Carthaginians, so the land route to Illyria was a much safer bet for Philip and his forces. With the Romans unable to send out troops to halt a land advance, much ground was gained and many cities captured by the Macedonians before the Romans could stop Philip's advance.

The greatest Roman fear was that Philip would be able to assist Hannibal, so his march had to be stopped somehow. Rome decided upon a strategic alliance with a group who already had experience of fighting Philip, and who were much better placed to keep control of his advance. The Aetolian League were old enemies of the Macedonians, having fought with them in many Hellenistic power struggles. In 211BC, an alliance was set up between the Aetolians and Rome, the terms of which make Rome's priorities and intentions at this time clear. In return for fighting with Rome against the Macedonians, the Aetolians were allowed to keep any towns they conquered along the way. Rome would take only those things that could be taken away – any navies, and spoils. Clearly, land was not what motivated Rome in this fight, it was the prevention of Philip assisting their greatest enemy, Hannibal.

Although the Aetolians did capture a few towns, the years following 211BC were uneventful in campaign terms, and there were few, if any grounds for continuing the war. Philip appeared to be heading back to Macedonia, and Roman fear of attack, and interest in helping to defend Hellenistic lands, waned. In 207BC Philip invaded Aetolia itself – to no Roman response. Proconsul Publius Sulpicius Galba Maximus sent no troops to liberate Aetolia, and by 206BC the Aetolians were suing for peace, having given Philip back all of the towns they had captured. Galba objected to this, and eventually sent a small force of 35 ships and 11,000 troops, but it was too little too late, and the Aetolians held firm to their new agreement to Macedonian terms. In 205BC, the treaty of Phoenice was drawn up, marking the formal end of the First Macedonian War. Under the terms of the treaty, Philip could keep all the lands he had gained, but had to pledge to not take action against Rome in the Adriatic. For Rome, this was essentially an agreement by Philip not to help the Carthaginians, who were certainly the enemy Rome feared most at this time, and towards whom Rome could now concentrate all her attention.

The Second Macedonian War (200–197BC)

Whilst Philip had been focusing on alliance with Carthage and war with Rome, another Hellenistic leader had been pushing back his boundaries and expanding his empire. Antiochus III of the Seleucid kingdom was already being called 'the great' by the Greeks, just as they had called Alexander, and his armies had been advancing through Asia Minor, capturing city-states on the way and leaving them as vassal states of his kingdom. Meanwhile, in the Hellenistic empire of Egypt, a child king, Ptolemy V, was on the throne, and the situation was precarious. Antiochus could not let this opportunity to control Egypt go unexploited, so he sought a treaty with Philip V, to aid him in gaining Egyptian lands. Philip was probably relieved that Antiochus did not have Macedonia in his sights, so he accepted the treaty, and they agreed to divide Egypt up between them.

Antiochus then turned in the direction of Coele-Syria, while a Roman presence in the west made Philip look east, to Thrace and Ptolemy's lands in the Aegean. In 201BC, Philip took troops across the Hellespont, with the intention of conquering Caria. He was driven back by an alliance of Pergamum, Rhodes and Athens, who then sent an embassy to Rome, to complain about Philip's campaigning, and appeal for Roman assistance against Philip. Rome's response was to send envoys to demand Philip and Antiochus stop their campaigns, and for Macedon to become a Roman province under the command of Publius Sulpicius Galba Maximus.

A coin showing the head of Ptolemy V Epiphanes from 210BC. Ptolemy V was the fifth ruler of the Ptolemaic dynasty, and he was made king at the tender age of five, after the death of his father and the murder of his mother. The ceremonies carried out at the coronation of the young king are detailed on the trilingual Rosetta Stone. Ptolemy V married Cleopatra I, and died aged 28 in a battle against insurgents. (© R Sheridan/AAA Collection Ltd)

Although Rome may have had little interest in Greek lands, she was interested in making sure the Hellenistic kingdoms were not united against Rome. Thus it was in Roman interests to stop any one empire becoming too strong. Although the Senate had been wary of war, especially at a time when Roman manpower resources were so depleted in the wake of constant warring with Carthage, Galba was intent upon it. There may also have been a feeling of wanting to teach Philip a lesson, for his foolish alliance with Rome's greatest enemy at that time – Hannibal. The first ultimatum sent in 200BC by envoy to Philip was ignored, as Philip promptly invaded Attica and attacked towns in Thrace. The rudeness of the second envoy so angered Philip that he cut short negotiations, and went back on campaign, sealing the onset of the Second Macedonian War.

Having alienated most of his Hellenistic neighbours, Philip was in a vulnerable position against Rome. Not only did he have few allies, but he had many enemies who would not hesitate in supporting a Roman attack on Macedon. By 199BC, Galba had inflicted a few minor defeats against the Macedonians, but more importantly the Achaean League, the Aetolians and the Athenians had all pledged their support to Rome. By 198BC, the consul in charge of Macedon was a young man, under 30, called Titus Quinctius Flamininus. He went to Greece and negotiated peace terms with Philip, who offered to give up the lands he had captured since 200BC, and to pay reparations. This was not enough for Flamininus, who demanded Philip relinquish all Greek lands, including Thessaly, which had been under Macedonian control since the middle of the fourth century BC. Philip refused to agree to these terms, as they effectively meant giving up any positions of power. Flamininus marched to Thessaly, taking two legions including the Cannae legion, who had been fighting with Carthage for 14 years, and had not seen their homes during that period. Flamininus also gathered reinforcements from Greek states along the war, including 6,000 Aetolians. The two armies met on the battlefield at Kynoskephalai (197BC).

A bust of Titus Quinctius Flamininus, the victor of the battle of Kynoskephalai in 197 BC. (© R Sheridan/AAA Collection Ltd)

The Macedonians fought in a phalanx formation, and they met the Romans in a head-on charge. At first, the Romans were unprepared for the ferocity of the Macedonians, but their strength as a phalanx was also to prove their undoing, when, having been overstretched by the Roman line in a second charge, the Macedonian phalanx fell apart. The more manoeuvrable manipular formulation used by the Romans meant the scattered Macedonians could then be picked off in small groups by the Roman maniples. The Romans emerged victorious, and seized control of the area. Philip was forced to give up all the lands he had acquired, with the exception of Macedonia, and Macedonia was ordered to pay a large reparation fee to Rome. Flamininus then went on to carry out some mopping-up campaigns, to isolate Macedonia and push her boundaries firmly back. Despite pressure from other Greek states to depose Philip completely, Flamininus instead went for a controlled containment, since a deposition would have removed one of the factors preventing another strong Hellenistic power from taking over. The final peace terms also attempted to put a stop to Antiochus' plans in Asia, since the Asian lands garrisoned by Philip and Antiochus were also to be handed over to Rome. In a perfect PR move, Flamininus eventually used the Isthmian games of 196BC to make the following announcement, as reported by Plutarch:

> ...the Roman senate and Titus Quinctius Flamininus proconsular general, having conquered King Philip and the Macedonians, restored to freedom, without garrisons and without imposts, and to the enjoyment of their ancient laws, the Corinthians, the Locrians, the Phocians, the Euboeans, the Achaeans of Phthiotis, the Magnesians, the Thessalians, and the Perrhaebians. At first, then, the proclamation was by no means generally or distinctly heard, but there was a confused and tumultuous movement in the stadium of people who wondered what had been said, and asked one another questions about it, and called out to have the proclamation made

> again; but when silence had been restored, and the herald in tones that were louder than before and reached the ears of all, had recited the proclamation, a shout of joy arose, so incredibly loud that it reached the sea. The whole audience rose to their feet, and no heed was paid to the contending athletes, but all were eager to spring forward and greet and hail the saviour and champion of Greece.

By granting this freedom, Rome had ensured her safety from one large powerful Greek state, but without incurring the cost and manpower of policing the states from garrisons within. Flamininus was hailed as a heroic strategist, and two years later, when the Roman forces left Greece in 194BC, Rome felt assured of her control over Philip as a client-king.

The Third Macedonian War (171–168BC)

As it turned out, the lack of understanding over each other's concept of 'freedom' was a significant contributory factor in the Third Macedonian War breaking out 25 years after the last one had ended.

In 179BC, Philip V died. The year before he died, he executed his youngest son Demetrius, having been convinced by his eldest son, Perseus, that Demetrius was becoming over-fond of Rome and that he was a potential threat to Philip's power. With Demetrius thus despatched, it was Perseus who took over control of Macedonia in 179BC. Perseus immediately set about making himself an enemy of Rome, by arranging strategic marriages, re-establishing old allegiances with the Achaean League, and pushing his boundaries back to the north and south, which went against the terms of earlier treaties. Neighbouring Hellenistic kingdoms, far from seeing Perseus as a potential ally, became increasingly suspicious of his actions and started reporting them directly to Rome. In 172BC, one of the most loyal allies of Rome, Eumenes, king of Pergamum, arrived in Rome with a long list of complaints against Perseus, many of them carefully casting the worst possible light on the leader of Macedonia. At first, the Senate were unswayed by these reports, as there was so little desire to go to war after nearly a century of fighting. However, despite Perseus himself sending envoys to Rome to argue that war was not their intention, the Senate became convinced by Eumenes after he was involved in an accident which he clamed was an assassination attempt. Coinciding with this accident, trouble was stirred up once more in Illyria, and the Romans quickly blamed Perseus, once more giving Rome grounds to go to war with Macedonia.

Rome immediately sent out envoys to the Greek states, to ensure their continued support, and troops were sent to Epirus to prepare for an attack on Macedonia. The Romans were keen to establish themselves in Greece in good time for the campaigning season, so a trick was played to delay Perseus. A consular legate called Quintus Marcius Philippus went to Perseus to suggest he try harder to convince Rome that Eumenes was wrong in his accusations. It was suggested to Perseus that negotiation might be possible.

This delaying tactic effectively achieved a truce over the winter, giving the Romans valuable time to get their legions ready in Greece for war the following year. Philippus then set about making sure that none of the Hellenistic leagues could assist Perseus. Meanwhile, in 171BC the Roman army landed on the coast of Ilyria under the consul Licinius Crassus.

Once war was declared, Crassus experienced defeat at Thessaly. He was furious, and blamed the Aetolians for their lack of support. The Romans set about sacking not only enemy Greek towns, but allied ones as well, as retribution for their lack of support causing, as Crassus saw it, the failure at Thessaly. This made the Romans most unpopular with their one-time allies in Greece. The behaviour of the Roman army at this time was undisciplined and uncontrolled, which reflected the lack of effective reform therein over the previous years. Greek towns were destroyed and inhabitants sold into slavery. It seemed that more effort was being put into plundering towns for spoils, than strategically preventing an invasion by Macedonia.

For the next few years, the war turned into a series of raids on towns, and complaints against corrupt Roman consuls, until by 168BC, finally, a consul was put in place who could restore discipline to a Roman army that seemed to have lost its own, and gone feral. Lucius Aemilius Paulus, the new consul, quickly brought the Roman army in line with reorganisation and intensive retraining. He amassed a large force, which marched northwards, to meet the Macedonians in battle at Pydna on 22 June 168BC.

The Macedonians may have restocked their ranks since their crushing defeat at Kynoskephalai in 197BC, but they had not yet abandoned the phalanx, which was once again to be their undoing. The broken ground of the battlefield at Pydna made the tightly packed phalanx formation almost impossible to sustain, and the Macedonian army suffered massive losses – nearly 25,000 dead. Perseus escaped, but found no allies prepared to stand up to Rome for him, and so he was forced to surrender. Paulus then seemed to lose the discipline which he had showed in his organisation of the Roman army, by encouraging the army to once more wreak revenge on those Greek states who had not aided Rome in its fight against Macedon, or who had ever aided the Macedonians. Thousands were killed or sold into slavery, and huge gold and silver reserves seized.

As for Macedon, since the Romans had proved their inability at keeping it contained as one kingdom, they split it up into four smaller republics, none of which could aid the other since they were denied the right to trade with each other or inter-marry – *commercium* and *conubium*.

The Macedonian army

Professionalisation of the army

It is clear that the Macedonian army had, at one time, been one of the most effective fighting forces in the world, since it was this army that Alexander the Great used to build his extensive empire. The effectiveness of the Macedonian fighting force was largely due to the reforms of Philip II, built upon by the military genius of Alexander.

THE BATTLE OF PYDNA

The battle of Pydna was the final shot of the Third Macedonian War, and is a classic example of how manipular warfare could prevail over a phalanx formation in uneven territory. That is not to say that the Roman victory was solely due to their battle formation, however – the strong command of Aemilius Paulus enabled the Macedonian weaknesses to be seized upon by the Romans. As the final battle of four years, it is ironic that the battle itself was over and done with within a single hour; however, the favourable conditions, terrain and fighting style of the Romans made victory swift and decisive.

In the summer of 168BC, the new Roman commander Aemilius Paulus wanted to meet Perseus and his army head-on in battle, but Perseus had entrenched his men in a strong position on the river Elpeus from which he would first have to be lured. The cunning Paulus staged a very visible movement of 8,200 infantry and 120 cavalry troops to the coast, under Scipio Nasica, to make Perseus believe that the Romans were planning an attack from the sea. When night fell, however, Scipio moved his entire force south over the mountains to Pithium. Roman plans were nearly wrecked when a deserter informed the Macedonian army of the Roman position, and a force of 12,000 was sent by Perseus under Milo to prevent the Romans from reaching the Macedonians. However, Milo's force were defeated, and retreated back to the Macedonian camp, where Perseus, fearful now of his supply chain being cut off, made the decision to move to ground better suited to his phalanx.

Meanwhile, Scipio's force was reinforced by the arrival of the rest of the Roman troop under Paulus. At this stage, the Roman army numbered 38,000 – around 33,400 infantry and 4,000 cavalry, including 22 elephants. The Macedonian force was of a similar size, being around 44,000 men, 21,000 of which were in the phalanx, 3,000 were *hypaspists* (see p81), and around 4,000 cavalry, the rest being peltasts (see pp82–83), allied infantry and mercenaries.

What exactly started the battle of Pydna is not clear, but many cite the catalyst as an escaped horse, chased by the Romans in the direction of the Macedonians, causing a small skirmish that in turn escalated. If, indeed, this is how the battle started, it may well have been Paulus who 'helped' the horse to escape, in order to choose for himself the hour the battle would start. It may not, then, have been a coincidence that the battle did take place in the afternoon, when the sun was behind the Romans, and shining into the faces of the Macedonians. The catalyst might also have been due to a few Romans getting a little too close to the enemy, and being fought back by Thracians from Perseus' army.

The Roman army was formed with its legions in the middle, flanked by allied infantry, then cavalry on each wing, with the elephants on the right. The Macedonians flanked their central phalanx with peltasts, *hypaspists* and other allied infantry and mercenaries. The Macedonian cavalry was split between wings, with the skilled Thracian cavalry and Perseus' own elite cavalry squadron on the right. Drawn up in this way, the advance of the heavy phalanx was very strong, and the Roman army looked, for a while, as if they would not be able to recover from being pushed back from the phalanx. However, as the Macedonian army continued to push forward, the ground on which they marched became more and more uneven, meaning the phalanx could not maintain its all-important hegemony, and small gaps started to appear. These Paulus seized upon, using the flexibility of the manipular formation to send small groups into these gaps, where they could then attack the enemy in their vulnerable positions, from the rear and in the flanks. This should not have been able to happen, as Perseus had light troops on the field that could have been sent forward to fill the gaps, but it seems Perseus had lost his grip of command on the field. His phalanx was unable to turn, since the men were too tightly packed to untangle their *sarissae* sufficiently. Some discarded their *sarissae* to afford them greater movement, but this meant they were only armed with their short sword, which was no match for the weapons carried by Romans. Gradually, more gaps appeared, and were taken advantage of by the Roman manipular army, until the phalanx was completely broken apart, and the surviving Macedonians fled, some say with Perseus and his cavalry at the front. Around 25,000 Macedonians were killed, including all of the elite guard. Reports of only 80–100 Roman dead may well be a gross under-estimate, but it is clear that the Romans suffered nowhere near the losses of the Macedonians, and were the clear victors, honoured by a triumph march when they returned to Rome.

Crucially, Philip II made soldiering an occupation that was sufficiently well paid to be a full-time role. This ensured a group of men who could devote the time required to training and drill, to make sure they fought as a well-trained, highly responsive cohesive unit. Until this professionalisation of the soldier, Macedonian troops were drawn as and when they were needed, after which time the soldiers returned to their peacetime roles as farmers, merchants and craftsmen, thus forgetting much of what they had learned. By continuing the training throughout periods of peace, the Macedonian army kept up their knowledge of tactics and manoeuvres that were so essential for an effective phalanx, and improved between battles, instead of losing their skills.

The Macedonian infantry

Infantry was the key component of the Macedonian army, like most armies at this time. Troops were drawn using a territorial system established in earlier reigns, each province of Macedonia providing one *taxis* or regiment. These *taxeis* were under the command of a local noble from each province, and were often named after their commander.

The phalanx

Philip II organised his army in a phalanx formation, as did Alexander, and then Philip V. The phalanx centred around a core of infantry, or *pezhetairoi*. The advantage of this formation was that it presented a very strong shield-wall, which could be almost impossible to penetrate from the front. Soldiers in a phalanx stood close together, so that the overall strength of the phalanx could be greater than its component parts. The main weapon of the Macedonian phalanx was the *sarissa,* a pike with a wooden shaft, a metal tip, and a butt-spike at the other end. The remarkable thing about the *sarissa* was its sheer length – Polybius says it was 14 cubits, which is over 6m long. For obvious reasons, the *sarissa* was no good for close-hand fighting, so the phalangites were also armed with a sword or dagger. The *sarissae* were presented in a variety of ways, giving the phalanx more opportunity to inflict damage upon the enemy, as well as defend themselves from enemy missiles and charges. Traditionally, the first five ranks of the phalanx held their *sarissae* projecting beyond the first line. The other 11 ranks held their *sarissae* vertically, to break up the effect of any missiles, and also to hide the manoeuvres of the rear ranks from the enemy, affording an element of surprise. If a soldier held his *sarissa* upright during battle it was a sign of surrender. However, the Romans were not aware of this at the battle of Kynoskephalai in 197BC, resulting in hundreds of surrendering Macedonians being cut down by advancing Romans.

Macedonian phalangites carried a small round shield, and wore helmet and greaves often made from bronze. There is evidence, however, that the back ranks of the phalanx wore little or no armour, affording them greater ease of movement. Armour would, of course, be less crucial in this position, unless the front ranks of the phalanx were destroyed.

The phalanx was a very effective formation for heavy head-on charges. In fact, in head-on battles a phalanx army was hard to beat due to the fact it acted almost as one huge impenetrable weapon. However, in rough or broken terrain, unsuitable for head-on charges, the very unity that gave the phalanx its strength also became its greatest weakness. As soon as the phalanx had been split up, it was unable to operate in the manner in which the phalangites had been drilled, and it became ineffective. The phalanx was particularly susceptible to attack from behind.

This is an early example of the Macedonian helmet, from the sixth century BC. The front ranks of the phalanx would have worn helmets, though the further back the ranks were, the less likely they were to wear, or need, armour. (© Ronald Sheridan/ AAA Collection Ltd)

The hypaspists

Hypaspist means 'shield-bearer' in Greek, and the role was closely associated with the king's personal guard. It is thought the regiment had originally been formed from the personal retainers of the King's Companions. The *hypaspists* acted as a flexible link between the cavalry and the phalanx, and were more lightly armed than the other infantry. The *hypaspists* seem to have been the only infantrymen to wear boots, and their tunics were let down at the shoulder to allow free movement of the right arm. There is evidence that they were

The tightly packed formation of the phalanx is clearly shown by this carving from around 400BC, showing hoplites with shields and spears. (© R Sheridan/ AAA Collection Ltd)

sometimes armed with spears, and sometimes *sarissae*, and carried round shields. Since they were more lightly armed than the *pezhetairoi,* they could be used for swifter action, and often accompanied the cavalry. The *hypaspists* were hand-selected from the *pezhetairoi* for their skill and merit.

Peltasts

Either side of the phalanx in battle formation were two flanks of peltasts. These were light infantry, their name coming from the *pelta* – a light wicker and animal-skin shield. Peltasts were originally Thracian infantry, armed with javelins and daggers. The lightness of armour allowed peltasts to evade the charge of heavily equipped troops, and yet hold an advantage over lighter troops, such as archers, in hand-to-hand fighting. Peltasts were also cheaper to equip than the regular phalangites.

Cavalry

Under Philip II and Alexander, the Macedonian state had been capable of raising large numbers of cavalry, principally because of the 'Companion' system of recruiting from noble

families within Macedonia and its ally states, deliberately supported by land-grants and by other devices, which extended the potential pool of propertied horse-owning cavalry recruits. Subsequent social change in Macedonia, coupled with lack of state finances, served to diminish the numbers of cavalry available for recruitment by the state. During their wars with the Romans, the Macedonians were rarely able to raise more than a few hundred horsemen. Consequently, the Macedonians came to rely more and more on their phalanx to achieve victory, but they rarely had sufficient cavalry available to secure its flanks. Rome frequently enjoyed a considerable superiority in cavalry during her battles with Macedonian and Greek armies, and this was a principal factor in Roman victories.

The Macedonian cavalry were armed with a long cavalry spear called a *xyston*, which had spearheads at each end, due to the fact it often shattered in battle – either end of the shattered half could then be used as a shorter spear. The *xyston* was used as a stabbing spear, and the cavalryman also carried a sword slung under his left arm (and thus frequently obscured by the cloak in surviving representations).

Had the Macedonians of the second century possessed an effective cavalry arm to protect the flanks of their phalanx and to attack the legions, the battles of the Macedonian Wars might have turned out very differently.

These bronze greaves from the fourth century tomb at Derveni would have been either purely ceremonial, or worn by a very wealthy warrior. The fact that they were included as grave goods shows their high value. (© R Sheridan/ AAA Collection Ltd)

Allied troops and mercenaries

Manpower

Perhaps the most important factor in the defeat of the Macedonian army by the Romans was Roman superiority in manpower. It was Rome's capability to mobilise such huge armies that defeated Macedon, rather than any innate superiority of the Roman military system. No matter how many armies the incompetence of Roman military commanders might lose, there was always a near-inexhaustible reservoir of manpower to draw on. The first years of the Third Macedonian War saw many Roman reverses, but these didn't matter; all that mattered was the last battle.

Philip was unable to use significant numbers of his troops against the Romans because he had to guard his eastern borders against constant incursions by the Maedi. He therefore made extensive use of foreign troops and mercenaries.

Thracian troops

Philip V of Macedon occupied all the cities in Thrace up to the Hellespont, and made extensive use of Thracians in his army. At the battle of Kynoskephalai in 197BC there were

2,000 Thracians in Philip's army. The Thracian peltasts won skirmishes against Roman and allied Greek troops, and helped to push back the Roman left wing. In 190BC, 10,000 Thracians from the Astii, Caeni, Maduateni and Coreli occupied each side of a narrow forested pass and waited for Roman troops to march along the Hebrus valley in south-eastern Thrace, having just left the battlefield at Magnesia. They waited until the vanguard had passed, then attacked the baggage train and, killing the escort, began to loot the wagons. The Roman vanguard and rearguard rushed to help, and fighting began at several points. The battle swayed from one side to another according to the terrain, the numbers involved, and the courage of the combatants. The booty hampered the Thracians, as most of them left their arms behind so that they could carry away more spoils. The unfavourable ground, on the other hand, made the Romans vulnerable to the barbarians. Livy says:

This painting shows the Kallinikos skirmish of 171BC, a prelude to the battle of Pydna three years later. The Thracian King Kotys and his bodyguard cavalry, in co-operation with the Macedonian cavalry, charge in wedge formation ('like beasts of prey long held behind bars' – Livy) at the Aetolian cavalry, who form the flank of a Roman army. King Kotys is in front, with a Thracian bodyguard to the right and a Macedonian cavalryman to the left. (Painting by Angus McBride © Osprey Publishing Ltd)

Livy says that the victorious Thracian troops returned to their camp after the Kallinikos skirmish, swaggering, singing and dancing, with severed Roman heads as trophies. On the left and right are Thracian infantrymen, and in the middle a Thracian slinger. (Painting by Angus McBride © Osprey Publishing Ltd)

> Many fell on both sides and night was already coming on when the Thracians drew off from the fight, not to escape wounds and death, but because they had as much plunder as they wanted.

When Perseus rebuilt the Macedonian army he was joined in 171BC by Kotys, king of the Odrysai, with 1,000 picked cavalry, and about 1,000 infantry. Perseus already had 3,000 free Thracians under their own commander in his forces; these fought 'like wild beasts who had long been caged' (Livy) at the Kallinikos skirmish that year, defeating the Roman-allied cavalry. They returned from battle singing, with severed heads as trophies. Their performance at the battle of Pydna (168BC) was less remarkable – they are only mentioned in the accounts when running away! Perseus' riverbank guard of 800 Thracians precipitated the engagement after an argument midstream over a baggage animal that had escaped its Roman groom. Thracian infantry also led the Macedonian army out of camp; and 200 Thracian and Cretan archers fought on the Roman side. Perseus lost this battle, and Thrace west of Hebrus was incorporated into Macedonia, which was partitioned. From then on Thracian kings used Roman troops to secure their regimes; they acted only with the approval of Rome, and their children were held hostage there.

Cretan archers

For centuries, Cretan archers had been used in Greek and Macedonian armies, due to the great skill the Cretans had with the bow. Cretan boys were trained in archery from the age of seven, so their ability and accuracy was finely honed by the time they reached a battlefield. Cretan archers were a highly prized addition to many armies at this time, and Alexander seems to have had a company of Cretan archers from the beginning of his reign. These Cretans could have been mercenaries, but it is more likely that they were an allied contingent supplied by those cities of Crete favourable to Macedon.

Cretan archers were quipped with a small bronze *pelta,* which enabled them to fight at close quarters, as well as provide missile fire. They also served under their own officers. During the battle of Pydna, Cretan archers were mixed with Thracian archers, suggesting that both were equally as effective and accurate. Polybius claimed that the Cretans were highly effective as skirmishers, and Philip often used them as such in his rearguard whilst the army were in the field.

LATE REPUBLIC 150BC–27BC

Dominating the entire Mediterranean world, Rome continued to expand her frontiers through the superiority of her armies.

At home, however, the government was showing signs of strain, designed as it was for a regional republic, not an international superpower.

Rome's guardian soldiers would soon appear in the city in a far more menacing form...

BRITAIN
GERMANY
BELGICA
GAUL
DACIA
CISALPINE GAUL
ILLYRICUM
THRACE
ITALY
MACEDONIA
SPAIN
MEDITERRANEAN
SICILY
MAURETANIA
NUMIDIA
NORTH AFRICA
N
0
250 miles
0
500 km
The Roman Republic after the Punic Wars
Additional territory added to the Roman Republic by 27BC

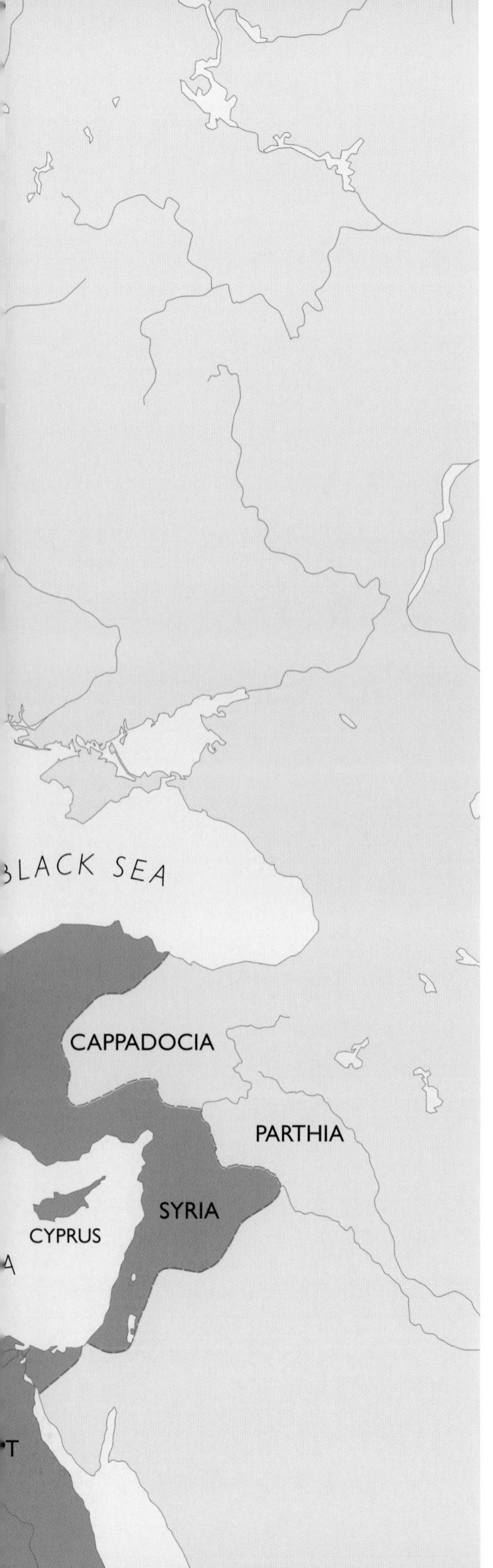

CHRONOLOGY

133	Start of Roman civil unrest
111	Start of war with Jugurtha
105	End of war with Jugurtha
104–100	Marius wins successive consulships
100	Birth of Julius Caesar in Rome
91–89	Social War; Roman citizenship granted to Italians
89–63	Three wars with Mithridates of Pontus
87–83	Marius and Sulla engage in civil war
82–81	Sulla is dictator of Rome
78	Death of Sulla
70	Pompey and Crassus are consuls
60	First Triumvirate: Julius Caesar, Pompeius Magnus (Pompey the Great) and Licinius Crassus
55	Triumvirate renewed for another five years Death of Lucretius
55–54	Caesar's expeditions to Britain
53	Crassus killed by Parthians at Carrhae
52–51	Caesar victorious in Gaul
52	Pompey is sole consul
49–46	Caesar and Pompey engage in civil war
48	Death of Pompey after battle of Pharsalus
47–44	Julius Caesar rules as dictator of Rome
44	Caesar is murdered
43	Second Triumvirate: Mark Antony, C. Julius Caesar Octavianus, M. Aemilius Lepidus
42	Brutus and Cassius commit suicide after defeat by Antony and Octavian
30	Antony and Cleopatra commit suicide after battle of Actium
27	Octavian becomes Augustus

Chapter 5
THE ROMANS

Background

By the end of the Third Punic War in 146BC, Rome had the bulk of Europe and some of Africa already sewn into the tapestry of her lands. Rome dominated the entire Mediterranean world, having defeated with ease the successor kingdoms that had emerged from the break-up of Alexander the Great's empire.

However, Rome was still a republic, organised as a regional, not a world power, and sooner or later the wealth and power gained from conquering new lands would become impossible to control by a government created to lead a small fledgling republic. The stability and unity of purpose which had so characterised Roman political life for centuries began to break down. Politicians started to employ violent means to achieve their ends, the disputes escalating until

A stone carving of Roman senators in procession. The Senate was the governing council of the Roman Republic, and the role of senator was much sought-after by citizens of Rome, as it brought with it power, fame and wealth. The Senate was supposedly designed to keep a check on any one family or individual becoming too powerful, but in reality the Senate contained many members of old patrician families of Rome, who had achieved their position through unashamedly self-promoting, and employing nepotism. (© R Sheridan/ AAA Collection Ltd)

they became civil wars fought on a massive scale. These violent clashes between legions constitute some of the major conflicts of the period, though there were still plenty of foreign wars taking place to keep the legions busy abroad. The impact of these foreign wars on the stability and development of the Republic are also marked factors of this period.

Foreign fighting

The Numantine Wars

Rome's first significant foreign threat during this period came from the territory of Numantia in early Spain. The Celtiberians had many times resisted Roman control in the region, repeatedly fighting back Roman attempts to take over Numantia, the town marking the centre of Celtiberian resistance to Roman rule. The Celtiberians had achieved many victories against the Roman army, and were even responsible for a serious decline in morale, as the length of service of Roman soldiers in Spain became greater and greater, with no immediate sign of achieving the victory that Rome so badly wanted. Scipio Aemilianus was eventually given control of the Roman army in Spain in 134BC, and he set about restoring the army to previous levels of discipline and mental and physical strength, before embarking on the decisive clash with the Numantians. Eventually, an eight-month siege of the town in 133BC, led by Scipio Aemilianus, sealed its fate, and its starving inhabitants could no longer hold back the forces of Rome. Numantia, like Carthage and Corinth before it, was razed to the ground, and those inhabitants who had not died from the siege, or taken their own lives to avoid Roman capture, were either sold into slavery, or forced to fight under Scipio to gain more wealth for the very power that had caused its destruction. Numantian lands were divided amongst its neighbours, to avoid any single power becoming too strong, and Scipio added 'Numantinus' to his own name.

However, Celtiberian resistance to Rome was not completely extinguished by this savage destruction of its major city, and it was not until the rule of Augustus, in 19BC, that the last Celtiberian uprising was successfully crushed.

The Mithridatic Wars

If Hannibal had been the nemesis of Rome at the end of the third century BC, the first century saw Mithridates taking on this role. Indeed, the defeat of Mithridates promised such reward for any commander able to achieve it that it caused the first military intervention in Rome. Sulla's decision to march on Rome with his legions in 88BC was as a direct result of his replacement by Marius in the Mithridatic Wars.

Mithridates was the king of Pontus in north-eastern Asia Minor, and his rise to power warned of his ruthlessness, involving, as it did, the murder of both his brother and mother, and the taking of his sister as his bride. As was inevitable of such a driven ruler, Mithridates' policies were aggressively expansionist, and he had Roman lands in Asia in his sights. In 89BC, Mithridates invaded the Roman Asian province of Pergamum, at a loss of far more than just land to the Romans. The Greeks who had been living under Roman rule saw a quick opportunity for defection, and just as Hannibal had done in the Second Punic War, Mithridates boosted his manpower with these disaffected ex-subjects of Rome, keen for revenge. In 88BC, Mithridates took Athens from Roman control, and led attacks on Rhodes. His zeal to rid Asia Minor of Romans knew no bounds, and Rome was about to get a taste of the lengths to which Mithridates would go. He ordered the execution of every Roman citizen in Asia Minor and the surrounding areas, and over 80,000 Romans were put to their death in the wholesale slaughter. If Rome had been angry at the loss of her provinces, it was nothing compared to the horror and wrath she felt at this massacre. In 87BC Sulla, having fought with Marius for the command against Mithridates, took five legions and marched to Athens. A bitter two-year siege of the town resulted in its eventual surrender and recapture by the Romans, and Archelaus, Mithridates' general, retreated with his forces to Macedonia where he met and joined up with another Mithridatic army. By the time Sulla's forces met Archelaus' army again in 86BC, the Romans were outnumbered three to one. Sulla overcame the differences in strength through his great skill in battlefield command at the battle of Chaeronea. Sulla routed the Mithridatic army, which fled as a force of only 10,000 from the original 120,000 who had started the battle.

Unable to return to Rome to claim a triumph, since he was still considered a public enemy after marching on Rome in 88BC, Sulla instead stayed in Asia Minor and entered into negotiation with Mithridates for the ending of hostilities – he wanted rid of the king of Pontus, so he would be free to devote his energies to enemies in Rome. Mithridates was ordered to give up the lands he had seized (no great hardship since most of them had already been taken back by the Roman forces), pay a tribute, release the prisoners of war, and provide Sulla with a large fleet and spoils with which to return to Rome. In return, Mithridates would be allowed to return to his original lands, as a friend of the Roman people, exactly as he had been before he had invaded Roman provinces in Asia.

Sulla, backed by a considerable force of men, now trained his sights on Rome, leaving behind L. Licinius Murena to take care of Asia for Roman interests. Murena reopened hostilities with Mithridates in 83BC, against the terms of the peace settlement, but after a few Roman defeats, this short war ended in 81BC, and peace reigned once more between Mithridates and the Romans. This was shattered in 74BC when the king of Bithynia, Nicomedes IV, died and left his kingdom to Rome. Mithridates could not countenance a new Roman province so close to his own lands, and so he invaded Bithynia, starting the Third Mithridatic War. A series of Roman generals, starting with Lucullus, experienced defeat and victory in engagements with the Mithridatic forces, until Pompey was sent out in 66BC. Sulla had died, and Pompey was his successor in Rome, keen for military glory to cement his political fortunes. It was after his defeat by Pompey in Armenia in 63BC that Mithridates eventually took his own life, heartbroken at his betrayal by his son, who led a rebellion against him.

The Gallic Wars

When Julius Caesar engineered for himself the governorship of Cisalpine Gaul (northern Italy) and Dalmatia in 59BC, there was no doubt that he would conduct campaigns to enhance his military reputation and political future. When the governorship of Transalpine Gaul (southern France) was added to his command, and the Helvetii in Switzerland began a huge migration, Caesar decided to campaign in Gaul.

Over the next few years the Romans made rapid conquests throughout Gaul. Few Gallic armies were capable of resisting the disciplined and well-equipped Roman legions, and Caesar was able to draw on an increasingly large and experienced army, as well as allies from Gaul and occasionally Germany to supply him with cavalry in particular. Within three years of leading his army into Gaul, Caesar was able to pronounce that the whole province was conquered and lead his army into Germany and across the Channel to Britain, expeditions that provoked shocked admiration back in Rome.

Gaul may have been conquered, but the Gauls were not. The last years of Caesar's command were spent dealing with sporadic revolts across the province, which were followed in 52BC by a major uprising. Finally the Gauls had found a leader who could unite them: Vercingetorix. It was at Alesia that the whole war in Gaul came to a climax, and when the army raised to relieve the besieged Gauls was repulsed, the war was effectively over. The relieving army dissolved and Vercingetorix surrendered. Although it was not until the reign of the first emperor, Augustus, that Gaul was properly pacified (and even after that there are indications of the occasional rumble into the mid-first century AD), the Gauls were never able to unite effectively again. Gaul became several Roman provinces, and Julius Caesar went on to fight and win a civil war.

Conflict at home

Marius and Sulla

In 88BC, Marius was given command of the army engaged in the wars with Mithridates. This, as we have seen, was a key appointment for any commander, as it offered the greatest of rewards – glory. Marius was not the original recipient of this golden ticket, however. His early protégé, Lucius Cornelius Sulla, had been given the honour of the command already that year, but while he was away completing his campaigning in Italy prior to embarking on his Mithraditic campaign, the situation changed. Having drummed up huge popular support, Marius had allied himself with a tribune with an axe to grind – Publius Sulpicius Rufus – who proposed a plebiscite on replacing Sulla as the commander of the armies against Mithridates. The people voted for Marius to replace Sulla, and an envoy was sent to inform Sulla of this news. Sulla took the news badly, as his stoning to death of the envoy suggested, and set about organising his five legions to do the unthinkable – march on Rome. For the first time in her history, Rome's streets were filled with armed citizen soldiers, heading for the Senate. Through fear of violence, the Senate gave in to Sulla's demands for his opponents to be outlawed, and Marius fled to Africa. Having secured support in the Senate (as much through fear as respect), Sulla left for Greece to fight the Mithridatic Wars. With victory in Greece secured, Sulla returned to Rome to find a new Marius in charge. In Sulla's absence, Marius had seized back control, died, and his son, also

POLITICAL BACKGROUND

Since much of the fighting engaged in by the Roman army at this time was essentially political, it is important to explain the origins of the political strife.

The Roman republican system was intended to prevent any individual or group within the state from gaining overwhelming and permanent power. The Republic's senior executive officers or magistrates, the most senior of whom were the two consuls, held power (*imperium*) for a single year, after which they returned to civilian life. A mixture of custom and law prevented any individual being elected to the same office in successive years, or at a young age, and in fact it was rare for the consulship to be held more than twice by any man. Former magistrates and the pick of the wealthiest citizens in the state formed the Senate, a permanent council that advised the magistrates and also supervised much of the business of government, for instance, despatching and receiving embassies.

The Roman political arena was fiercely competitive, as senators pursued a career that brought them both civil and military responsibilities, sometimes simultaneously. It was very rare for men standing for election to advocate any specific policies, and there was nothing in any way equivalent to modern political parties within the Senate. Each aristocrat instead tried to represent himself as a capable man, ready to cope with whatever task the Republic required of him, be it leading an army or building an aqueduct. Men paraded their past achievement and – since often before election they personally had done little – the achievements of past generations of their family. Vast sums of money were lavished on the electorate, especially in the form of games, gladiator shows, feasts and the building of great monuments. This gave great advantages to a small core of established and exceptionally wealthy families who, as a result, trended to dominate the senior magistracies. The higher magistracies and, above all, the consulships offered the opportunity for the greatest responsibilities and therefore allowed men to achieve the greatest glory. The consuls commanded in the most important wars, and in Rome military glory always counted for more than any other achievement. The victor in a great war was also likely to profit from it financially, taking a large share of the booty and the profits from the mass enslavement of captured enemies. Each senator strove to serve the Republic in a greater capacity than all of his contemporaries.

However, in the late second century BC the system began to break down. Rome had expanded rapidly, but the huge profits of conquest had not been distributed evenly, so a few families benefited enormously. The gap between the richest and poorest in the Senate widened, and the most wealthy were able to spend lavishly to promote their own and their family's electoral success. It became increasingly expensive to pursue a political career, a burden felt as much by members of very old but now modestly wealthy families as by those outside the political elite. Such men could only succeed by borrowing vast sums of money, hoping to repay these debts once they achieved the highest offices. The risk of failure, which would thus bring financial as well as political ruin, could make such men desperate. At the same time, men from the richest and most prestigious families saw opportunities to have even more distinguished careers than their ancestors by flouting convention and trying to build up massive blocks of supporters. Both types were inclined to act as *populares*, an abusive term employed by critics to signify men who appealed to the poorer citizens for support by promising them entertainment, subsidised or free food, or grants of land.

In addition to internal strife within the Senate, tension was caused by the fact that Italy's economy and society had been changed by Roman expansion and the influx of huge numbers of slaves. The population of Rome itself had swollen to 1,000,000 by the end of the first century BC, a high proportion of them without steady employment, and this produced a dangerous instability.

This statue of Vercingetorix is from Alise-Sainte-Reine, Cote-d'Or, in France. Caesar said of Vercongetorix:

> Himself a man of boundless energy, he terrorised waverers with the rigours of an iron discipline.

(© R Sheridan/AAA Collection Ltd)

called Marius, had been passed control in his place. The armies of Sulla and Marius met in bloody civil war at the Colline Gate in 82BC, and Sulla emerged the victor. For nearly two years, Sulla ruled as dictator with absolute power (an emergency magistracy concentrating power in his hands), and only laid this down when he went into voluntary retirement.

Pompey and Caesar

The chaos of the civil war and the rapid collapse of the Sullan constitution after his retirement in 79BC fostered a continuation of political disorder, and eventually the renewal of open war in 49BC. This period also had a profound influence on the careers and attitudes of the main protagonists in 49–45BC. Caesar himself first rose to prominence during Sulla's dictatorship, narrowly avoiding execution by the dictator when he publicly celebrated his relation by marriage to Marius at a family funeral.

However, a far more dramatic role was played by Cnaeus Pompey, who in 83BC came to the support of Sulla at the head of three legions raised from his family's estates and veterans who had served under his late father, Pompeius Strabo. At the time Pompey was

There is evidence that Julius Caesar suffered from epilepsy, and seizures, or *defectio epileptica*, are mentioned in many Roman sources, such as Suetonius and Appian, Plutarch even states that Caesar was affected by an epileptic seizure whilst he was fighting in the battle of Thapsus. (© AAA Collection Ltd)

only 23 and, having never held public office, had no legal authority on which to base his power. Fighting with distinction in Italy, Sicily and North Africa, Pompey was granted the title 'Magnus' ('The Great') by Sulla, though this may have been more than a little ironic. After Sulla's retirement, the Senate continued to employ the services of this private citizen and his personal army. Employing Pompey, rather than a legally appointed magistrate under their control, set an exceptionally bad precedent. Probably the Senate felt that, since Pompey and his legions existed, it was better to use him than risk his turning against them.

In 71BC Pompey returned victorious from Spain, and decided to stand for the consulship the following year. He was too young, and had held none of the normally

WHO IS SPARTACUS?

Although inextricably linked in popular imagination to Kirk Douglas in the Stanley Kubrick film of 1960, the real Spartacus was born some two thousand years earlier, a native of Thrace. Spartacus had served in the Roman army as a mercenary, but he was later sold as a slave, and bought at auction by the owner of a gladiator school in Capua. In 73BC, Spartacus escaped the school with 77 other men, and fled to the hills around Mount Vesuvius. Over time, more escaped slaves, gladiators and convicts joined Spartacus' band, and before long there were 70,000 disaffected rebels. Having first dismissed the small scale of Spartacus' army, the Senate soon realised that they were a force to be reckoned with, and sent an army of 3,000 Roman soldiers to suppress the uprising. Spartacus' army defeated the Roman force, as well as the next one sent to quash them of 6,000 men, much to the horror of Rome. Spartacus' plan seems to have been to lead his army northwards through Italy, cross the Alps and then disperse when they got to Gaul. During this journey Spartacus gave final proof to Rome, if proof were needed, that his army were a serious threat, when they massacred a Roman army of two legions – a total of 10,000 men, at Mutina (modern-day Modena), under the governor of Cisalpine Gaul, Cassius Longinus. Although their advance seemed to have been proceeding well, Spartacus seems to have changed his mind and he and his rebel slave army marched south to seek plunder. It was clear that a decisive move was needed to prevent this slave rebellion from getting any further out of hand, so Crassus was appointed to organise the defeat of Spartacus' army. Crassus was a wealthy man, and built up a large force, which pursued Spartacus' army down to the Italian peninsula, effectively trapping them there. When a Roman prisoner was crucified by the rebel slaves, the Senate recalled Pompey from Spain and Lucullus from northern Turkey, to combine their forces with that of Crassus. Spartacus' army was eventually defeated on its way to the port of Brundisium, and Spartacus died on the battlefield. Six thousand of the rebel slaves were crucified along 200km of the Appian Way between Capua and Rome under Crassus' orders. They hung there as a warning to other slaves that the might of Rome would eventually catch up with any rebellion, though Spartacus and his army had certainly given the Roman army a run for their money.

required junior magistracies, but he kept his legions outside the city as a scarcely veiled threat. Marcus Licinius Crassus, who had just returned from suppressing Spartacus' slave rebellion, took the opportunity to retain his own army and in turn declared himself a candidate for the consulship.

Crassus was exceptionally wealthy, his fortune based originally on property confiscated from Sulla's executed opponents. The Senate was forced to permit their candidature and the Roman people, who were on the whole well disposed to both men after their successes, duly elected Pompey and Crassus as consuls for 70BC. Thus Pompey at the age of 36 entered the Senate directly as a consul, an utterly unprecedented action. His military record was already spectacular, but, given his age, he clearly expected to be given further important tasks.

Pompey's first major achievement was to suppress the pirates plaguing the Mediterranean. He orchestrated the command for this campaign in 67BC, as he knew it would bring early glory. A combination of careful organisation, massive resources, and a willingness to accept the surrender of pirate communities and resettle them elsewhere allowed Pompey to achieve victory in under two months. In 66BC, again by popular vote, Pompey was sent to Asia to continue the fighting against Mithridates of Pontus. The war was virtually over before Pompey arrived, so it took little time for him to complete the defeat of Mithridates, who committed suicide when his own son turned against him. Pompey then proceeded to campaign throughout the near east. After a three-month siege, Pompey took Jerusalem. He and his officers went into the Holy of Holies in the Great Temple, although they declined to take any of its treasures.

This was a great propaganda success, the Roman aristocracy always striving to be the first to do any spectacular deed. Pompey disbanded his army, and returned to Rome to celebrate an especially lavish triumph. Now he had two main political objectives: the first was to gain formal approval for all of his reforms in the eastern provinces; the second was to secure grants of land for the soldiers who had served him so well. However, despite his military greatness, Pompey was no politician, and opposition from Crassus amongst others meant the argument over his requests dragged on for nearly two years and was finally resolved in a manner that astounded most senators.

The First Triumvirate

In 60BC Julius Caesar returned from Further Spain, where he had campaigned with success against local tribes. Six years younger than Pompey, Caesar's career had been fairly conventional up to this point, although his lavish spending on games and public feasting, combined with his rakish lifestyle, had won him numerous political enemies. Having won the right to celebrate a triumph, Caesar hoped this honour would permit him to win the consulship for 59BC. Around this time Caesar made approaches to both Crassus and Pompey and managed to reconcile them. Together the three men formed a secret political alliance, which is known by historians as the First Triumverate. To cement the alliance, Pompey married Caesar's daughter, Julia, a union which, for all its political inspiration, proved to be a very happy one. In return for supporting his candidature, Caesar undertook to gain land for Pompey's veterans and to secure the ratification of his Eastern Settlement. Caesar won the election, and was granted special command of three provinces, Illyricum, Cisalpine Gaul and Transalpine Gaul (modern-day Provence in southern France) for five years. Caesar departed for his provinces in 58BC, never to return to Italy until the beginning of the Civil War (about which more is explained in Chapter eight). Very much the junior partner of the triumvirate, Caesar needed military glory to rival Crassus and, especially, Pompey. At first he appears to have contemplated a Balkan war against the Dacian King Burebista, but the news of the migration of a Gallic tribe towards Transalpine Gaul shifted his focus away from Illyricum. Over the next years Caesar campaigned throughout Gaul, twice bridged the Rhine and marched into Germany, and led two expeditions across the sea to Britain. That island remained unconquered, but the euphoria over Caesar's expeditions could be compared to the excitement that greeted the moon landing in 1969. Caesar won massive glory in his Gallic campaigns (about which more can be read in Chapter six), and produced his *Commentaries*, probably published in annual instalments, to celebrate his achievements. As well as gaining glory, Caesar became one of the wealthiest men in the world, from plunder and the sale of slaves, hundreds of thousands of whom were captured during the conflict.

The figures of a Gallic prisoner, flanked by Roman soldiers can be clearly made out on this Roman triumphal arch from Carpentras, in Provence, France. (© R Sheridan/ AAA Collection Ltd)

In 55BC, after some rivalry, Crassus, Caesar and Pompey were once again elected to the consulship, and granted provinces: Caesar's command of his existing provinces was extended for another five years; Pompey was given both Spanish provinces (but in an unprecedented move was allowed to remain in Rome and command through subordinates); Crassus was given Syria, from which he planned to lead an invasion of Parthia, for it seems that he felt the need to rival the conquests of his colleagues. Aged almost 60, he was considered rather old for active command by Roman standards, and there were doubts about the legitimacy of a war with Parthia, but the triumvirs were too strong for any opposition to stand much chance. In 54BC Crassus left to join the army in Syria, and the following year he was defeated at the battle of Carrhae. Crassus was killed when his army was forced to retreat. Rome was still torn apart by political rivalry, and in 52BC, the Senate appointed Pompey sole consul and charged him with restoring order, for the first time permitting troops to guard Rome itself.

Prelude to war

In 52BC Pompey married the daughter of Publius Metellus Scipio, a known opponent of Caesar. Pressure on Caesar mounted, as incoming consuls lobbied to have him replaced in his province, since the war in Gaul appeared to be over. Pompey opposed these moves, but not particularly strongly – his attitude appeared increasingly ambivalent and the extension of his Spanish command gave him military might to match against Caesar. The latter was being forced into a corner. He had either to give up his command and trust Pompey to protect him from the inevitable wrath of his rivals, or to fight. Caesar's large, veteran army lay on Italy's own border, and many Romans already feared that this force would be turned against the state in a bid for dictatorship. Eventually, Pompey's supporters persuaded him to recall veterans from his old army, and take command of two legions, I and XV. In the meantime, Caesar wrote to the Senate, reminding them of his military achievements on Rome's behalf, and offering to lay down his command, provided that Pompey did the same thing. If he did not, then Caesar felt that he was obliged to retain his legions as protection against the faction opposed to him. The letter also contained the scarcely veiled threat that he was also willing to free Rome from the tyranny of Pompey's faction. His offer was rejected, and on 7 January 49BC the Senate met and passed its ultimate decree, the *senatus consultum ultimum*, which called on the magistrates to use any means to defend the state. Disguised as slaves, Caesar's supporters hid in carts and fled north to join Caesar. In the days to come, Pompey and the Senate began to prepare the war effort against Caesar. The news reached Caesar at Ravenna on 10 January. He spent the day watching gladiators training and held a previously arranged dinner in the evening, but secretly issued orders for several parties of soldiers to travel in civilian clothes carrying concealed weapons to Ariminum (modern-day Rimini), the nearest town in Italy. With him he had only a single legion and apparently some 300 cavalrymen – they travelled by night, and reached the river Rubicon, which marked the boundary of Caesar's province. Commanders were barred by law from leading troops outside their province

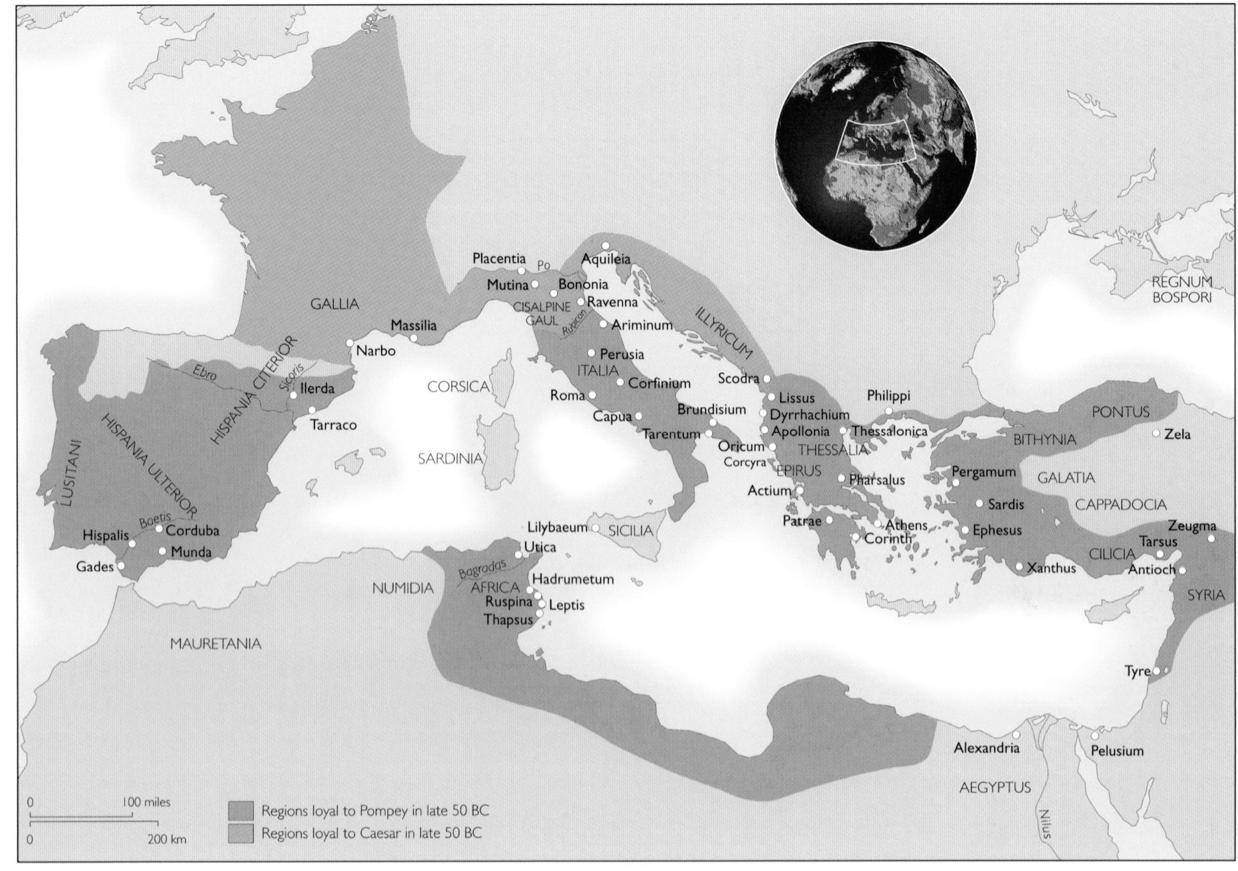

The Roman world in 50BC.

without the Senate's express permission, so crossing the river would turn Caesar into a rebel. After deliberation, Caesar crossed the Rubicon, uttering the famous line '*alea iacta est*' – 'the die is cast'.

The Second Triumvirate

Caesar marched on Rome, had himself made dictator and defeated his opponents in the Balkans, Egypt, Asia Minor, North Africa and Spain. In 44BC he was made dictator for life and prepared to march against Parthia, but he was assassinated by the Liberators led by Brutus and Cassius. In 43BC the Caesarian factions headed by Mark Antony, legate of Caesar, and Octavian, adopted son and heir of Caesar, clashed in battle. However, at the close of the year Antony, Octavian and a third commander, Lepidus, united to form a second triumvirate, to concentrate power in their hands and eradicate their opponents. But intense friction remained between Antony and Octavian. Lepidus was eased out of power, and by 40BC the Roman world was effectively divided into eastern and western halves held by Antony and Octavian. A final conflict for total control was inevitable, and in 31BC the unlikely Octavian triumphed over the charismatic Antony and his lover Cleopatra at the battle of Actium. Octavian pursued the despairing Antony to Egypt, forcing him to commit suicide. In 30BC the civil war finally ended.

Roman military reform

The rise of the professional army

The conversion of the Roman army into a professional force during this period fundamentally altered its relationship with the rest of society. Until this time the legions had been militia forces, all citizens who possessed a certain property qualification being obliged to serve when called upon by the Republic. The wealthiest, able to provide themselves with a horse and the necessary equipment, served as cavalry; the moderately well off as heavy infantry; the poorer as light infantry; and the poorest rarely served at all. In a real sense the army represented a cross-section of Roman society under arms. For these men service in the army was not a career but a duty to the Republic. As men of property – most were farmers – they easily returned to civilian life after each period of service. However, as the Empire expanded, wars tended to last longer and be fought further away, while there was a growing need for permanent garrisons to protect conquered territory. A decade of service in a garrison in one of the Spanish provinces could well mean ruination for the owner of a small farm. Service became increasingly unpopular and the eventual solution was to turn to men who were willing to make the army their profession. A soldier's pay was low, the conditions of his service extremely harsh, and a military career only tended to be attractive to the poorest citizens, who in the past had not been obliged to serve. Such men proved excellent soldiers, but when the war ended and their legion was disbanded they had nothing to return to in civilian life. The Senate refused to acknowledge this situation, maintaining that military service was a duty requiring no formal reward, and made no provision to provide for discharged soldiers. Individual commanders began to demand land for their veteran soldiers, wanting to settle them in colonies on conquered territory. Soldiers started to become more loyal to generals who offered such rewards than to the Republic that neglected them. This transferral of direct and unquestioning military loyalty from the Senate as a whole to the generals as individuals was to prove fatal to the Republic.

A snapshot of the Roman army at the time of the Gallic Wars

Social background

The Roman army that campaigned in Gaul in the first century BC was to all intents and purposes a professional one, with many soldiers in the legion regarding their military service as a career. The soldiers were equipped, trained and paid by the state, often serving for many years at a stretch. Gallic warfare, however, was based on the values of a warrior society. The Roman conquest of Gaul was therefore a clash between two cultures employing very different methods of waging war.

Recruitment and service

Recruitment to the legions was based on a mixture of conscription and volunteering, the only qualification for service being citizenship, at least in theory. Recruits were supposed to be at least 17 years old, although the majority were in their early 20s when they joined up. Roman ideology preferred recruits from rural backgrounds, rather than from towns and cities with their softening and corrupting influences. The legionaries signed up for military service of no fixed length, although they could expect to be discharged with a grant of land on which to settle after five years or so continuous service. Military pay was not especially good, but there were plenty of opportunities for enrichment, particularly on a lucrative campaign like Caesar's conquest of Gaul, with the likelihood of generous amounts of booty.

While the legions were armed and equipped uniformly, and were principally heavy infantry, the variation in type of forces a successful army needed was provided by 'auxiliary' units raised from other provinces of the Roman empire, or from neighbouring states and tribes friendly to Rome. Caesar was so successful in his early campaigns in Gaul and his military prestige so great that he was able to attract auxiliary units from the Germans, as well as support from Gallic tribes, who provided him with another source of cavalry that was particularly valuable when the loyalty of the Aedui wavered in 52BC.

Auxiliaries used their own fighting techniques; they were not trained in the Roman style of fighting, and were commanded by their own officers, usually members of the ruling elite of the tribe or state from which they were recruited.

Before the reforms of Marius, Pliny says that the legions of the Republican army had five animal standards: eagle, wolf, minotaur, horse and boar. Each standard belonged to a different type of solder, from the *hastati* to the *triarii*. By choosing the eagle standard as a single symbol to unite the whole army, Marius was showing that they were now one body of men, equal within the eyes of their commander. (© R Sheridan/AAA Collection Ltd)

Organisation and logistics

The Roman army in Gaul included slingers from the Balearics and archers from Crete and Numidia, who provided lightly armed mobile troops to increase the firepower of the army, particularly at a distance or in a siege. Additional infantry was provided by Gallic tribes in the same way as cavalry, and would have consisted of groups of warriors from tribes who were allied to Rome. The wealthiest of these warriors were probably armed and equipped in a way very similar to the Roman legionaries, but the Gauls placed greater emphasis on individual prowess and prominent displays of courage in battle, rather than the discipline and training of the legions.

Auxiliaries provided the Roman army's main cavalry force. The cavalry Caesar employed in Gaul, consisting mainly of Gallic or Germanic elites, was not always reliable or effective, and sometimes they lacked discipline, particularly early on in the campaigns.

THE MARIAN REFORMS OF THE ARMY

Marius was perhaps the first military leader who held greater command over his legions than did the Senate. By the time Marius was first made consul in 107BC he had already made his mark on the battlefield. A natural commander, Marius had won important battles against the armies of the Numidian King Jugurtha in the Jugurthine Wars of 110–105BC, effectively turning the fortunes of Rome around in the war, and eventually masterminding a triumphant Roman victory. His own success having been achieved on the battlefield, Marius easily commanded the respect of his men, but it was the changes brought about in the army during his command that cemented Marius' popularity. The military reforms carried out by Marius constitute a watershed in the development of the Roman military. Aware that a superpower, as Rome now was, required a huge army to service and protect it, Marius abolished the laws that had prevented a large part of the Roman population from taking positions in the army. Under Marius' reforms, ownership of property was no longer a requirement for soldiers. By boosting army numbers with this landless proletarian class Marius also ensured he had a bedrock of men who would be less opposed to, and even keen to carry out, long periods of continuous service, having no farms at home to worry about. These men became full-time professional soldiers, with no need to supplement their wages with a private income, meaning they could devote all of their time to training and campaigning.

A serious defeat with heavy loss of Roman life at the hands of the allied Germanic tribes of Cimbri and Teutones in 105BC was the spur for further reforms by Marius. The Assembly once more looked to Marius to prevent such severe losses being repeated – over 80,000 soldiers were apparently killed by the fierce Germanic tribes – and Marius did not disappoint them. He abolished the age distinctions, grouping the soldiers together into units called cohorts. All soldiers were armed with the same weapons, paid for by the government, offering a previously unseen uniformity (and therefore perhaps predictability) to the way they fought as an army. The weapons they carried were the *pilum* (javelin), which Marius improved to make break at the neck on impact, and the *gladius* (sword). In addition to these weapons, the soldiers carried all their supplies and equipment on their backs, leading to their nickname of 'Marius' mules'. The cohorts still fought in a flexible manipular style, but the centuries could be rearranged in different groupings, and the cohorts into different lines, affording greater flexibility to the army from battle to battle.

Marius made the legions more permanent, and gave them a symbol under which to unite – the eagle standard. Marius also made the army a more attractive career prospect by promising fitting reward for service. No longer would battle-weary veterans return to a retirement of financial ruin. Veterans were instead promised land for service, meaning that the future was one less thing that they had to worry about.

Marius' reforms were crucial to the army being a force fit for purpose at this time. However, they ultimately spelled disaster for the Republic, granting, as they did, power to individuals through the backing of an army, rather than the backing of the Senate. In this way, individuals could rise to power by force alone, bypassing and eventually attacking the Senate itself. Armies turned to their commanders for their orders, and not their government, and effectively became personal weapons. It would not be long before these armies were used against each other in civil war.

Images of fighting were common in ancient Rome including, as in this case, on sarcophagi. This late second-century AD sarcophagus from Rome has a stylised depiction of battle between Romans and barbarians that conveys the confusion and urgency of pitched battle. (© M Andrews/AAA Collection Ltd)

By the end of the campaigns the cavalry was a powerful force that contributed to Caesar's victory in the Civil War. The German cavalry sometimes worked in concert with light infantry, which allowed the holding of terrain in addition to the useful mobility of cavalry.

Logistical support was generally well organised, with a supply system reliant on shuttling provisions from a supply-base to the campaigning army. The army made use of Gaul's navigable rivers to move supplies around, but the poor road system and the speed of Caesar's movements led to difficulties. Although Caesar could call on his Gallic allies and later the subjected tribes for supplies, his movements and the direction of the campaign were often heavily influenced by logistical demands. An understanding of this lay behind the Gallic scorched-earth policy in the revolt of 52BC. When the legions were in winter quarters, Caesar ensured they were garrisoned in the territories of recently conquered tribes to serve the dual purpose of ensuring a strong military presence in newly reduced territory, and punishing those who resisted Rome by forcing them to feed the occupying army, a penalty that could have affected a tribe's ability to support its own population.

Fighting style

The Roman legionary's equipment did not make him reliant on his neighbour's shield for protection in combat as in a Greek phalanx operation, as he fought as an individual, but he was dependent on the strength of his unit. If his comrades in his century, cohort or legion gave way, he would eventually become exposed to attack on the flank or rear. The might of the Roman army lay in the strength of its formations, and that was based on unit morale, discipline and training. Roman soldiers were not automatons in a 'military machine'; they were trained to think and use their own initiative as well as follow orders. The training and discipline instilled in the soldiers meant that Roman units could move over battlefields in

These figures illustrate legionary fighting techniques. The top left-hand figure is a typical heavy-armed legionary throwing his heavy *pilum* prior to charging with his sword. The legionaries relied on the shock and confusion caused by the *pila* volley to maximise their own rapid sword charge, when each legionary would aim to collide with an opponent and stab him as he fell back. The top right figure shows a dedicated light-armed legionary. His flat oval shield is more manoeuvrable than the regular *scutum*, and his light javelins allow him to fight in advance of the battle-line or deliver missile support over the heads of his comrades. The bottom left-hand figure is a regular legionary advancing without armour. Caesar, Tacitus and Dio all refer to heavy infantry relieved of their body armour to increase speed and manoeuvrability in battle. The bottom right-hand figure is a legionary in a crouch stance. This was possibly an option for a legionary wishing to get under the guard of an opponent armed with a slashing sword. (Painting by Angus McBride © Osprey Publishing Ltd)

formation and even retreat while maintaining a defensive formation, an invaluable technique in warfare for minimising casualties.

In combat with opponents with slashing swords, the Roman legionaries threw their *pila* and then moved in very close for hand-to-hand combat. The large *scutum* protected most of the legionary's front and left side, his short *gladius* was ideal for stabbing in close-quarter fighting, and he could even punch at the enemy with the metal boss of his shield. If the legionaries moved in close enough, they could literally cramp the style of their opponents, while still giving themselves the small amount of room they needed to operate effectively.

Weapons, equipment and armour

Legions were uniformed at state expense, and were well equipped for their military roles. Each legionary, with his mail coat and bronze or iron helmet, was armed as well as the most wealthy and successful Celtic warriors, and this must have given them a huge psychological

A detail from the Altar of Domitius Ahenobarbus, from the first century BC. The armour and equipment used by the infantrymen and cavalrymen can be clearly seen. (© R Sheridan/AAA Collection Ltd)

Although these soldiers are from slightly later in the first century AD, they are organised in a way typical of the late Repubican army. Here we see a front century formed in four ranks of 20, with the centurion, identified by his helmet crest, positioned on the extreme right. The standard bearer is at the centre of the formation to prevent him from being killed during the first clash and stop the standard from falling into enemy hands. The inset reveals the regular 'chessboard' formation of the legionaries. Having advanced within range of the enemy the front ranks would have thrown their lead-weighted *pila* and are charging at the run with drawn swords. The three figures positioned behind the century are the *optio* (centurion's deputy), *cornicen* (trumpeter) and *tessarius* (watchword officer). The *optio* and *tessarius* are positioned to use their long staffs to shove legionaries back into line and prevent any attempt by the rear rankers to flee. (Painting by Angus McBride © Osprey Publishing Ltd)

advantage when facing the Gauls. The large shield or *scutum* provided additional protection. The legionary's principal weapons were the *pilum* (javelin) and short sword, the *gladius*. The short *gladius* was a brutally efficient tool for killing: a short stab at the torso or especially the belly of his opponent, who may well have been fighting without armour, and he would have been killed or badly injured with damage to internal organs and serious bleeding. Though Roman solders were trained to stab with their swords, that did not stop them from slashing with them, and the fine quality and perfect weighting of the *gladius* meant that they could easily hack off limbs.

The Celtic-style saddle allowed Caesar's cavalry to be as effective as later, stirruped cavalry, despite the absence of stirrups. Cavalry troops might vary considerably in their

The Roman cavalryman shown in this Germano-Roman relief wears a mail shirt. The lack of stirrups is evident – the use of the Celtic saddle made such things unnecessary. (© R Sheridan/AAA Collection Ltd)

equipment, since they equipped themselves, but a wealthy cavalryman might have a mail shirt and helmet, an oval or hexagonal shield which was more manoeuvrable on horseback than a rectangular one, a spear and a long sword, which was ideal for running down those fleeing from battle, one of the principal roles of the cavalry.

Chapter 6

THE NUMANTINES

Numantine campaigns against Rome

Background

The central area of Spain, known today as the Meseta or Plateau, was inhabited in early Roman times by peoples who are known today as 'Celtiberians', because of the fusion of Celtic and Iberian cultures. Their great tribes were the Lusitani, the Vettones, the Vaccei, the Carpetani, the Arevaci, the Pellendones, the Belli and the Titii. Each of these tribes had its own distinct personality. Usually peaceful and benign towards strangers, the Celtiberians were formidable warriors when menaced or provoked.

The Numantine Wars

Defeat under Nobilior

When in late summer 133BC the gates of the smouldering city of Numantia opened and a staggering crowd of human ghosts emerged to surrender to a Roman army, the moment marked the end of a ten-year war which had cost Rome unbearable humiliations.

This pottery horse or donkey is an example of Celt iberian zoomorphic art from Verdolay. (© Prisma/AAA Collection Ltd)

The tribes and major places of central Spain in Roman times.

The first conflict between Numantia and the Romans is thought to have taken place in 197BC, when the consul Cato was forced by a dangerous outbreak in central Hispania to make the first incursion into the Plateau – Meseta – region, though with little success. Repulsed before he got very far, Cato marched with seven cohorts towards the Ebro river, and established camps on a mountain some 6km from Numantia, called today 'La Gran Atalaya' – 'the great watchtower'. The site of the base he set up there was to be used by all his successors in their operations against Numantia.

After decades of ignored complaints about the rapacity of Roman authorities in Hispania, the main towns of Celtiberia, such as Segeda, the capital of the Belli tribe, decided to prepare themselves for war. Led by the chieftain Carros, they began to enlarge and repair the walls of the city; and the inhabitants of neighbouring villages, including those of the nearby Titii tribe, were forced to take shelter in the strengthened fortress. Roman protests, and attempts to recruit auxiliaries for the war against the Lusitani tribe, were rejected. At this time the Lusitani frequently displayed before the Celtiberians the weapons, standards and other booty they had captured from the Romans, and mocked the Celtiberians for their passivity.

These Iberian warriors are reconstructed from contemporary ceramics. This group certainly represents an elite type of warrior, from the level of armour and equipment, and possibly they are *auxilia* serving with the Roman armies in Spain. (Painting by Angus McBride © Osprey Publishing Ltd)

Rome, foreseeing a hard fight, raised a 30,000-strong consular army instead of the more common army of around 10,000 to 15,000. Command was entrusted to Quintus Fulvius Nobilior, a man of aristocratic lineage whose father had combat experience in Hispania in the 190s, but who proved to have learned little from the example. Having fought his way to Numantia, the most influential centre in the region, Nobilior probably foresaw a classic clash of armies on open ground, but he was disappointed: it is no accident that even today the word 'guerrilla' is written in Spanish the world over. Having neglected proper reconnaissance, Nobilior's force was ambushed whilst in column formation, with a loss of a third of the Roman troops. The date was 23 August 153BC, and when news of the disaster reached Rome that date was declared a *dies ater* – a 'sinister day' – and ever afterwards no Roman general would willingly accept battle on 23 August.

Nobilior's next battle against the Celtiberians achieved great effect with his use of the elephant – they panicked the Numantines, who started to flee, until a large stone from the walls of Numantia struck one of the elephants and it ran amock, stampeding the others. As the maddened beasts raged through their ranks the Roman soldiers gave way in confusion, and the day ended with 4,000 Romans and three elephants dead, at a cost of 2,000 Numantine lives. Nobilior continued to carry out operations in the area, but the only result was a steady attrition of his forces. With his remaining 5,000 men he decided to winter in the camp on the Gran Atalya; and over the coming months there his army was further reduced by cold, famine and sickness.

Reforms of Scipio

This unfortunate campaign was typical of several other Roman attempts on the Numantine area, and the series of humiliations finally provoked Rome into sending to Hispania probably her finest living soldier: Publius Cornelius Scipio Aemilianus Africanus, grandson of the victor over Hannibal, and himself the destroyer of Carthage in the Third Punic War. The Senate waived the legal ban on any man holding two consulships within ten years, and Scipio was given the 'extraordinary' appointment as consul of Hispania Citerior for 134BC. He was not, however, given an army of size commensurate with his rank, and was only allowed to raise volunteers. Scipio found the Roman armies in Hispania to be in a terrible state, with an almost complete breakdown in morale and discipline. Scipio set to work, driving camp followers and hangers-on from the camps, forbidding luxuries, and reducing personal baggage to a minimum, along with transport facilities. Dress and rations were reduced to austere levels; Scipio set an example by adopting, and ordering for all personnel, the rough woollen *sagum* worn by the Hispanic tribesman in the country where they would be fighting. He instituted an intense training programme of drills, route marches, and practice fortifications and assaults.

On the march, the general made a point of bringing up the rear of the column, indicating his suspicion that too many legionaries were ready to drop out at the first opportunity. Each man was ordered to carry a month's wheat ration, and no less than seven rampart stakes. Physical punishment with the officers' vine sticks was reintroduced for all

A group of warriors from different Hispanic tribes await the right moment to spring an ambush on the Roman column in the valley below. Large confederations of warriors from several tribes were by no means unknown during the Spanish wars. (Painting by Angus McBride © Osprey Publishing Ltd)

offenders, including Roman citizens. Significantly, much attention was paid to reconnaissance tactics.

In May 134BC, Scipio began his march in the direction of Numantia, choosing the long route, to avoid some of the worst 'ambush country', and gathering support from neighbouring tribes as he went, discouraging them from aiding the Numantines. Finally, Scipio arrived before Numantia in late August or early September. Here he met up with Jugurtha, a prince of Numidia and at that time an ally of Rome, who supplied several war elephants with 'turret crews' of slingers and archers. By now Scipio's forces totalled almost 60,000 men, although he had brought only 4,000 with him from Italy.

The siege of Numantia

By calculating the size of Numantia, we can make an educated estimate of an effective Numantine garrison of around 2,500 warriors. To this we may add around 1,000 warriors who came to shelter in the city from the outlying villages, giving around 3,500, one-twentieth of the Roman strength. It may be thought surprising that Scipio did not launch an immediate assault, in view of his numerical superiority. However, he did not have complete confidence in much of his army, and the respect inspired by the Numantines in previous campaigns was not

SIEGE FORTIFICATIONS OF NUMANTIA

Numantia was on top of a hill 1074 metres above sea level, known today as Muela da Garray. Little remains of what were once strong defensive walls surrounding at least three roughly concentric fortified precincts at different levels, all strengthened by large square towers with a diameter of about 5.7m. When Scipio arrived the walls were partly demolished on the southern and western sides, though here the defenders had thrown up improvised fortifications with stakes, pointed stones and ditches.

Scipio's first step was to raise an initial palisade around the vulnerable north-east sector of the city's approaches: the rivers, in autumn flood, made a good enough obstacle on the west and south. The palisade, reinforced with stones and earth and by a half-metre ditch with pointed stakes at the bottom, took some 16,000 stakes and stretched some 4,000m. In view of the relatively treeless terrain, Scipio's foresight in making his men carry stakes with them was vindicated. The palisade was raised in a single day. Next, Scipio began the construction 100m behind the palisade of the 'wall of circumvallation': one of those awesomely thorough, patient feats of military engineering that explain Rome's mastery of the world. It was a stone wall, 4m thick at the base and 2.4m thick at the top, 3m high from ground to rampart-walk, defended on the inside by a V-section ditch 3m deep. When complete it is thought to have stretched nearly 9km – double the perimeter of Numantia itself. Every 30.85m (the interval called a *plethron*) there was a square, four-storey wooden tower, the upper floors for sentries and signalling, the lower for war machines. In each of the 300 towers was at least one catapult, throwing balls of 1 or 2lbs weight or shooting bolts over ranges of around 300m. These light catapults were supported by 50 heavy *ballistae* or stone-throwers emplaced in the various camps, to bombard the walls and visible concentrations of the defenders. To support the construction of the wall two camps were built opposite one another, and in permanent communication by red flag signals during daylight and by lantern signals at night. Scipio established his headquarters in one of these camps during the siege.

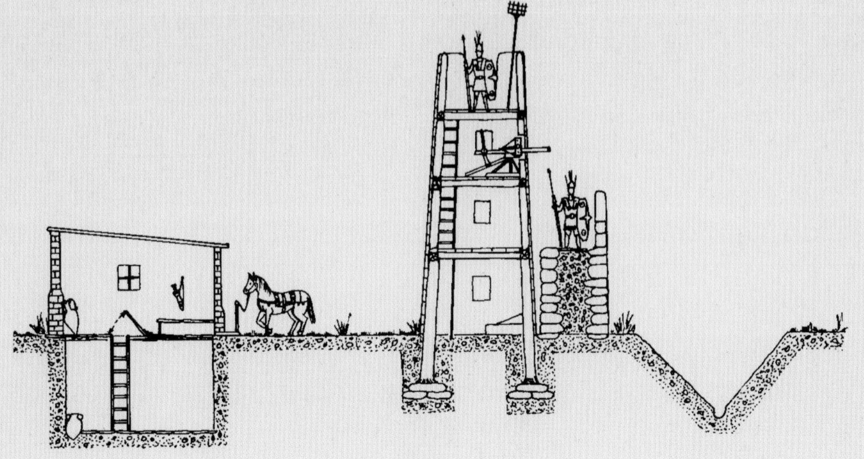

This view through the wall of circumvallation constructed by Scipio at Numantia shows, on the left, a house with one store at ground level and a second dug down into the ground beneath it, for insulation. In the centre is one of the artillery and watch towers, built about every 30m round the wall of circumvallation. The wall itself was faced with stone, and protected with a V-section ditch on the Numantine side. (Drawing by Rafael Treviño Martinez © Osprey Publishing Ltd)

to be taken lightly. Polybius, who was an eyewitness, writes that Scipio '...did not consider it reasonable to engage desperate men, but preferred rather to encircle them and starve them into surrender...'. This encirclement was on an enormous scale, as Scipio spent until November overseeing the construction of walls, camps, dams, booby-traps, ditches and artillery stages.

This scene shows one of the desperate attacks on the Roman walls of circumvallation carried out late in the final siege of Numantia by the starving defenders. (Painting by Angus McBride © Osprey Publishing Ltd)

Since the Numantines were not archers, but spearmen and slingers, the 'no man's land' between Numantia and the Roman walls was 500m, meaning the Numantines were unable to harass the Roman positions without leaving the protection of the walls of the city.

Once the construction and preparations were complete, Scipio settled down to starve the Numantines out. He toured the whole perimeter daily, to keep his men alert. The 3,000 or so Numantines launched repeated attacks on different sectors of the circumvallation, covering these sorties with diversionary attacks elsewhere, but with their limited numbers these attempts must have stretched their manpower to the utmost. They also attempted to lure the Romans into open battle, but Scipio, against the urging of his officers, refused to rise to the bait. The only result of these attacks was to wear down the strength of the Numantines.

With the situation inside the city deteriorating, as supplies became exhausted and all hope of outside help was abandoned, a noted Numantine citizen named Retogenes Caraunios made a last desperate attempt to summon assistance. One dark night, with five friends and five servants, he climbed the Roman wall by means of a rope ladder, killed the sentries and – with five companions – managed to seize horses and ride for help, the others returning to the city. He rode to a number of Vacceian towns, appealing for help, but for fear of Roman reprisals he was refused by all except the citizens of Lutia (Cantalucia). There some 400 young warriors agreed to come to the aid of Numantia. Their decision was taken against the advice of the council of elders who, to avert Roman reprisals, sent word to Scipio's camp. Receiving the intelligence at 2pm, Scipio marched immediately for Lutia to demand the surrender of the warriors. Since they had already left, the Lutians surrendered 400 innocent youths, who suffered the amputation of their right hands. Next morning Scipio was back on the walls before Numantia.

The surrender of the Numantines

With this collapse of the last desperate effort to bring help to the besieged city, the starving Numantines in spring 133BC sent an embassy of five men, led by one Avaro, to negotiate terms with Scipio. The Roman general, who was well aware of the state of the garrison from questioning prisoners, demanded unconditional surrender and the confiscation of all weapons. This last demand was enough to bring talks to a halt, since the Hispanic warrior regarded the giving up of his weapons as the ultimate shame. When the embassy returned to the city and repeated Scipio's terms, Celtiberian arrogance reached its paroxysm. The messengers were accused of treacherously dealing with the Romans for their own personal benefit, and were butchered on the spot. Stark starvation now faced the townspeople; bread, meat and animal forage had all been exhausted, and the survivors were passing from eating the boiled hides of animals to outright cannibalism, first of the dead, then of the ill, and finally of the weak. There are numerous classical accounts of the last days of Numantia. Valerius Maximus, writing in the first century AD. says of the Numantine Theogenes:

> Only the fierceness of his race could give such vigour of mind. Being superior to all others in honours, dignity and wealth, when the cause of the

> Numantines was lost, [he] placed firewood everywhere and set fire to his houses, which were the most beautiful in the city. Then he appeared before his fellow citizens, naked sword in hand, and forced them to fight each other in pairs: the vanquished being thrown, after decapitation, into the fires. When all others had submitted to this terrible death-law he threw himself into the flames.

This attitude seems to have been general, as Florus wrote in the second century AD:

> The Numantines, possessed of the most furious rage, determined to take their own lives, destroying themselves, their leaders and their homeland by iron, poison and the fires that they set everywhere. Only when all human courage was exhausted did [the survivors] decide to surrender.

Scipio ordered them to deposit their weapons in an agreed place, and for the survivors of the holocaust to congregate at another spot on the following day. When the Numantines asked for one more day it was granted; and in this interval many more of them, reaching a climax of desperation, committed suicide rather than endure the fall of their city. The next day they surrendered their weapons and on the third day the last of the survivors gave themselves up. The Romans watched as they staggered from the gates: filthy, ragged, emaciated, with long, tangled hair and beards and nails like talons, but with a piercing hatred in their eyes. Scipio chose 50 of them to be set aside for his triumphal procession in Rome; the rest were sold into slavery. Numantia was demolished, and, as in the cases of

The Celtiberian city of Numantia was near what is now Soria in Castile-León. This wall of tiles from Soria shows the much-portrayed suicide of Numantians in the face of the Roman siege. Artists have been inspired by this desperate scene for centuries. (© R Sheridan/ AAA Collection Ltd)

Carthage and Corinth, its reconstruction was forbidden. A cavalry unit was permanently garrisoned in the area to prevent the reoccupation of the ruins. Numantia fell at the end of July, or the beginning of August 133BC, after a nine-month siege, and Scipio received his triumph in Rome in 132BC, where he was honoured with the additional title 'Numantinus'.

The fall of Numantia was not the end of Iberian resistance; many other cities continued to hold out for many years. It took until after the campaigns of Augustus, in 19BC, before the last focus of resistance in the Iberian peninsula was snuffed out.

Numantine troops

The Celtiberian warrior

Celtiberian social organisation is difficult to discover. Broadly it seems that ultimate authority was wielded by the council of elders led by the eldest man of the tribe. In time of war, after the necessary deliberations, the command of the fighting men was entrusted to a single military leader, who was responsible for the conduct of operations and who received full support from the tribe. Celtiberian warriors were feared by their enemies, which led to them also being employed as mercenaries by many of them, having, as they did, the reputation of being the finest mercenary infantry available. Their appearance was that of fierce but fit men, making something, as they did, of the cult of a trim physique, accentuated at the waist by the wearing of tight, broad belts. Most Celtiberians fought as light infantry, which led to them being at a distinct disadvantage against armies of many better-armed and armoured infantry, but at an advantage in the type of guerrilla warfare used by the Iberians, where speed and agility were crucial.

The Celtiberians enjoyed gymnastic exercises, and 'gladiatorial' combats ranged from friendly contests to fights to the death to settle various differences between warriors. They also practised horsemanship, hunting and ambushes – indeed, any activity which would qualify them as warriors. Unusually, we learn that it was common for warriors to carry a small receptacle containing a quick-acting poison extracted from the roots of the plant *Ranunculus sardonia,* which they used to swallow to give themselves a quick death if all hope was lost. This poison also produced a contraction of the lower jaw, giving the victim the appearance of a sinister – literally 'sardonic' – smile. This was apparently terrifying to the Roman legionaries, who thought that the dead man was defying them from beyond the grave.

Balearic slingers

Balearic slingers were used by Celtiberian armies, these warriors being famous all over the ancient world for their skill in handling their simple but terrible weapons, which were capable of great accuracy, and of crushing metal helmets and cuirasses. Their skill with the sling was developed from childhood, when they began intensive training at the hands of their fathers. One of the first toys they were given was a sling; Strabo claimed that when they began to show familiarity with it, a piece of bread was placed on a stake, and the trainees were not allowed to eat it until they had knocked it to the ground. It is easy to

This depiction of the surrender of the few surviving Numantians to Scipio Aemilianus is by Federico de Madrazo, 1815–1894. (© Prisma/ AAA Collection Ltd)

understand the high degree of mastery shown in adulthood by slingers trained by such methods. A little-known detail is that each man used three slings of different sizes and lengths, to throw missiles to short, medium and long range. The sling was carried wound around the brow, as a hair-band. It was made of black rush, animal hair, or animal sinews banded together.

The missiles of small and medium size were made of lead or ceramic material; for the heavier ones we may presume that any suitable stone picked up on the battlefield would have been used. Common sense suggests that slingers must also have carried a sword and *caetra* shield (see p122) for personal protection at hand-to-hand ranges. Considering that the sling was cheap and easy to make and handy to carry, it may have been used as a secondary weapon by spear- and sword-armed warriors.

The cavalry

The horse enjoyed great importance in the social and military activities of the ancient Iberians. The horse was honoured as a divinity, and sanctuaries were dedicated to it. Presumably in a public demonstration of the affection and respect in which they held these animals, Iberian riders decorated their horse furniture in a liberal, even exaggerated manner, with bells and ornaments in bright colours.

The Iberians made widespread use of the cavalry in all their campaigns – a good example of their effectiveness is provided by the campaigns of Hannibal, whose army included large contingents of Spanish horsemen. They not only fulfilled the traditional, rather peripheral role of light cavalry as a force to distract the enemy, but also proved capable of defeating in battle the best Roman cavalry when led by able commanders. Spain was rich in wild horses, described in many Roman texts as being very fast and of great beauty, while being of moderate size. Strabo praised their stamina, as they were usually ridden by two men over long distances. The riders used saddle pads of wool, linen or hide, secured by a broad leather girth. Some of the earliest examples of horseshoes come from central Spanish burials, and they may well have been invented by Celtiberians. This invention considerably increased the military potential of cavalry, and influenced the organisation of armies: in Iberian armies the proportion of horsemen ranged from 20 to 25 per cent of the total force, in the Carthaginian manner, while Roman armies counted no more than around 10 to 14 per cent cavalry.

The Celtiberians had an advanced knowledge of horsemanship, and trained horses and riders with care. One exercise was to train the horse to kneel and remain still and silent on the appropriate signal, a useful skill in the context of the guerrilla warfare which they often pursued. In battle the horsemen sometimes played the role of 'dragoons', dismounting to fight on foot alongside their hard-pressed infantry in an emergency. On other occasions they formed a ring with the horses in the centre, presumably to protect these valuable creatures from injury. Their mounts apparently had some kind of picket pin attached to the reins, to allow the rider to tether them in battle. The armament of the cavalry does not appear to have differed significantly from that of the foot soldiers, comprising spears and swords; and the *caetra* was the favoured shield, being hung on the side of the horse when not in use.

Arms, armour and equipment

Weapons

A Celtiberian man's most valuable possessions were his weapons, and on many occasions negotiations with the Romans were broken off due to Roman attempts to confiscate weapons. The swords used by the Celtiberian warriors are of two simple types: straight or curved. The straight type was the style adopted by the Romans – the famous double-edged *gladius Hispaniensis* discussed more in Chapter three – and the curved was the *falcata*. Both were widely admired and feared as examples of highly skilled craftsmanship, deadly in the hands of their highly skilled owners.

Several vase paintings from the time also clearly show the use of spears and javelins, and there are references to Celtiberian warriors throwing spears with blazing bundles of grass tied to the heads, not at buildings but in order to break up the close-order infantry formations. The conventional spear seems to have been used by foot and mounted warriors alike.

Armour

The body protection used by Iberian warriors was basically similar to that of other peoples of the ancient world, but with local characteristics. The head was simply protected by a helmet of some kind, varying from a simple leather cap to more elaborate examples, of mixed construction or entirely of metal. Ancient historians made a clear distinction between two types of Iberian infantry: the *sculati* or heavy and the *caetrati* or light, the reference being to two types of shield. The *sculati* carried the classic long *scutum* of Celtic origin, and the *caetrati* carried the *caetra*, a Latin corruption of a local name for a small, round buckler. The combination of the *caetra* buckler and the *falcata* sabre was apparently the most favoured battle equipment among Iberian warriors. Body armour seems to have been made from various materials, including simple fabric such as linen, thickly woven panels of esparto grass, hardened leather, and metal plate, scale and mail.

Fighting style

The kind of guerrilla warfare practised by the Celtiberians was considered entirely legal and honourable among some tribes. Diodorus tells us that:

> there is a custom characteristic of the Iberians, but particularly of the Lusitans, that when they reach adulthood those men who stand out through their courage and daring provide themselves with weapons, and meet in the mountains. There they form large bands, to ride across Iberia gaining riches through robbery, and they do this with the most complete disdain towards all. For them the harshness of the mountains and the hard life they lead there are like their own home; and there they look for refuge, being impregnable to large, heavily equipped armies.

These wandering bands rarely attacked members of their own tribes, but understandably the Romans were unwilling to grant any colour of honour to their activities, and always referred to them simply as bandits.

Strabo accuses the Iberians of being incapable of forming large confederations, and there was a general failure to exploit victory after success in battle. An army's cohesion might be maintained for some time after a victory, but in the case of defeat the warriors dispersed very quickly, producing among the Romans the sensation of fighting against an intangible enemy. In set-piece battles on open ground the Romans also suffered the unpleasant surprise produced by Iberian tactics which differed considerably from the hoplitic methods usually encountered by the Republican Roman army.

After a great deal of preparatory chanting and ritual dancing, the Celtiberians would attack *en masse* and in apparent disorder. At a pre-arranged signal the attack was halted, and the warriors would retreat, giving an appearance of defeat. This sequence might be repeated over and over again during several days, and each withdrawal obliged the Romans to mount a pursuit, while maintaining their formations. Finally, after several attacks of this kind, it sometimes happened that the Romans lost their discipline, or their nerve, and broke formation to pursue the retreating warriors. At this point the Iberians would quickly regroup, mounting a counterattack and frequently decimating the legionaries in detail – who, being more heavily equipped and armoured, were less agile in individual combat.

This sort of fighting, known among the Romans as *concursare*, has been described by some as a simple absence of tactics. However, there had to be some kind of co-ordination to allow these sudden advances and retreats to occur simultaneously in the confusion of battle, without leaving groups of warriors isolated and outnumbered. Rounded horns made of ceramic materials have frequently been found by archaeologists in Celtiberian regions, and some believe that they may have been used to transmit signals in battle.

The typical short sword of the Iberian cavalryman is shown in this denarius coin, of the second century BC. (© R Kawka/AAA Collection Ltd)

Chapter 7

THE GAULS, GERMANICS AND BRITONS

Gallic campaigns against Rome

Background

The typical patterned trousers of the Gallic Celts can be seen from this small Roman bronze of a prisoner from Gaul. (© R Sheridan/AAA Collection Ltd)

On 28 March 58BC the Celtic tribe of the Helvetii left their homes in Helvetia (Switzerland) and, along with their neighbours, the Raurici, Tulingi, Latobrigi and Boii, began a migration west. The purpose of this mass movement of tribes, including men, women, children and livestock, was to move to western Gaul, to the lands of other Gallic tribes on which they intended to settle after defeating the inhabitants and forcing them to move on. The migration of the Helvetii did not come as a surprise to anyone, as extensive planning began in the late 60s BC, as the Helvetii were feeling the pressure of space. Hemmed in by the mountains of Helvetia, they had little opportunity to expand their territory to cater for a growing population and to display their military prowess by occupying enemy land. In 61BC, the Helvetii started building up three years' supply of grain for the journey and for sowing the new lands they planned to take over in western Gaul. In the spring of 58BC the Helvetii burned their towns, villages and surplus grain to rule out the possibility of abandoning the migration, and with thousands of wagons started west, towards the Gallic lands west of the Rhône, and towards the Roman province.

Gauls and Romans were concerned by the prospect of this migration. The movement of several thousand people would cause huge damage to the lands they passed through, and could destabilise the whole of southern Gaul as tribes chose whether to join the Helvetii in a bid for land, or to oppose them. Some tribes would have looked towards Rome for assistance, and in 60BC the Senate had sent ambassadors to Gallic tribes in an attempt to discourage them from joining the Helvetii. The proposed migration threatened the security of Rome's allies, including the Aedui and the Allobroges, as well as Gallia

The porch from a Gallic shrine at Roquepertuse, Provence. The niches allowed the display of human skulls, the kind of practice that fuelled Roman prejudice of the 'barbarian' Gauls, and the alleged brutality of Gallic cults. The skulls are of fit, healthy men, which suggests that they were killed in war. The Celts believed that the dwelling place of the immortal soul was the head, so to possess an enemy's head was to possess his soul. (© R Sheridan/AAA Collection Ltd)

Narbonensis (Provence) with its desirable fertile lands. In Roman thought, Germans were less desirable neighbours than Gauls. Rome did not want upheavals on her northern borders and the preparations for the migrations led to thoughts of war in Rome.

The migration of the Helvetii

A Roman war in Gaul was becoming inevitable by the late 60s, and the consul of 59BC, Julius Caesar, was eager to make his mark militarily. Caesar, as the new governor of Cisalpine and Transalpine Gaul, was duty bound to protect his provinces, which were directly in the path of the migrants. The Helvetii asked Caesar for permission to cross Roman territory, and when he refused they turned north to continue their migration without trespassing on Roman land. Although the Helvetii were now no longer a direct threat to Rome, Caesar followed them swiftly into free Gaul, and made an unprovoked attack on the Helvetii at Bibracte (Autun). Perhaps hoping to cut the Romans off from their supplies, the Helvetii decided to give battle and attacked the Roman rearguard. Caesar

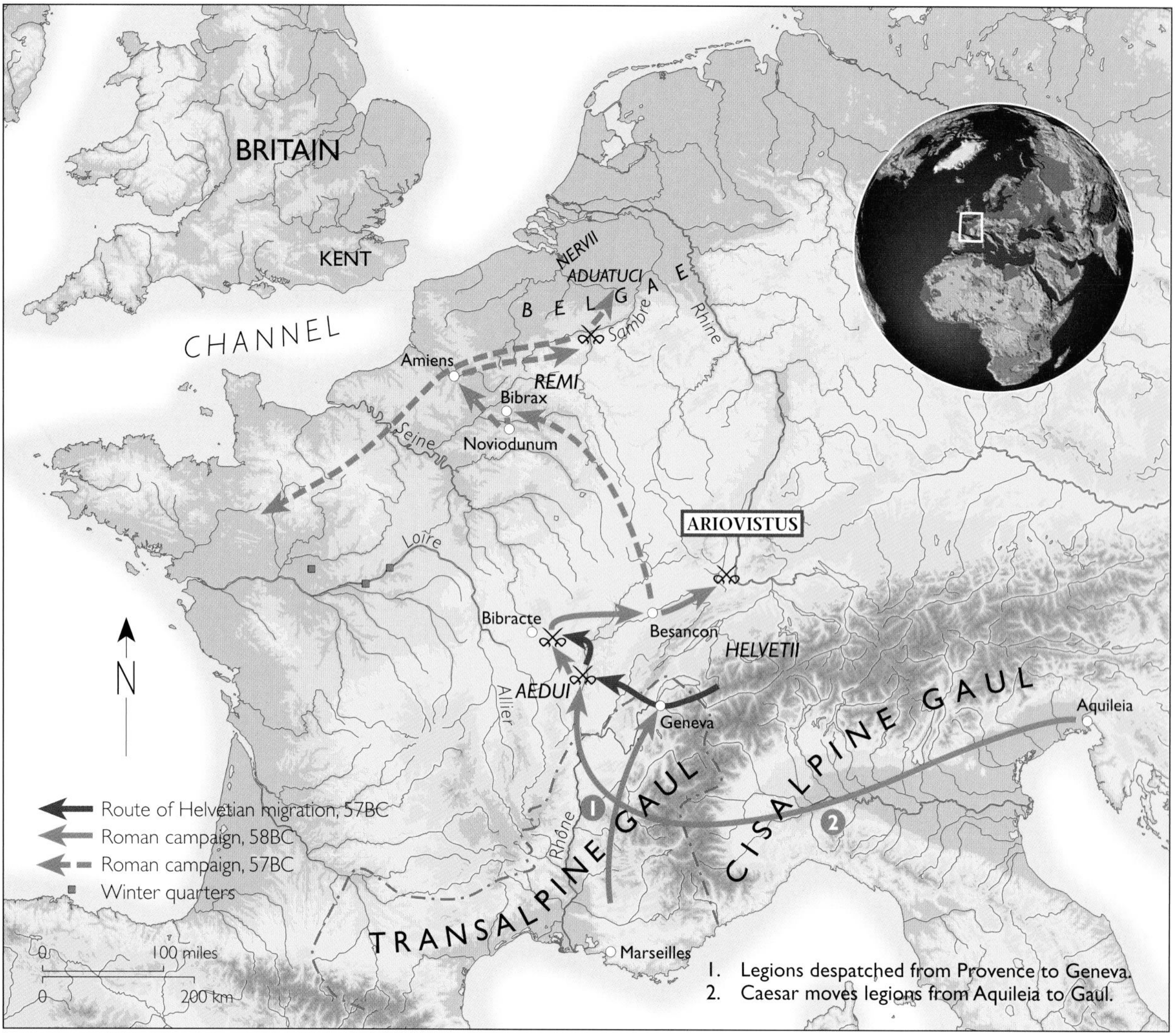

Campaigns of 58 and 57BC.

deployed on a slope under cover of a cavalry screen, and the Romans inflicted a sound defeat with heavy losses. Concerned that Germanic tribes might move into the lands vacated by the Helvetii, Caesar ordered the survivors home – he claims that of the 368,000 who set out on the migration, only 110,000 returned.

Germanic and Belgic tribes

In 58BC Caesar turned on the German tribes who occupied land on the left bank of the Rhine under their king Ariovistus. Caesar needed a good reason for attacking a king who was a 'Friend and Ally of the Roman People', and claimed that the Germans were raiding allied Aeduan territory and other Gallic tribes had asked for help. After a pitched battle in Belgica (Alsace), the flexibility of the Roman army of cohorts ensured victory over the Germanic Suevi led by Ariovistus, with reported losses of 80,000 Germans. By early 57BC, if he had not already resolved to do so, Caesar had decided to conquer the whole of Gaul. Some Gallic tribes were persuaded to form alliances with Rome because of the protection and influence that such a relationship would bring within Gaul. The Aedui in central Gaul were encouraged to remain Caesar's staunchest ally by his willingness to let them expand their influence over defeated tribes. The Remi in northern Gaul preferred to fight with Rome than against her, providing Caesar with intelligence during the campaign. However, the majority of Belgic tribes feared Rome's growing power in the region and prepared to resist, soliciting help from the Germans. Caesar claims they could raise an army of 200,000 warriors. Caesar raised two more legions, bringing the total to eight (32,000–40,000 men, plus auxiliaries), and at the start of the campaigning season, headed for northern Gaul. The resistance of the Belgae was overcome, their chronic disunity causing them to break up into tribal groups, which were defeated piecemeal. A later alliance between the Nervii, Atrebates and Viromandui saw Caesar survive a dangerous battle by his coolness in command, which allowed him to turn the fearless impetuosity of the Celts against themselves. This successful engagement broke the power of the Belgae to such an extent that even German tribes beyond the Rhine sent envoys to Caesar offering submission. In the same year Caesar's lieutenant Publius Licinius Crassus subdued Amorica (present-day Normandy and Brittany). At the end of the second year, Caesar reported that Gaul was at peace and the Senate in Rome voted him an unprecedented 15-day public thanksgiving, which greatly increased his political and military reputation. He returned again to northern Italy to spend the winter; his legions were quartered in northern Gaul, the tribes there being forced to provide for the soldiers. In 55BC the tireless Caesar wiped out the Germanic Tencteri and Usipete, who had crossed the lower Rhine the previous winter. He bridged the Rhine near Koblenz and raided on the German bank; and in the same season he led a small expeditionary force to Britain.

The British expedition

It should be remembered that to the Gauls, Oceanus Britannicus (the Channel) was probably just a particularly marked geographical frontier between closely related Belgic peoples. There was constant contact across it, and Rome was already profiting by this to follow her usual method of 'softening up' potential future conquests, by interfering in tribal and dynastic quarrels. Caesar writes that before he crossed Oceanus Britannicus he had received envoys from some British tribes offering submission to Rome, and that they were

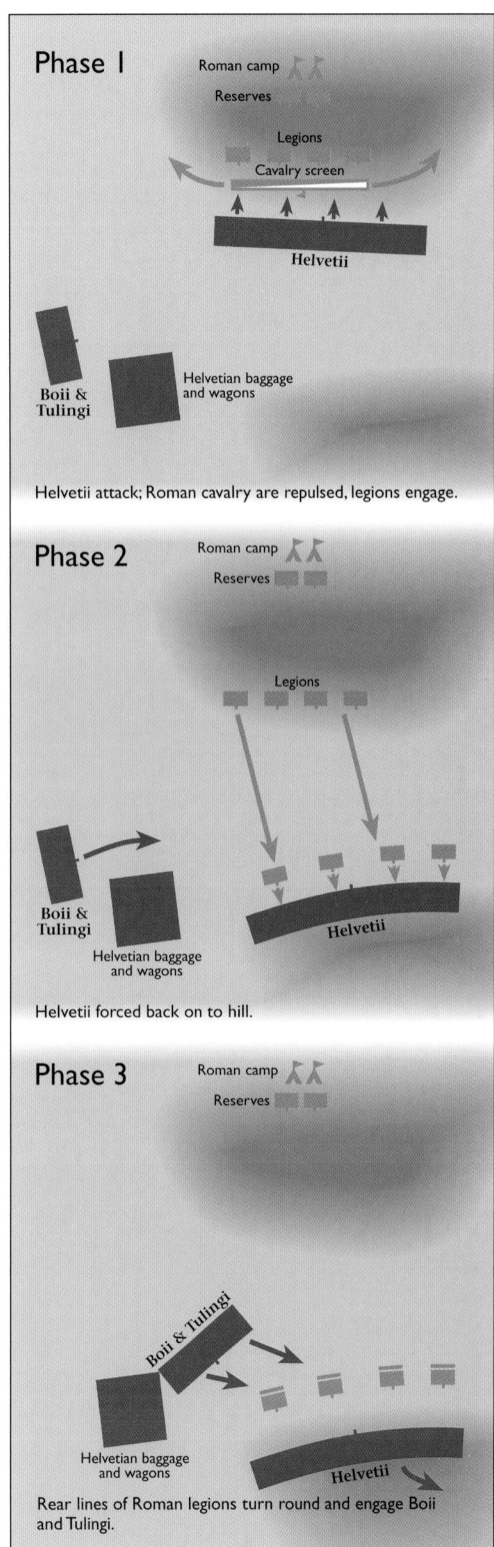

The battle against the Helvetii, 58BC.

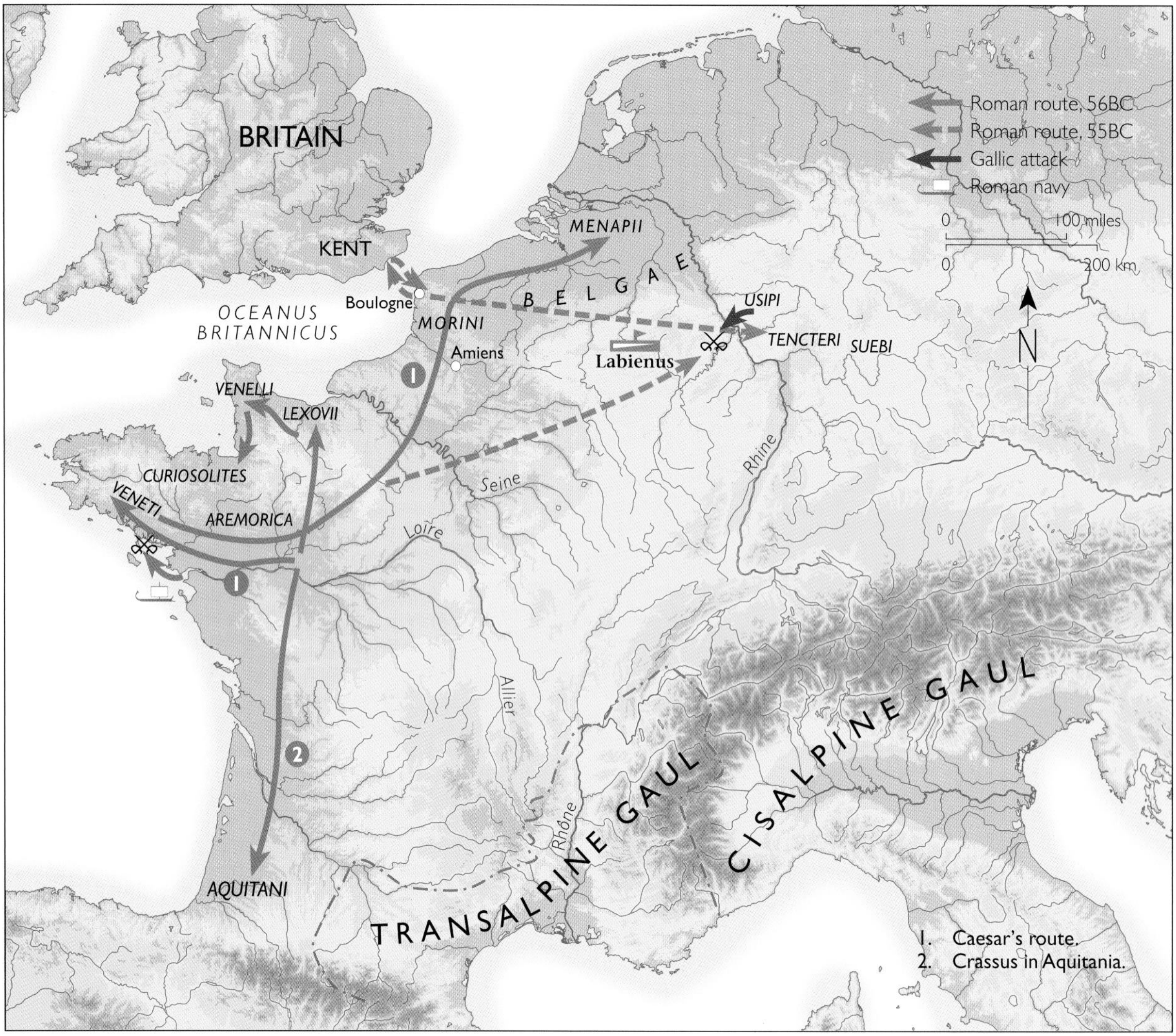

Campaigns of 56 and 55BC.

accompanied on their return to Britain by one Commius, supported by Caesar as the chief of a powerful southern British tribe, the Atrebates. Commius was ordered to urge other tribal leaders to trust Rome, and to warn them of Caesar's coming. Caesar's expeditions into southern Britain in 55BC and again the following year were certainly not planned as invasions; he lacked the resources for occupation, and the most important military reason for making the crossings was probably to discourage support for the Britons' rebellious cousins in northern Gaul. The second expedition was more successful then the first, resulting, as it did, in the capitulation of various tribes, the seizing of hostages and spoils, and the paying of annual tributes to Rome, but the main purpose of both expeditions was publicity.

The crossings of Oceanus Britannicus caught the imagination of the Roman public more sharply than even the bridging of the Rhine. Caesar became a hero, and a public thanksgiving of 20 days was decreed in Rome, very satisfactorily trumping any popularity that Crassus and Pompey had been able to achieve in the capital.

Before Caesar's campaigns, Roman naval actions had been confined to the Mediterranean. The trireme illustrated on this denarius from 49BC was ill suited to working in the tidal waters of the Atlantic seaboard and campaigns had to be halted until suitable conditions or vessels were available. (© R Sheridan/AAA Collection Ltd)

The last uprising of Vercingetorix

The disunity of the Gallic Celts had allowed Caesar to pick off the tribes one by one, despite the fact he enjoyed no great superiority of forces, and had even enabled him to enlist the very effective Gallic cavalry as allies in various campaigns. These years had, nevertheless, seen very determined attempts to resist Roman expansion, and in the winter of 53/52BC the great revolt which had been threatening erupted, perhaps because the tribes finally realised that co-ordinated resistance could prove effective against the Romans, and possibly because a tribal council that Caesar had held the previous year indicated that Gaul was now being treated as a province of Rome.

Vercingetorix, the charismatic young son of Celtillus of the royal house of the Arverni, was fanatically anti-Roman, and a leader of real ability; and he was willing to use any means to his end. He built a coalition of Gallic tribes around his own leadership, and urged a 'scorched earth' policy, so as to avoid pitched battles and sieges while cutting the Romans off from supplies. Villages were burned to the ground, wells poisoned, roads destroyed, and the countryside stripped of crops and livestock. Caesar's troops were subjected to ambush and attack from all sides, and their supply lines and stores were constantly being destroyed.

VERCINGETORIX (72–46BC)

An ambitious young noble of the Arvernian tribe whose father had been executed for attempting to make himself king, Vercingetorix was ejected from the tribe by his uncle and other tribal leaders. They opposed his attempt to raise rebellion, but he was nonetheless able to raise a force and take control of the Arveni, then succeed where no other Gallic leader had, by forging an army under single leadership to resist Rome. His authority was so great that he was able to maintain Gallic morale even after a couple of reverses.

Plutarch wrote this account of the surrender of the proud Gallic chieftain:

> The leader Vercingetorix put on his finest armour and equipped his horse magnificently, then sailed out of the gate. After riding several times around Caesar who was sitting on a dais, he then dismounted, took off his armour, and set himself at Caesar's feet where he remained in silence until Caesar ordered the guard to take him away and keep him for his triumph.

A coin of Vercingetorix who made himself king of the Arverni tribe and was able to unite the Gallic tribes under his sole leadership, to create serious opposition to the Romans. (© R Sheridan/ AAA Collection Ltd)

Knowing Vercingetorix to be in the vicinity, Caesar besieged Gergovia near Clemont-Ferrand, a strong position easily defended from behind ten-foot perimeter walls built on the crest of a range of hills. The garrison repulsed an attempted storming, and the Gallic army was able to launch an overwhelming attack from outside the walls on the troops occupied with the siege. By the time Caesar retired from the field that night he had lost 700 men and 36 centurions – his first outright defeat in Gaul.

A major ambush followed, but Vercingetorix was unable to control his hot-headed followers, and what had been intended as a feint attack to separate a Roman column led by Caesar from its baggage train turned into a fatal reality. In their battle-madness the Gallic Celts charged anything in their path, and were methodically slaughtered in the customary manner by the superbly disciplined legions. Vercingetorix retired with his own forces to Alesia on the Seine (modern Alise-Ste-Reine). He was followed by Caesar with about 3,000 infantry and a force of mercenary Germanic cavalry. While Vercingetorix stayed inside Alesia, the centre and figurehead of Gallic resistance, Caesar made use of every resource of Roman military skill in preparing the containing defences – a complicated series of dry ditches were dug; a tributary of the Seine was diverted to fill a moat; and large areas were sewn with caltrops and 'lilies' (sharp stakes sunk in pits). Walls were built facing both inwards towards Alesia and outwards towards any would-be relieving army of Gauls;

The reconstructed Roman siege-works of Alesia. Archaeological investigations at Alesia have shown that these defences were nowhere near as extensive or complete as Caesar claimed. Nonetheless, they were highly effective in repelling a joint attack by those besieged in Alesia and the Gallic relieving army. (© M Andrews/AAA Collection Ltd)

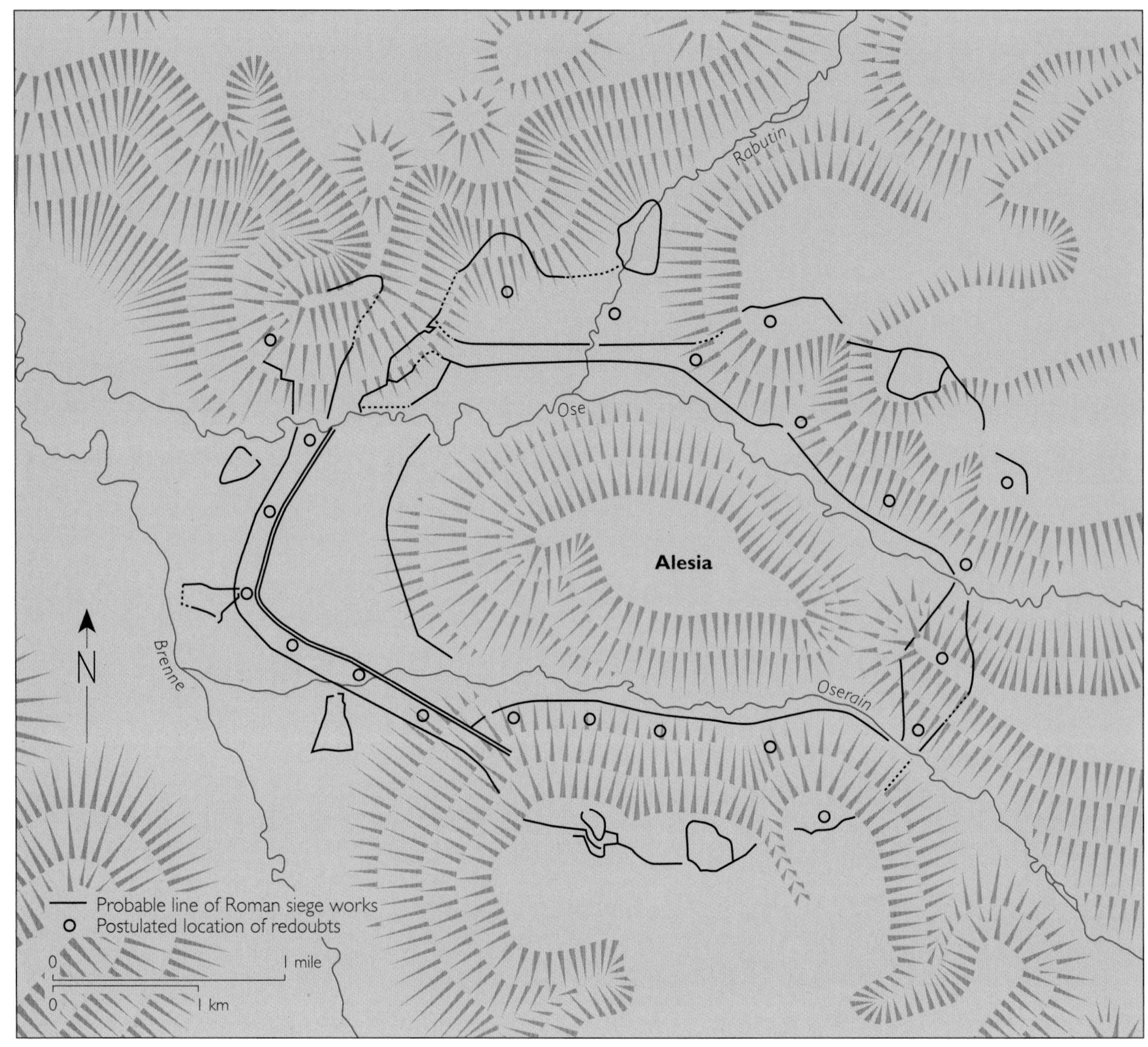

The siege of Alesia.

the outer rampart was all of 15 miles long. Caesar's besiegers thus occupied a ring around the town, defended front and rear.

After a month's siege the defenders of Alesia expelled the women, children, old and sick from the town to save useless mouths. They were not allowed to leave the site by the Romans, and presumably gradually perished in the no-man's land between the armies. Soon afterwards a Gallic relief army appeared outside Roman lines, and Caesar's army was subjected to attacks from both inside and outside. During one furious attack, Caesar himself finally took the Gallic attackers in the rear with four cohorts and part of the Roman cavalry. The Gauls broke off their attempt on the wall, and those who were not cut down were taken prisoner. Disheartened, the Gallic relief army began to melt away, and on the following day Vercingetorix and his tribal chiefs were delivered up to the Romans, and the garrison's weapons handed over, while the general sat before his inner fortifications.

Over the next two years Gaul was brought under Caesar's control so completely that there were to be no further national risings, even during the Roman civil wars of 49–31BC. The utmost ruthlessness was shown towards any sign of resistance. The new province's tax yield amounted to four million *sesterces*; a Gallic legion was raised, and some Gallic leaders were placed on Caesar's staff. Many Gauls fled to Germany, Switzerland, Eastern Europe and Britain.

Vercingetorix was kept in chains reserved for Caesar's eventual triumphal procession, for six long years. In 46BC his shrunken frame was dressed once more in his best armour; and after being paraded in Caesar's triumph Vercingetorix, a prince of Gaul, was ritually strangled.

Gallic troops

A warrior's appearance and status

The appearance to southern European eyes of Celtic warriors must have been unforgettable – their height, white skin, muscularity, fair hair and blue eyes. Their abundant hair was left uncut by most warriors. In some cases it was plaited so as to hang on either side of the forehead. The Sicilian-Greek Diodorus describes how some Celts smeared their hair with thick lime wash and drew it back from the forehead to produce a weird effect, like the flying white mane of a horse. Drooping moustaches were popular, and there are also depictions of bearded warriors.

The Celtic fashion of wearing trousers was particularly noted by Greek and Roman writers, and the colourful chequered and striped patterns of the Gauls' trousers were probably made of wool or linen. Tunics with long or short sleeves were worn with a waist belt or girdle; over this was worn a cloak. Braiding and fringes were attached separately. Leather shoes completed the turnout.

Neck rings, known as torcs, were worn by chieftains and many warriors, made of gold, electrum, silver and bronze. Most surviving examples are of exquisite workmanship. Large numbers of these torcs must have fallen into the hands of victorious Roman forces in their wars with the Gauls; perhaps more significant is the Romans' copying of this and other fashions from their deadly but impressive enemies. Bronze brooches, often embellished with studs mounted with coral or exquisitely enamelled, are found in warrior graves singly or in pairs, in the region of the chest where they had held a cloak in place.

One of the best insights into the character of the Celtic warrior was written by Strabo, a Greek geographer who lived around the beginning of the first century AD. He wrote:

> The whole race, which is now called Celtic or Galatic, is madly fond of war, high spirited and quick to battle, but otherwise straightforward and not of evil character. And so when they are stirred up they assemble in their bands for battle, quite openly and without forethought; so that they are easily handled by those who desire to outwit them. For any time or place, and on whatever pretext you stir them up, you will have them ready to face danger,

Roman marble copy of an original bronze statue forming part of a group erected at Pergamene by Attalos I. The statues commemorated Attalos' victory over the Celts of Asia Minor (the Galatae) in 240BC. This superb piece is now known as 'The Dying Gaul'; note the torc, the moustache, and the spiky effect of the hair, perhaps lime-washed? (© R. Sheridan/ AAA Collection Ltd)

> even if they have nothing on their side but their own strength and courage ... To the frankness and high-spiritedness of their temperament must be added the traits of childish boastfulness and love of decoration.

In most Gallic tribes, raiding neighbours was the warrior's principal means of acquiring wealth and position, and tribes sought to extend their influence over smaller neighbours. The bravest tribes, and therefore the most secure, were those with wide influence and many dependent tribes. Tribes might form alliances with neighbours or even, in the case of the Sequani, with the Germans, in order to increase their own military prowess. Gallic war bands consisted of groups of warriors belonging to an elite class, following their chieftain and concentrating on raiding; larger-scale armies of the kind faced by the Romans in Gaul were probably less common, and may have included peasants, the dependent farmers who would not normally have been involved in regular warfare.

Training

From early puberty the young man of the warrior caste progressed through the martial arts of the Celt, with the accompaniment of hunting, feasting and drinking. As a fully fledged warrior he would support and be supported in battle by a close age group of his own peers, who had been with him throughout his training for manhood. In this way many young men developed a strong man-to-man bond; and Didorus, Strabo and Athenaeus all remark that homo-erotic practices were accepted among Celtic warriors.

Gallic cavalrymen of the first century BC. Many Celtic horsemen fought without helmets or body armour, and it seems most likely that during their life-or-death struggle with Rome some of the poorer warriors must have acquired items of captured Roman equipment that escaped ritual destruction. These riders would normally throw their javelins immediately before contact; the heavier thrusting spear would be used at close quarters, and finally the sword might be drawn. (Painting by Angus McBride © Osprey Publishing Ltd)

The infantry

The Gaul, whether on foot or mounted, was primarily a swordsman. The mass of infantry warriors was the most formidable part of a Gallic army; they fought as 'heavy' infantry, coming into direct contact with enemy troops. After some time spent slashing the air with their long swords, pouring abuse on the enemy, rhythmically banging their weapons on their shields and tossing their standards to the harsh braying of war trumpets, the tall swordsmen rolled forward like an incoming wave and began a screaming run towards enemy lines. At about 30 metres they began to discharge their javelins; within seconds individual warriors were using their powerful physique to break up the opposing ranks.

If this first assault failed, a whole series of these attacks would be mounted, separated by short rest periods. The charges would last until the enemy was battered into defeat, or the Gauls became exhausted and retired, or just stood their ground in defiance.

Celtic infantry and cavalry on the Gundestrup Cauldron. The warriors have animal motifs on their helmets, which would have made them stand out on the battlefield, and they are accompanied into battle by the carnyx, a long trumpet-like instrument made of bronze. (© R. Sheridan/AAA Collection Ltd)

The cavalry

Gallic nobles and their immediate following filled the ranks of the cavalry. We may suppose that most wore metal helmets, and carried spears and javelins. Cavalry tactics were normally simple: a shower of javelins were thrown, and followed up by a charge using spears and swords. Gallic cavalry, manned by the wealthiest warriors, was particularly effective and scored significant victories against Caesar's more numerous auxiliary cavalry in the first couple of campaigning seasons. The lack of stirrups was no bar to powerful cavalry; the design of the Celtic saddle, with a pommel on each corner of the seat unit, provided its rider with a secure mount from which to throw spears, thrust with a spear or slash with a sword, and implement shock tactics. The horsemanship of the cavalrymen and their co-operation with the light infantry who regularly worked alongside the German cavalry was clearly impressive, and indicative of at least some training, which we hear little about in any sources.

The British charioteer's body is painted with designs in woad – his passenger is a Belgic nobleman, fully armed with a set of javelins, sword and 'infantry' shield. The Celtic chariot was by all accounts an extremely fast and manoeuvrable vehicle; the Celts delighted in performing stunning tricks of daring and skill at high speed. The warrior was able to fight against horsemen from the chariot platform, but would dismount to fight on foot against infantry. The charioteer would stand off, ready to swoop in and pick up his nobleman in an emergency. (Painting by Angus McBride © Osprey Publishing Ltd)

Use of chariots

When Caesar engaged with the Celtic tribes in Britain, he found they were still using chariots, something that had gone out of fashion on the Continent, and their speed and agility caused the Roman infantry serious difficulties. The chariots served as battlefield 'taxis' for the wealthiest nobles, dropping them off at the fighting, and collecting them up again if they were injured or needed to withdraw from the battle. Caesar leaves us this impression of Celtic chariot tactics from *De Bello Gallico*, his memoirs of the Gallic Wars written in the mid-first century BC:

> In chariot fighting, the Britons drive all over the field hurling javelins, and generally the terror inspired by the horses and the noise of the chariot wheels is sufficient to throw their opponents' ranks into disorder. Then, after making their way between the squadrons of their own cavalry, they *[the high class warriors riding in the chariots]* jump down and engage the enemy on foot. In the meantime the charioteers retire a short distance...and place the

> chariots in such a position that their masters, if hard pressed...have an easy means of retreat...By daily training and practice they attain such proficiency that even on a steep slope they are able to control the horses at full gallop, and check and turn them in a moment. They can run along the chariot pole, stand on the yoke, and get back into the chariot as quick as lightning.

Slingers and archers

Firepower was available in the form of slingers and archers, although these men were probably not members of the warrior class, as this form of warfare was not really regarded as 'heroic'. Slingers were sometimes involved in open warfare (such as the Gallic ambush of a Roman column in 54BC), but more often in the defence of hill forts, along with archers. In preparation for the general revolt of 52BC, Vercingetorix called up all the archers of Gaul; they were probably Gauls of the lower classes, but were vital to the success of the strategy of the revolt.

Arms, armour and equipment

Warriors equipped themselves according to their wealth and status: the braver and more successful, the more likely they were to be able to adorn themselves with beautifully decorated and high quality equipment. Only the wealthiest warriors would have possessed mail coats,

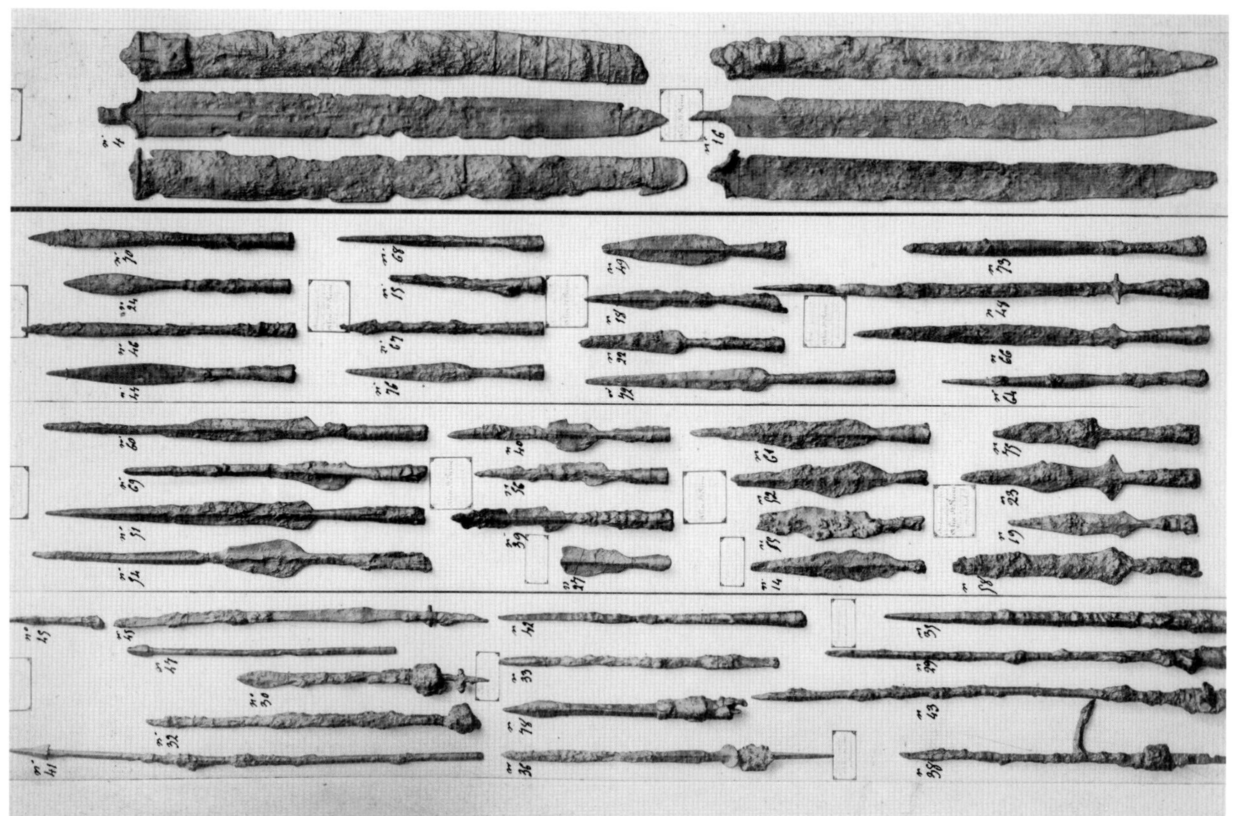

Finds of weapons from the Roman siege at Alesia. The site was explored by Napoleon III in the 19th century and many of these iron spearheads, *pilum* shafts and catapult bolts were found at Monte Rea where the fiercest fighting took place.

but such aristocrats could have been equipped in a way very similar to a Roman legionary, with the mail armour providing reasonably good protection from the slashing blows of the long Celtic swords, a bronze or iron helmet, sword and shield.

Helmets, like mail coats, were probably very rare and worn only by the wealthiest warriors, but stylistically they were very similar to some Roman helmets; indeed, the *coolus* helmet which evolved into one of the main elements of the Roman imperial army was originally a Gallic design.

Celtic warriors were primarily thought of as swordsmen in the ancient world, and Gallic Celts carried spears and swords, the latter around 90cm long, considerably longer than the Roman *gladius*. They were designed primarily for slashing rather than stabbing, and pointed to a fighting technique that required plenty of room for the individual to wield his long weapon. The Greek historian Polybius, writing in the second century BC, claimed these long swords had a tendency to break on impact:

> ...they are effective only at the first blow; thereafter they are blunt and bent so that the warrior has not time to wedge it against the ground and straighten it with his foot, the second blow is quite ineffective.

However, Polybius' claims are unfounded, and archaeological evidence shows that many Gallic swords were made of high-quality iron and they were extremely effective weapons. The sword was usually suspended on the right hip from a sword belt of leather or a chain of linked iron rings.

Spears and javelins of bronze and iron took various forms and sizes, and bows were evidently used in some areas by some warriors. The sling – the simplest and cheapest of all missile weapons, but one demanding long practice for accuracy – was also used, and great dumps of sling ammunition have been found on some Celtic sites. The effectiveness of the sling stone should never be underestimated. Large 'cobblestones' hurled at great speed could inflict fatal crushing injuries even upon soldiers protected by metal helmets, and many hits must have produced major limb fractures.

The Gallic elongated rectangular shield was probably made of hide or wood like the Roman *scutum*. Some shields may not have been particularly thick or strong, which may explain why Caesar reports that the Roman *pila* were able to pierce several of them simultaneously; the bronze shields that survive from antiquity may have been for decorative or ceremonial purposes and not actually for use in battle. Given that the majority of warriors probably lacked body armour, and indeed some may have chosen to fight without armour to stress their courage and military prowess, the shield was a vital piece of protective equipment. When their shields were put out of action by the Roman *pila*, the Gauls became dangerously exposed to the Roman attack.

Organisation and strategy

Very little is known about the organisation of Gallic armies and their workings in pitched battle, although they seem to have relied heavily on the effectiveness of infantry and cavalry charges at the start of battle to break the enemy lines. Pitched battle, even on a small scale, provided one of the best opportunities to display military prowess and so was an important way of making war, but not all Gallic tribes were so keen on meeting the enemy in the open, especially when that enemy was as powerful as Rome, so the strategies of the tribes varied. While some stronger tribes and coalitions like the Nervii were eager to meet the Romans in pitched battle, others like the tribes of Aquitania in south-western Gaul relied more on hit-and-run tactics and attacking the invaders' supply lines, as Vercingetorix planned to do during the revolt of 52BC.

Large Gallic armies could not remain in existence for very long, and unless a decisive engagement quickly occurred, such an army would usually have to disband because of lack of supplies. The Belgic army in 57BC, which combined many different tribes, was forced to dissipate for this reason when a decisive engagement with Caesar was not forthcoming.

The professional Roman army had many advantages over the armies of the Gallic warrior societies and it was not surprising that several tribes quickly went over to Rome, or that under the leadership of such an effective leader as Caesar, the conquest of Gaul was completed remarkably quickly.

Fighting style

Gallic and Roman fighting styles were the complete antithesis of each other. For both cultures, victory in pitched battle was the ultimate accolade for a warrior or soldier, and also for tribal chieftains and Roman generals. To show courage on the battlefield was expected; to die in battle was glorious. By the mid-first century BC, when Caesar began his conquest of Gaul, Romans and Gauls had been fighting each other on and off for centuries. In their literature the Romans betrayed both a fear of their barbarian neighbours, and a sneaking admiration for the way they fought. Gauls were perceived as much larger than Romans (they are portrayed as being of almost giant stature in some accounts); certainly they probably were generally a little taller than the average Italian legionary, and the Romans seem to have been rather defensive about being shorter than their adversaries.

The Gallic fighting style allowed the warrior to display himself on the battlefield, either through fighting naked or by wearing elaborately decorated armour, and he showed off his valour by fighting as an individual. The warrior's long sword required him to have a fair amount of space around him on the battlefield in order to operate properly. The Celtic sword was essentially a slashing weapon, and in the hands of a tall Gallic warrior with a long reach, could be a deadly blade, particularly against shorter opposition with short swords. But the Gallic warriors fought as individuals; though training and especially experience must have provided them with some understanding of tactics, and commands could have been communicated on the battlefield through musical instruments, they did not possess the same degree of training to fight as a unit as the Roman soldiers did. When forced to retreat, they could not always maintain ranks and withdraw in good order, something that required considerable training and absolute trust in one's fellow soldiers.

BATTLE AGAINST THE NERVII, 57BC

Caesar employed eight legions, two of which were still marching, and an unknown number of auxiliary infantry and cavalry. The Nervii had at least 60,000 warriors of the Nervii, Atrebates and Viromandui.

Faced with a sudden attack, the Roman legionaries did exactly the right thing. Their training and discipline kicked in, and they grabbed arms and automatically created a line of battle. The two cavalry forces were already engaged, with the Gallic cavalry mauling the Romans. Despite the battle line being cut up by the hedgerows, the Roman held the line fast and withheld the Belgic onslaught. The Roman centre was successful and the left wing repulsed the Atrebates, pursuing them across the Sambre. This success left the half-built Roman camp and the right wing of the battle line exposed, and the Gauls captured the camp.

Meanwhile, the Roman right wing was outflanked by the Nervii, several of the officers had been killed and the ranks had become too packed together to operate effectively: the situation was critical. Taking up position on foot with the front rank soldiers, Caesar ordered the ranks opened up and the two legions to form a square so they could defend themselves from attack on all sides. His own presence helped to stiffen resistance until help arrived in the form of the X Legion, which had been sent back to assist after capturing the enemy encampment, and the two rookie legions of the rearguard that had finally arrived. The combined force of five legions turned the tide of battle and obliterated the Nervii who refused to surrender or withdraw.

Caesar's over-confidence had led to a dangerous situation, but his personal bravery and the experience of his army had turned it into a significant victory.

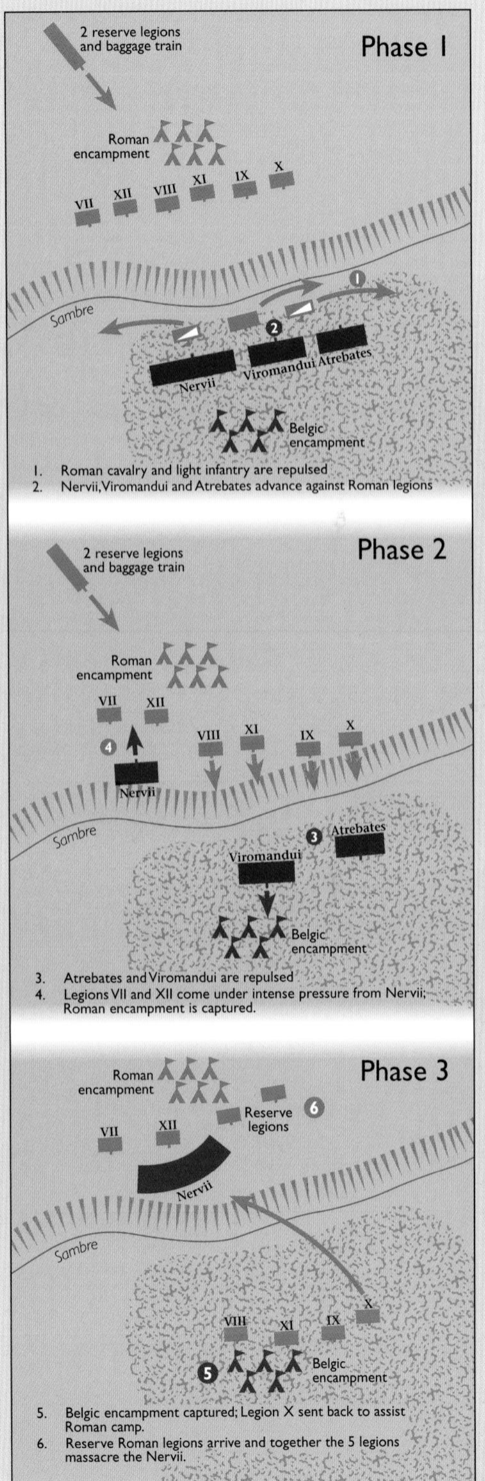

The battle against the Nervii, 57BC.

The Battersea Shield, found in the Thames at London. This bronze shield may just have been for ceremonial purposes, but it is the same design as the wooden versions used in battle. The Celtic shield, like the Roman *scutum*, provided good protection to the infantryman. (© R. Sheridan/AAA Collection Ltd)

This made them vulnerable to outflanking manoeuvres and to cavalry attacks on retreating warriors. Lack of space to swing their swords could also cause havoc in the Gallic ranks. When forced together, Gallic warriors could not use their swords properly, and this made them vulnerable to an enemy who could operate at very close quarters with deadly efficiency.

Chapter 8
LEGION AGAINST LEGION

The civil wars of Rome

Background

In 49BC Julius Caesar, faced with the choice between being forced out of politics altogether or starting a civil war, invaded Italy. His success effectively tolled the death knell of the Republican political system, for after his victory he established himself as sole ruler of the Roman world. Caesar was murdered because his power was too blatant, and his assassination returned Rome to another period of civil war, which ended only when Caesar's nephew and adopted son Octavian defeated his last rival in 31BC. It was left to Octavian, later given the name Augustus, to create the regime known as the Principate, a monarchy in all but name, returning stability to Rome and its empire at the cost of a loss of political freedom.

The Via Sacra ran through the heart of Rome, at this point passing through the Forum. This route was followed by the triumphal processions honouring successful generals. (© Dr S. Coyne/AAA Collection Ltd)

Caesar seizes control

Once Caesar made the decision to cross the Rubicon into Roman territory in 49BC, much of Rome was filled with dread about the bloodshed that they believed would follow. The precedent of every civil war fought in the last 40 years gave them good reason to fear. In Gaul, Caesar and his legions had fought very aggressively and often with extreme brutality, some sources claiming that over a million people had been killed in less than a decade. Perhaps, as some modern commentators claim, many expected the legions to behave in no less harsh a manner now that they had burst into Italy, and Cicero on one occasion even wondered whether Caesar would not prove more like Hannibal than a Roman general.

Caesar's army moved quickly, and he seized towns largely unopposed. The advance of his army was not accompanied by massacre or atrocity, however, and his soldiers were under strict orders not to loot. Caesar was trying to show that he was still willing to compromise. Messages went back and forth as he suggested various compromises. Pompey and his allies replied by saying that they could not negotiate while Caesar commanded troops on Italian soil, and that he must return to Cisalpine Gaul before anything could be discussed. Pompey did offer to leave for Spain once Caesar had laid down his command, but Caesar refused the offer, perhaps not trusting the Senate, or maybe feeling that he had gone too far to withdraw at this stage. Even so, both sides continued to claim publicly that they still hoped for a negotiated settlement, and were only thwarted by the enemy's intransigence.

The suddenness of Caesar's advance surprised and unnerved his opponents, just as he had intended. Pompey left Rome in the second half of January, declaring that it could not be defended. He was followed by most of the magistrates, including the consuls, who left in such haste that it suggested panic. Many Romans were still uncertain about just how firmly committed each side was to fighting, and this open admission of military weakness made many wonder whether Pompey could really be relied on to defend the Republic.

The early clashes between Caesar and Pompey's armies went badly for Pompey, and were opportunities for Caesar to gain more troops, and garner support in Italy for his now-notorious clemency (*clementia*), a policy to which he would adhere throughout the conflict in marked contrast to his opponents who employed the more brutal methods normal in past civil wars. In less than two months Caesar had seized control in Italy. Pompey had escaped, with the best of his soldiers, and many leading senators. Caesar sent Curio with two legions to secure Sardinia and then Africa. Caesar himself decided to set out for Spain overland and defeat Pompey's legions there. In a matter of months, and through a mixture of boldness and skilful manoeuvre, Caesar had overrun Spain at minimal loss to himself.

In Africa, Curio encountered the governor, Publius Attius Varus, who had declared against Caesar. He was supported by the Numidian King Juba, who commanded a large, if sometimes unreliable army. Curio had little military experience – none at all of high command – and was considered brilliant but unreliable by most of his contemporaries.

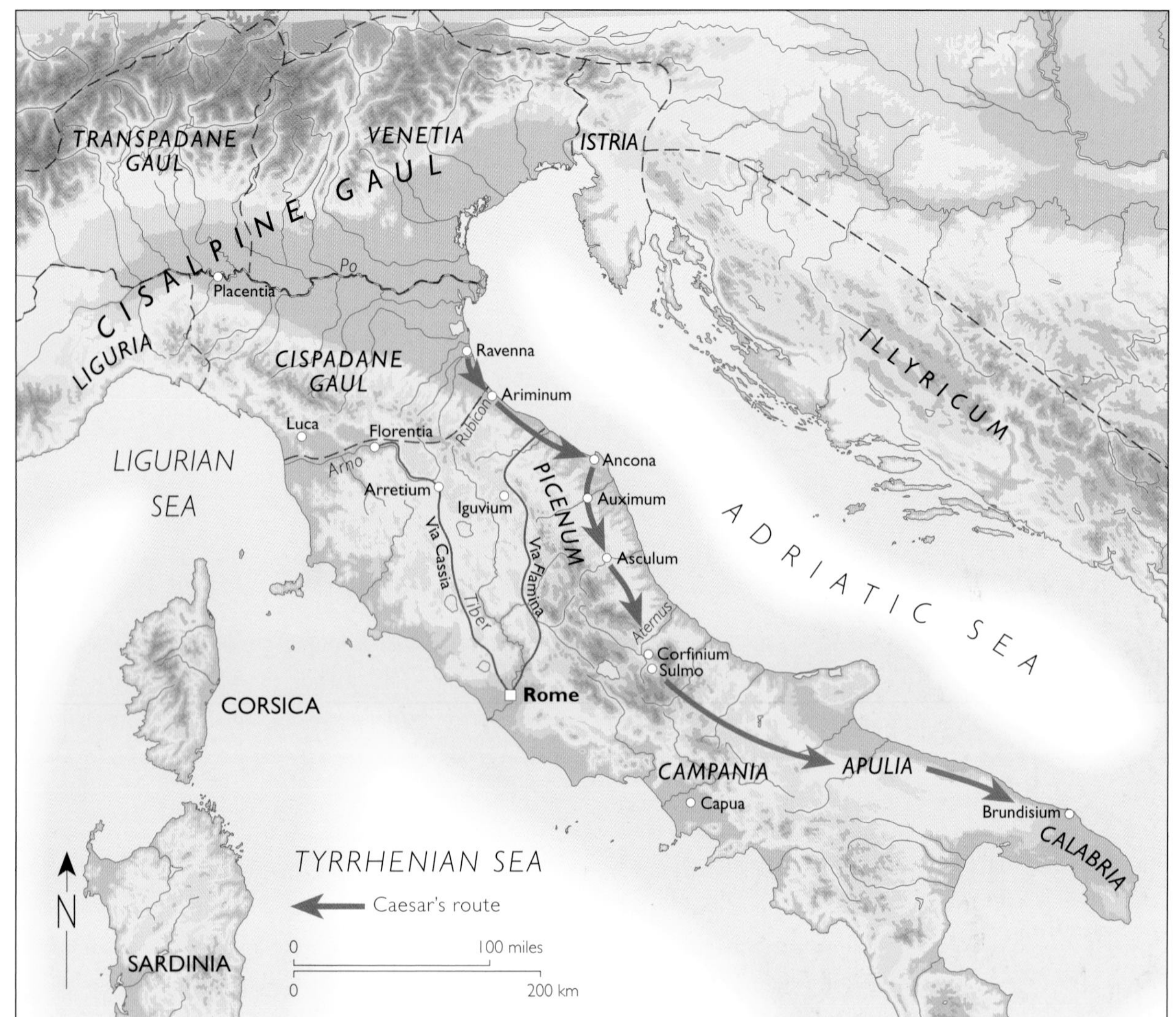

The Italian peninsula and Caesar's advance.

Acting on false intelligence, Curio launched an attack on what he believed was a small detachment of Juba's army. In fact, the bulk of the king's forces was there, and the Romans were ambushed and virtually annihilated. Curio was surrounded with the remnants of his troops on a hilltop and died fighting. Only a small fraction of the army escaped to Italy. This was not the only bad news reaching Caesar in late 49BC, for Mark Antony, a tribune who supported Caesar, had suffered a lesser defeat in Illyricum.

Caesar spent a short time in Rome, having been appointed dictator before he arrived, and held the post for 11 days, using his powers to hold elections in which he was voted to the consulship. He was eager to move against Pompey, and near the end of the year went to join his army of some 12 legions along with 1,000 cavalry which had been assembled at Brundisium. Caesar exhorted his soldiers by saying that this next campaign would be the culmination of their labours. The crossing of the Adriatic was a great gamble, for Caesar had no significant naval force with which to oppose the vast Pompeian

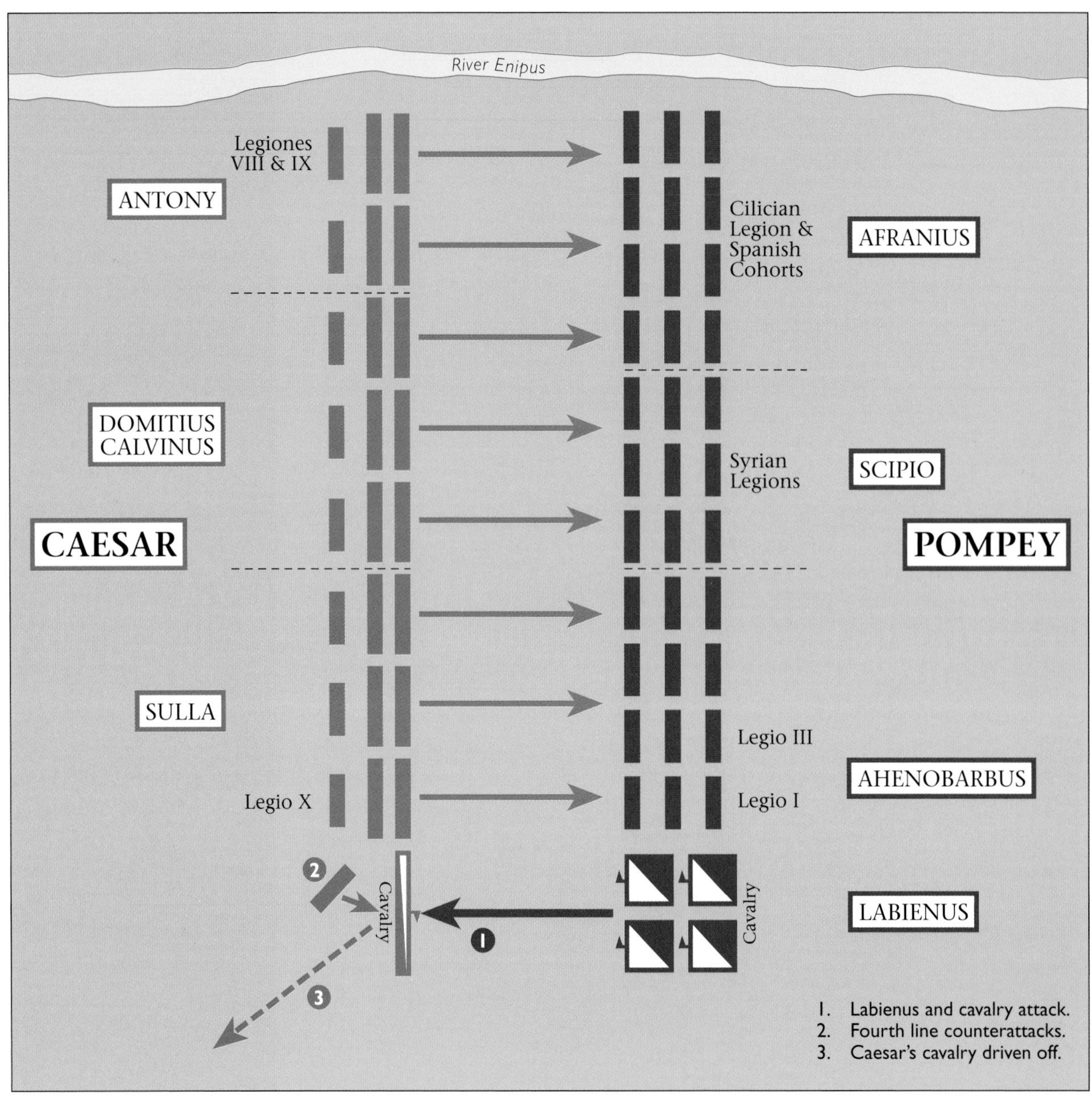

The battle of Pharsalus, phase 1.

fleet, yet the enemy did not expect Caesar to move in winter when the weather was poor, and Caesar landed without opposition at Paeleste in Epirus. However, Bibulus, commander of the Pompeian fleet, intercepted some of Caesar's transport ships, isolating Caesar from the remainder of his army under Mark Antony, and leaving him severely outnumbered by the enemy.

Caesar was isolated, with few supplies, and his men had to make do with the little they had brought with them and whatever could be gathered from local communities. Finally, on 10 April, Mark Antony managed to bring the remaining legions across the Adriatic – Pompey reacted too slowly and failed to prevent the union of the two forces. Caesar's supply problems

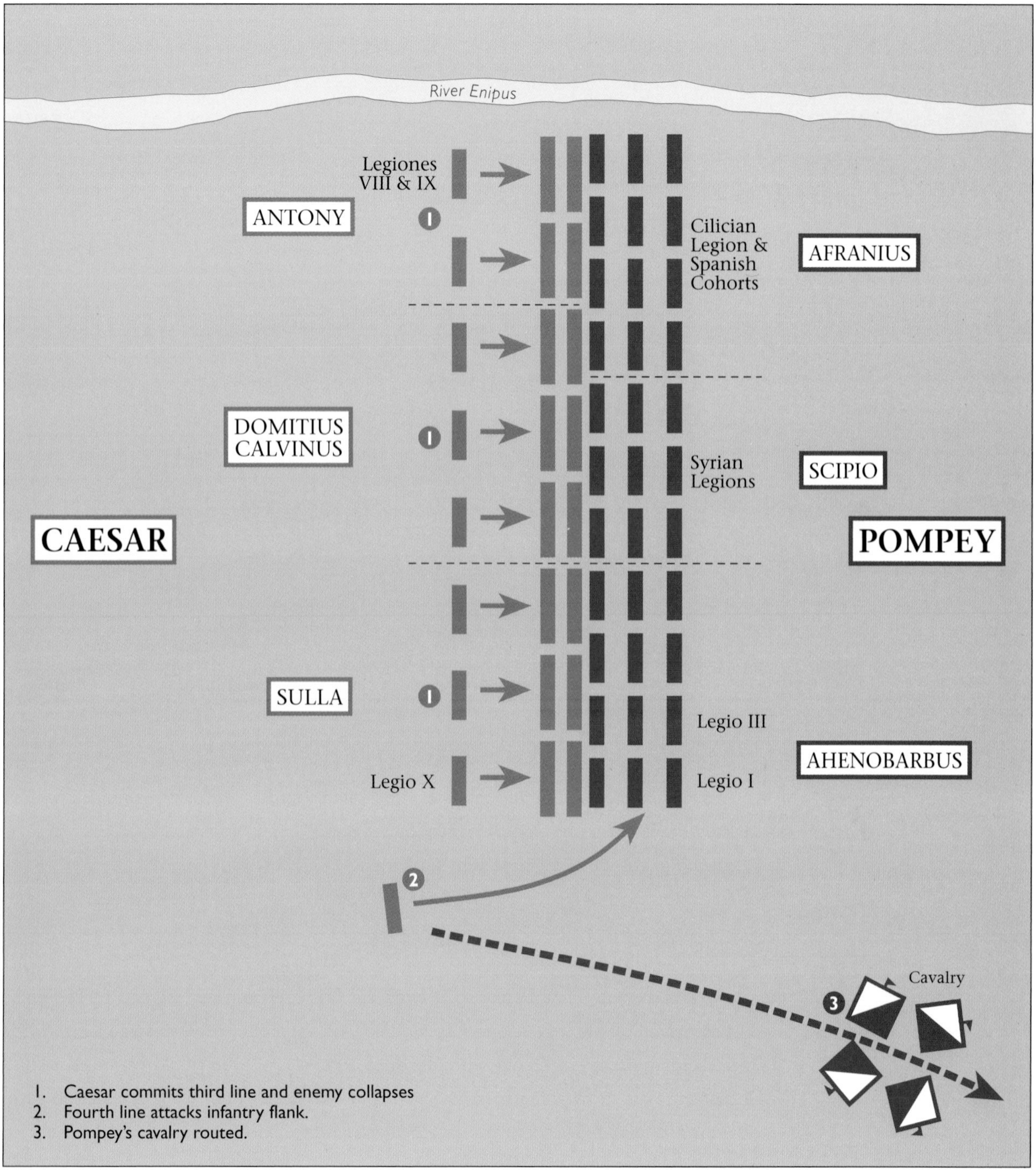

The battle of Pharsalus, phase 2.

continued to hamper his progress, and his army experienced some defeats in skirmishes against the Pompeian enemy. Pompey now had several options. One would have been to use his fleet to cross to Italy, now largely unprotected, but this would still mean that Caesar had to be defeated at some future date, and might be seen as running from his opponent. His personal belief was that they ought to shadow Caesar's army, but avoid open confrontation, hoping to wear him down by depriving him of supplies. This was a well-known Roman strategy, often known by the nickname of 'kicking the enemy in the belly'. However, there was massive pressure from the senators with the army to bring matters to a swift conclusion by bringing the enemy to battle. In early August the two armies camped near each other on the plains of Pharsalus. Several days were spent in the manoeuvring and formal challenges to battle that so often preceded the battles of this period. The pressure on Pompey to fight grew stronger and stronger. Finally the two armies clashed again at the battle of Pharsalus, a defeat for Pompey despite his superior numbers. This was a deeply humiliating defeat, and saw Pompey leave for the coast directly afterwards.

Defeat of Pompey and war with Egypt

Caesar rested only a very short time after the victory, before rushing in pursuit of Pompey; until he had been taken or killed there could be no end to the war. News arrived that Pompey had gone to Rhodes and then taken ship for Egypt, hoping to receive aid in rebuilding an army.

A 16th-century plate showing the battle of Pharsalus. If contemporary accounts are accurate, Pompey's command at Pharsalus was remarkably spiritless, and his behaviour, being the first rather than the last to despair and leave the battlefield, utterly inappropriate for a Roman general. Caesar also says that his men were astounded by the luxuries that they discovered in the Pompeian camp, items more suitable for effete Orientals than true Romans, although this could well be propaganda. (© R. Sheridan/AAA Collection Ltd)

Egypt was wracked by its own civil war at this time, for the old King Ptolemy XI Auletes (or 'flute-player') had left the throne jointly to his son Ptolemy XII – a boy of about 14 – and his eldest daughter Cleopatra.

The boy king was dominated by his advisers, Pothinus the eunuch and Achillas the commander of his army, a force that effectively included two Roman legions which had been in the province since 55BC and had largely 'gone native'. Pompey's ship arrived on the coast near Ptolemy's camp and he appealed to the young king for support. Since the king was unwilling to support a loser and eager to win favour with the victor, Pompey was lured ashore and murdered, the first blow being struck by a centurion who had served under him in his Asian campaigns.

Caesar landed at Alexandria on 2 October 48BC, and was met by a deputation from Ptolemy that presented him with Pompey's head and signet ring. Caesar is supposed to have wept, distraught at the loss of his former friend and missing the opportunity of pardoning him. This emotion may have been genuine, as indeed may his alleged desire to spare Pompey, but it is equally possible that he simply wished to distance himself from the cruelty of an act from which he derived political benefit. Nevertheless, he gave honourable burial to Pompey's remains, then marched in pomp to the palace. This display enraged the volatile Alexandrians and provoked some rioting. Caesar's soldiers responded with force and, since the late king had recommended his children to Rome, declared that both sides in the Egyptian Civil War should disarm and submit to his arbitration. Some time in the next few days Cleopatra visited Caesar. The most famous story is that she was wrapped up in a carpet or blanket and carried secretly into the palace by a faithful Greek attendant, before being unrolled in front of a mesmerised Caesar. Cleopatra was 21 – more than 30 years younger than Caesar – exceptionally attractive, if not quite flawlessly beautiful, highly educated, intelligent, and with a fascinating personality. This began one of the most famous romances in history.

It was not long before Ptolemy's advisers felt that their cause could not compete with his sister's for Caesar's favour. Leading their army to support the mob of Alexandria, they besieged the palace, blockading Caesar's men for six months. His soldiers were close to panic when the water supply was cut off, but new wells were dug inside the compound and the crisis averted. Reinforced by *legio* XXXVII, composed of former Pompeians, Caesar became bolder and attempted to seize the whole of the Pharos Island, on which the great lighthouse, one of the Seven Wonders of the World, was built. After a near-disastrous naval engagement which caused confusion and panic among Caesar's troops, almost leading to his drowning, Caesar regained control and his army was reinforced by that of King Mithridates of Pergamum, who had marched overland from Asia Minor to Egypt. In the next engagement, Ptolemy fled but drowned when the boat carrying him to safety capsized. Caesar returned to relieve Alexandria.

The war in Egypt was over, but for more than half a year Caesar had been out of contact with the rest of the world. The surviving Pompeians had had time to regroup, and the Civil War would drag on. Caesar remained in Egypt for two months, allegedly feasting with

From Alexandria, this is the only known representation of the Pharos lighthouse, one of the Seven Wonders of the Ancient World. According to the Arab traveller Abou-Haggag Al-Andaloussi who visited the lighthouse in 1166, it was 117m high (384ft), and hollow, with the internal core being used as a shaft to lift the fuel needed for the fire. There was a huge mirror at the top which reflected sunlight during the day. During the night, fire was used as the warning light. (© R. Sheridan/AAA Collection Ltd)

Cleopatra. At one stage the queen is supposed to have taken him on a luxurious cruise down the Nile. Militarily and politically, Caesar's inaction for this long period makes no sense. Perhaps he had never had a clear plan for what he should do once he had won the Civil War, or perhaps he was exhausted and could not resist a time of rest in fascinating company.

Veni, vidi, vici – the Zela campaign

It was not until late May or early June 47BC that Caesar finally stirred himself to move. There was bad news from Syria, and he sailed there with *legio* VI, leaving the rest of his army to garrison Egypt. Caesar marched against Pharnaces, son of King Mithridates, and cause of his father's suicide, having led a rebellion against him. Seeing the disorder caused within the empire by the Civil War, Pharnaces decided to invade the heartland of Pontus, a

Although Cleopatra was famed as the most beautiful woman in the world, it seems this was probably exaggerated. Plutarch says this:

> Her actual beauty was not in itself so remarkable; it was the impact of her spirit that was irresistible. The attraction of her person, joining with the charm of her conversation and the characteristic qualities of all she said or did, was something bewitching. It was a delight merely to hear the sound of her voice.

(© R. Sheridan/AAA Collection Ltd)

territory 'lost' to Rome. Caesar met Pharnaces at Zela, and won a hard-fought battle, which decided the war within days of the beginning of the campaign. Caesar is said to have commented on how lucky Pompey had been to make his reputation as a commander fighting such opponents. Later, when he celebrated his triumph over Pontus, the procession included placards bearing just three Latin words: '*Veni, vidi, vici*' – 'I came, I saw, I conquered'.

Although the eastern Mediterranean was now settled, many problems had developed elsewhere during Caesar's absence. Cassius' behaviour in Spain had provoked rebellion, while in Africa, Scipio, Africanus, Labienus, Cato and many other die-hard senators had raised an enormous army supported by King Juba. There were difficulties in Italy, too, made worse by the lack of communication from Caesar while he was in Egypt. There was also another mutiny among Caesar's veterans, news made all the more bitter because the ringleaders came this time from Caesar's own favourite, the *legio* X. The older soldiers wanted to be discharged and others complained that they had not received the rewards promised once their labours were at an end. These were their public grievances, but boredom may have played as big a part in provoking the outbreak, for throughout history armies have been more prone to mutiny when they are inactive. Caesar arrived back in Italy just as the mutineers were gearing themselves up to march on Rome. His behaviour amazed them when he rode into their camp and addressed them and asked what they wanted. Already stunned, the veterans were horrified when he addressed them as Quirites – civilians rather than soldiers – instead of comrades. It was an incredible display of Caesar's charisma and self-assurance, for soon the legionaries and especially Legio X were begging him to decimate them and take them back into his service.

Caesar was impatient to embark on the African campaign, and spent the bare minimum of time in Rome before hurrying across to Sicily, then on to Africa. A difficult campaign against Scipio's army, reinforced by that of King Juba, saw Caesar's troops suffering at the hands of Numidian cavalry, but Caesar eventually triumphed at Thapsus, specially targeting the enemy elephants with his slingers and archers, panicking the animals who fled, trampling their own troops. Cato committed suicide, as did Juba. Scipio fled by sea, but drowned when his ship sank. Africanus was captured and executed. However, Labienus and Pompey's two sons escaped to Spain to continue the struggle.

Caesar went back to Rome. In the past he had held the dictatorship for just long enough to hold consular elections, but now the Senate voted him into the office for ten years. He held four triumphs over the Gauls, Egyptians, Pharnaces and Juba respectively. Yet, in November 46BC he had to leave for Spain to fight the final campaign of the Civil War.

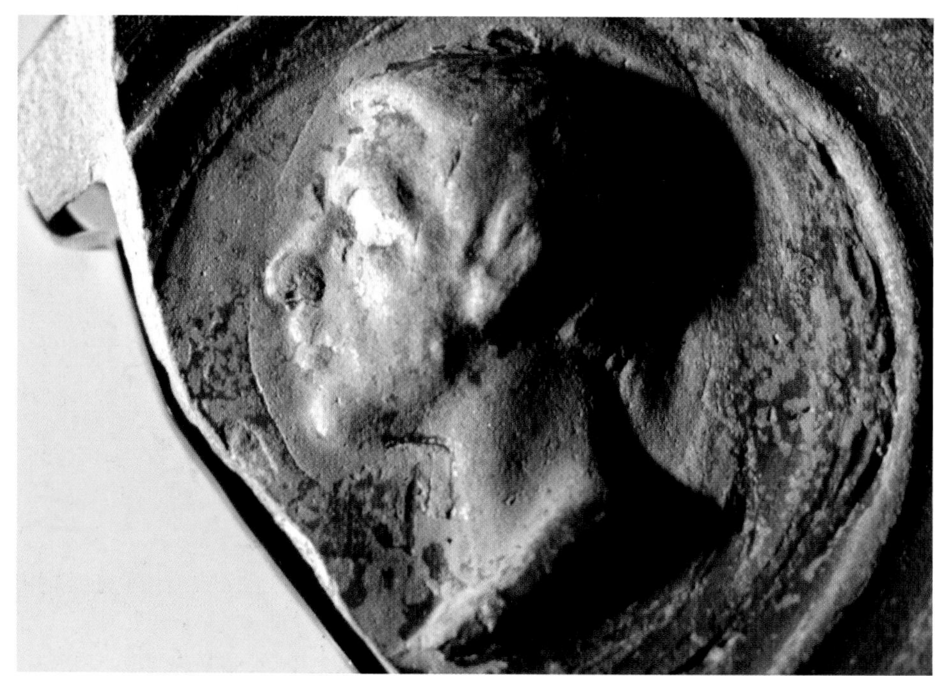

'It is said of Cato that even from his infancy, in his speech, his countenance, and all his childish pastimes, he discovered an inflexible temper, unmoved by any passion, and firm in everything ... to go through with what he undertook. He was rough and ungentle toward those that flattered him, and still more unyielding to those who threatened him. It was difficult to excite him to laughter, his countenance seldom relaxed even into a smile; he was not quickly or easily provoked to anger, but if once incensed, he was no less difficult to pacify.' (Plutarch) (© R. Sheridan/AAA Collection Ltd)

DECIMATION

Decimation was one of the most serious punishments that could be meted out to the Roman army. It involved the tenth man of each legion being condemned to death, with the execution being carried out by his peers, usually through a violent beating. Decimation was sometimes used as a punishment for legions that had deserted or fled a battlefield against orders. Polybius describes it thus:

> This is inflicted as follows: The tribune takes a cudgel and just touches the condemned man with it, after which all in the camp beat or stone him, in most cases despatching him in the camp itself. But even those who manage to escape are not saved thereby: For they are not allowed to return to their homes, and none of the family would dare to receive such a man in his house. So that those who have once fallen into this misfortune are utterly ruined...
>
> If the same thing happens to large bodies, and if entire maniples desert their posts when exceedingly hard pressed, the officers refrain from inflicting the bastinado or the death penalty at all, but find a solution of the difficulty that is both salutary and terror-striking. The tribune assembles the legion, and brings up those guilty of leaving the ranks, reproaches them sharply, and finally chooses by lot sometimes five, sometimes eight, sometimes twenty of the offenders, so adjusting the number thus chosen that they form as near as possible the tenth part of those guilty of cowardice. Those on whom the lot falls are bastinadoed mercilessly in the manner above described; the rest receive rations of barley instead of wheat and are ordered to encamp outside the camp on an unprotected spot. As therefore the danger and dread of drawing the fatal lot affects all equally, as it is uncertain on whom it will fall; and as the public disgrace of receiving barley rations falls on all alike, this practice is that best calculated both to inspire fear and to correct the mischief.
>
> The Histories VI.37.2-4, 38.1-3

The Spanish campaign

Cassius had proved both incompetent and corrupt as governor of Spain, alienating his own troops and the local population. By the time he was replaced by Caius Trebonius the situation was almost beyond redemption and the new governor was expelled by mutinous soldiers. Pompey's elder son Cnaeus arrived and was rapidly acclaimed as commander of the rebellious legions. He was soon joined by other Pompeians, including his brother Sextus and Labienus. A huge army of 13 legions and many auxiliaries was raised, although the quality of most of the new units was highly questionable.

Caesar travelled rapidly, as was his wont, covering the 1,500 miles to Corduba in just 27 days, and whiling away the trip by composing a poem, *The Journey*. He had eight legions, the old soldiers of *legio* X, and 8,000 cavalry. The early stages of fighting included a number of fierce skirmishes, but Cnaeus Pompey was reluctant to risk a battle. It was already proving the most brutal campaign of the entire conflict.

The Pompeians were suffering a continual trickle of deserters. Men accused of publicly stating that they thought Caesar would win were arrested, and executed or imprisoned. In the middle of March, Caesar met Cnaeus Pompey at Munda. The fight was fierce and determined, but Caesar prevailed, despite the fact that his army was fighting uphill. Munda was blockaded, the legionaries grimly fixing the severed heads of Pompeians to spikes topping their rampart. The mopping-up took several months. Caesar had won the Civil War, but now it remained to be seen whether he could win the peace. Unfortunately, he would not be given the time to find out.

On 15 February 44BC, Caesar's dictatorship and other powers were extended for life. A month later he was stabbed to death by a group of senators that included men who had served him for years, as well as pardoned Pompeians.

Becoming an empire

The Second Triumvirate

Directly after Caesar's murder, Octavian, adopted son and heir of Caesar, formally took the name Caius Julius Caesar Octavianus and returned to Italy to rally a few of Caesar's veterans. He was just 19, but incredibly self-confident. Mark Antony failed to take him seriously, and anyway saw him as a rival for the loyalty of Caesar's supporters rather than as a useful ally. It was round about this time that Antony and Cleopatra brought the child Caesarion into the public eye, presenting an actual son of Caesar to counter the adopted heir. Antony soon left for Cisalpine Gaul, taking charge of an enlarged army, with which he was in a position to threaten Rome. To those senators who hoped for a return to peace and stability and were broadly sympathetic to the conspirators, Antony was clearly the greatest threat to peace, for Caesar's other subordinate, Lepidus, was cautious by nature and unlikely to act of his own accord, even though he had command of the legions in Transalpine Gaul and Nearer Spain. Octavian was seen by the Senate as a useful figurehead to draw support away from Antony. Yet Octavian was building up his power, and rallied a force of veterans from *legio* VII and VIII, and was soon joined by two more legions that were nominally under Antony's command, but answered the call of Caesar's heir.

After clashes between Antony and Octavian's armies in Cisalpine Gaul, the two joined forces along with Lepidus, and together at the head of a huge army – altogether nearly 43 legions, though not all were present – they seized Rome, and on 27 November 43BC had a tribune pass a law by which they became triumvirs with consular powers to restore the state for five years. The need to avenge Caesar figured heavily in their propaganda, and the dead dictator was formally deified and a temple constructed for his cult. A comet seen in 44BC was proclaimed as a clear sign that Caesar had ascended to heaven after his murder, and from now on Octavian was regarded as the son of a god.

THE IDES OF MARCH

Caesar planned to leave Rome on 18 March 44BC and, given the scale of his planned campaigns, would be most unlikely to return for several years. Brutus, Cassius and the more than 60 other conspirators decided that they must act. They were a disparate group, but had preserved their secret for several months. On the morning of 15 March (a date known as the Ides) there was some dismay when Caesar did not arrive at the Senate on time. Eventually he came and the Senate rose to greet him. The conspirators clustered round his chair, using the excuse of pleading for the recall of Publius Climber. For a while the charade went on, but when Caesar stood to leave and tried to shake them off, the conspirators drew their knives, Casca striking the first blow from behind. Caesar died of multiple stab wounds. There was a final irony about his death, for Caesar's own Senate House had not been completed, and the old *curia* still lay in ruins from its destruction by Clodius' men. As a result, the Senate had assembled in a temple attached to Pompey's theatre complex. When Caesar fell, his body lay at the foot of a statue of Pompey.

Octavian emerges as champion

The success of the triumvirate could not last long, as each member became more concerned about their own realm of power. An abortive rising by Lepidus in Italy was swiftly defeated by Octavian, but Octavian displayed his father's clemency by sparing Lepidus and allowing him to live out the rest of his life in comfortable retirement as Pontifex Maximus, Rome's most senior priest. In the meantime, Antony's obsession with Cleopatra was growing after her assistance in his ultimately disastrous war with the Parthians. Octavian's propagandists seized on this opportunity to depict Antony as a man so dominated by a sinister eastern seductress that he had betrayed his Roman origins. Octavian portrayed himself as the champion of all Italy against the eastern menace. War finally came in 31BC, and culminated in Antony's defeat at the naval battle of Actium. He and Cleopatra both escaped to Egypt, and committed suicide shortly afterwards.

Octavian was now unrivalled master of the Roman world, commanding an enormous army of some 60 legions. Militarily he was more secure than either Caesar or Sulla, but his actions soon showed that he had learned from the failures of both. When he returned to Rome in 29BC he formally laid down his powers, dissolving the triumvirate. Eventually he created the system known as the Principate, but this evolved gradually and there were more than a few false starts along the way. At first his power was still too blatant, for he held the consulship each year and there was resentment, especially whenever he left the city, but in time Octavian's public position was made to seem less monarchic. He made considerable effort to disassociate himself from Octavian the triumvir, and eventually he became, instead, Augustus, a name with deeply traditional associations, and the Father of his Country (*pater patriae*). To all intents and purposes Augustus was a monarch, for his power could not be opposed by any constitutional means, yet he managed to maintain the illusion that he was not the master of the state, but its servant, a magistrate like all the other magistrates save that his authority, and his continued services to the state, were greater.

The Roman armies

Rome's civil wars split the state into factions, and the army with it. Since there were no ethnic, ideological or social differences between the rival sides it was inevitable – even more than in any other civil war – that the organisation, tactical doctrine and equipment of their armies was virtually identical.

The legion

The main strength of the Roman army lay in the legions, units with a paper strength of about 5,000. In this period, a legion consisted entirely of heavy infantry. In theory the legions were

This frieze from the headquarters building of the legionary fortress at Mainz in Germany dates to over a century after the Civil War, but it gives a good idea of the classic fighting stance of the legionary – crouching slightly to gain the maximum protection from his shield, with his left leg advanced and sword thrust underarm. (© R. Sheridan/AAA Collection Ltd)

recruited only from Roman citizens, but during the civil wars many non-citizens were enlisted to bolster numbers. In his *Commentaries,* Caesar frequently emphasised the heterogeneous nature of the enemy armies, but he had himself formed an entire legion, *legio* V Alaudae, from Gauls, only later giving them the franchise as a reward for distinguished service. Given the dominance of the Roman military system, some allied kings had remodelled their armies after the Roman style. King Juba of Numidia included four legions in his large army, while Deiotarus of Galatia formed two that would later be amalgamated and formed into Legio XXII Deiotariana as a fully fledged part of the Roman army.

These Roman swords are from the first century AD, and show the popular *gladius*. (© R. Sheridan/AAA Collection Ltd)

The inevitable war between Antony and Octavian began in 32BC. Antony moved west to defend Greece and Macedonia but found his fleet blockaded in the Gulf of Ambracia by Agrippa. His land army of 19 legions was cut off by Octavian on the promontory of Actium, at the mouth of the Gulf. On 2 September 31BC, Antony and Cleopatra fought their way free of the blockade but most of their fleet was destroyed during the battle. The fleet was manned by four legions, and 5,000 legionaries died in the battle. The surviving ships surrendered and the army went over to Octavian. Having fled to Egypt, Antony despaired and took his own life, leaving Octavian in control of the whole of the Empire. This painting shows a veteran marine from one of the legions of the fleet, surrounded by details of his weapons and armour. (Painting by Angus McBride © Osprey Publishing Ltd)

The basic tactical unit of the legion was the cohort of some 480 men. There were ten of these in each legion, and the cohort in turn was subdivided into six centuries of 80.

Recruitment

Traditionally, all Roman male citizens between the ages of 17 and 46 were liable for military service. Most recruits to the legion were between 17 and 23, with the peak age of enlistment

A first century BC relief of two Roman legionaries, carrying swords and shields, wearing armour and helmets. Mail armour can clearly be seen worn by the legionary on the right. (© R. Sheridan/AAA Collection Ltd)

being 20, but recruits as young as 13 and 14, and as old as 36 are known. The majority of legionaries claimed origin *(origio)* in a town or city, but few actually came from urban centres. Most cities were centres of agricultural trade and had substantial rural territories attached to them. Some parts of the Empire were particularly devoid of urbanisation and in many cases origins were simply spurious, granted at enlistment with Roman citizenship.

Peasant farmers had been the backbone of the citizen militia of the Republic, and the country remained the favoured source of recruits until the late Empire. Recruits with agricultural backgrounds were preferred for their endurance and because they were unaffected by the sleazier distractions of city life. Vegetius, writing in the late fourth century AD, said of rural recruits:

> They are nurtured under the open sky in a life of work, enduring the sun, careless of shade, unacquainted with bathhouses, simple-souled, content with a little, with limbs toughened to endure every kind of toil, and for whom wielding iron, digging a ditch and carrying a burden is what they are used to from the country.

Many legionaries, if not the majority, were conscripts, and not necessarily educated to any great standard. The levy of such recruits was necessitated by the huge scale of the civil wars.

Training

Legionary recruits trained daily for four gruelling months. Training began with practising the military steps. Recruits were required to march 29km in five hours at the regular step, and 35km in five hours at the faster step, loaded with a pack about 20.5kg (45lb) in weight. This burden was merely for acclimatisation; the weight of his arms and armour alone could be far greater. Strict maintenance of the ranks was enforced during drill, the centurions and training officers using their staffs to beat any laggards. Once the recruits could march in time and follow the commands relayed by the trumpets and standards, manoeuvres were practised endlessly. They practised different formations: the hollow square, wedge, circle, and the *testudo* ('the tortoise' – a mobile formation entirely protected by a roof and wall of shields). They were trained in overcoming obstacles, in charging and breaking off combat, in changing lines and relieving engaged units. The recruit was also taught to spring out of the line – this might prove useful in combat.

Weapons training was conducted with swords, javelins and shields made of wood and wicker but twice the weight of the real thing. These weapons were used against 1.8m (6ft) practice posts. The instructors emphasised covering the body effectively with the shield while using the sword point instead of the edge, for this caused deeper wounds and was more efficient than slashing. Weapons training might occur twice a day.

If possible, recruits were also taught to swim so that a campaigning army's advance would not be impeded by rivers. They were also given cursory instruction in archery, the sling and riding, so that they had knowledge of all arms.

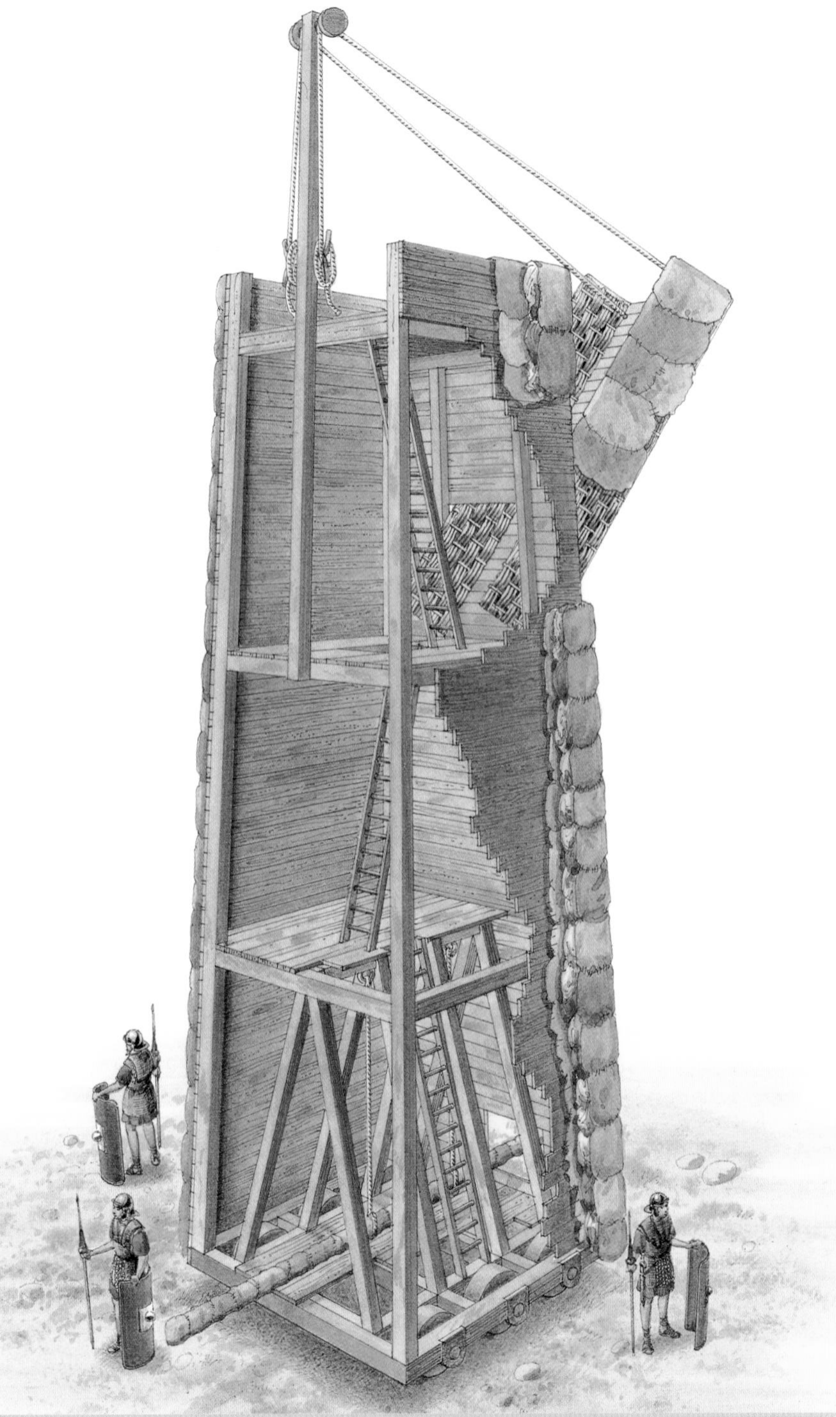

None of the historical accounts of Roman siege towers actually describes the machines, except occasionally to record the height. However, the Roman writer Vegetius writing in the late fourth century AD preserves a description of a tower that he perhaps borrowed from a lost work of the late first century AD. Within the tower, three distinct levels are specified: the lower level, housing a battering ram; the intermediate level, supporting a boarding bridge; and the upper level, accommodating missile troops. (Painting by Brian Delf © Osprey Publishing Ltd)

POMPEY VS CAESAR – EFFECTIVENESS OF ARMIES AND GENERALS

By the end of the Gallic campaigns, Caesar commanded ten legions. The majority of these troops were seasoned veterans, utterly devoted to Caesar and confident in their own and their commander's ability. In support were bands of excellent Gallic and German cavalry. To match against this Pompey had seven legions garrisoning his Spanish provinces, although these had little actual combat experience. There were also two legions that had not yet left for the east and were still in Italy, but as both had recently served under Caesar their loyalty appeared questionable. However, Pompey boasted that he had only to stamp his foot in Italy for more legions to appear, and was also sure of the loyalty of the eastern provinces which he had reorganised just over a decade before. In the long term, Pompey could probably claim greater resources than Caesar, but it would take time to mobilise these into field armies.

In 49BC, Pompey was almost 58, but remained an extremely fit and active man, and others marvelled at the energy he showed in joining the training exercises of his soldiers. His military record was extremely good, even if he had made something of a habit of arriving in the last stages of a conflict to claim the credit largely won by someone else. He was certainly a brilliant organiser, as his campaign against pirates, as well as, more recently, his supervision of Rome's corn supply, had shown. In his youth he had been a bold commander, on several occasions leading charges in person, but his aggression, in a properly Roman way, had always been based on sound preparation. However, although he was six years older than Caesar, Pompey had spent the last decade in Rome, and had not served on campaign since 62BC. His performance during the Civil War would suggest that he was past his best as a general. He was not helped by the presence of so many distinguished senators in his camp. Unlike Caesar, whose followers were undistinguished and whose authority was unchallenged, Pompey was always under pressure to alter his plans. Most of the senators who flocked to his cause had more prestige than ability, and on more than a few occasions proved a positive hindrance.

Caesar failed to attract any distinguished supporters from the senior members of the Senate. Now in his early 50s, he was still very much at the peak of his ability, and was fresh from a decade of successful fighting in Gaul. His strategy during the Civil War, as in Gaul, was based on rapid offensives, sometimes in the face of great odds. Though often criticised for recklessness by modern commentators, it is important to emphasise that such boldness was characteristically Roman, and should not conceal that much preparation underlay these enterprises. Although subject to occasional epileptic fits, he was in other respects an extremely healthy and active man, capable of massive effort and rapid long-distance travel. Caesar promoted and lavishly rewarded any soldiers who distinguished themselves, but even more than this it was his remarkable charisma that ensured that his soldiers were devoted to him. Throughout the war, desertions from the Pompeian forces were common, but all of our sources claim that there were no defections in the other direction. Fighting a war to protect his honour and status, Caesar's objective was clear and obvious, giving the Caesarian war effort a unity of purpose not displayed by the other side. Yet it also meant that it was much easier for him to lose. If Caesar was killed, or his army defeated so heavily that he was discredited, then the war would effectively have been over. Only the Pompeians could suffer defeat after defeat and still prolong the struggle.

It is hard now to say whether Pompey or Caesar was the better general. The vast bulk of our evidence comes, directly or indirectly, from Caesar's own version of events. His *Commentaries* obviously present his own actions in a favourable light, while dismissing those of the enemy. However, they also provide evidence that allows the wisdom of some of Caesar's decisions to be questioned. Yet, for the Romans the answer was obvious, for the most important attribute of a great general was that he won his wars. Caesar defeated Pompey, and in the end there was no more to be said.

Although painted in the early 20th century, this depiction of the Roman Senate with Crassus and Cataline by Maccari helps us to visualise the arena in which many of Rome's greatest battles were fought through words and deeds. (© Prisma/AAA Collection Ltd)

Weapons and armour

All legionaries were equipped with the same basic defensive gear, consisting of a bronze helmet (most often of Montefortino or Coolus patterns), cuirass (usually mail but sometimes of scale), and a large semi-cylindrical body shield constructed from three layers of plywood to give it both flexibility and strength. The latter seem most often to have been oval in shape, but it is possible that the transition to a more rectangular shape was already underway. Such shields were heavy – reconstructed examples weighing in at 10kg (22lbs) – but offered good protection. They could also be used offensively, the soldier punching forward with all his bodyweight behind the shield's bronze boss. We are told that one of Caesar's soldiers, in spite of having his right hand chopped off almost as soon as he had boarded a warship, was able to clear the deck of enemies by knocking them down with his shield during the fighting off Massila.

A soldier's other offensive equipment consisted of a short sword, the famed *gladius*, sometimes a dagger, and the *pilum* or heavy throwing javelin. The *pilum* consisted of a wooden shaft just over a metre long (four feet), topped by a narrow iron shank about half a metre in length (two feet) and ending in a pyramid-shaped point. When thrown, all of its great weight was concentrated behind this small tip, giving it formidable penetrative power. It was designed so that once it punched through an enemy's shield, the slim iron shank would slide easily through the hole made by the point, and had the reach to wound the man behind. Soldiers may have carried two *pila* on campaign, but only one on the day of battle itself.

Organisation and deployment

In battle, a legion most often formed in three lines, four cohorts in the first line and three in the second and third. Intervals were maintained between each unit and the cohorts from the next line stationed to cover these gaps, creating something resembling a chequerboard formation. However, since all cohorts were armed uniformly, the legion was perfectly capable of fighting effectively in other formations, and we also hear of armies in four or two lines, although a single line was considered too brittle to be employed save in dire need. The legion was a very flexible force. Its structure and size made it an important subunit within the battle line, but one or several cohorts could as easily be detached for smaller operations.

The doctrine of the period was to deliver a massed volley at very short range – some 13.5m or so – and follow this up with a charge, sword in hand.

The cohort is traditionally viewed as the primary tactical unit of the legion. This is certainly the impression given by Caesar and Tacitus, who tell of formations and tactics based around the cohort. However, it has been suggested that the cohort could not function as a tactical unit because it had no commander or obvious standard of its own, leaving the century as the primary tactical unit. When Caesar and Tacitus speak of cohorts moving in a battle we should view them as groupings of centuries fighting in support of each other.

As with all armies throughout history, theoretical unit sizes were rarely reflected in the field. At Pharsalus in 48BC the cohorts of Pompey's legions averaged around 400 men apiece, while Caesar's force was little more than half that size. Campaign attrition reduced one of Caesar's legions to less than 1,000 men during the Egyptian campaign.

Allies and auxiliaries

The legions were the mainstay of any army, especially decisive in pitched battles, but both sides supplemented their numbers with allied soldiers or auxiliaries, fighting in their own traditional style. Such troops were especially useful in providing cavalry and light infantry. In most cases they were locally recruited and led by their own native chieftains. At first Caesar's auxiliaries came primarily from the Gallic and German tribes, and Pompey's from his provinces in Spain and his many clients in the east, but as the war progressed, troops were recruited wherever possible and the pattern became more complex.

EARLY EMPIRE 27BC–AD235

The early imperial period of Rome's history was marked by threats to the security of the now-immense empire, and internal struggles as the city tried to reconcile the monarchic powers of an emperor with the republican ideals of its forebears...

BRITAIN
GERMANY
BELGICA
GAUL
DACIA
CISALPINE
GAUL
ILLYRICUM
THRACE
ITALY
MACEDONIA
SPAIN
MEDITERRANEAN
SICILY
MAURETANIA
NUMIDIA
NORTH AFRICA
N
0 250 miles
0 500 km
The Roman Empire in the time of Augustus
Additional territory added to the Roman Empire by the time of Hadrian
Roman territory under Trajan, later lost

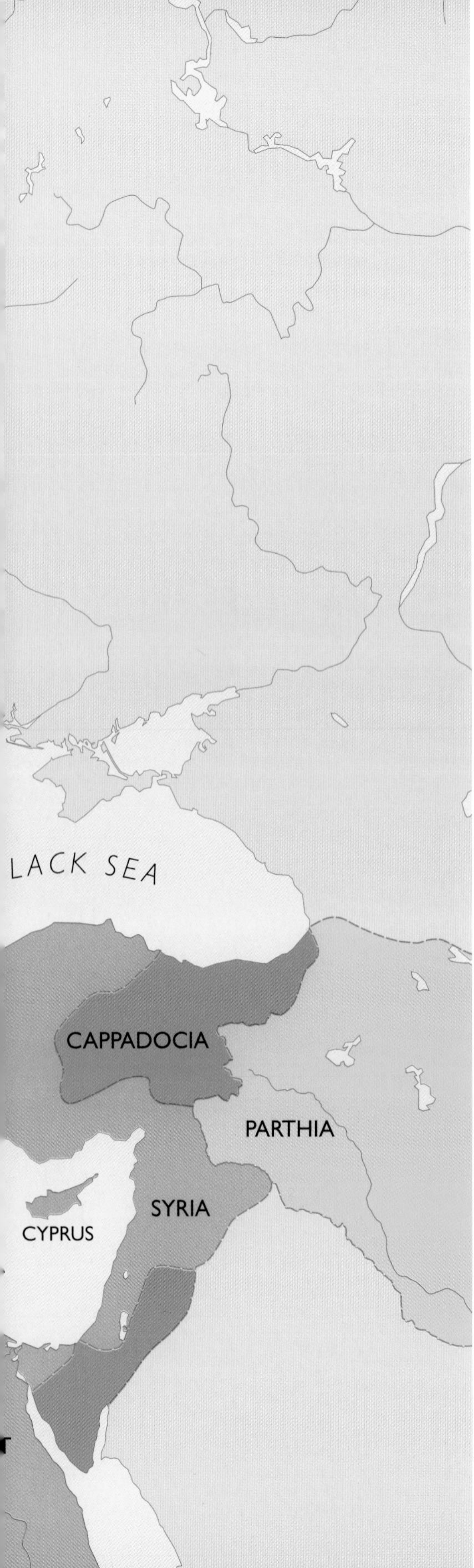

CHRONOLOGY

27BC	Octavian becomes Augustus, first emperor of Rome
AD14	Death of Augustus, accession of Tiberius
37–41	Reign of Caligula as emperor
41–54	Reign of Claudius as emperor Conquest of parts of Britain
54–68	Reign of Nero as emperor
68	Galba becomes emperor
69	Year of the four emperors: Otho succeeds Galba; Vitellius succeeds Otho; Vespasian succeeds Vitellius
69–79	Reign of Vespasian as emperor
79–8	Reign of Titus as emperor
81–96	Reign of Domitian as emperor
96–98	Reign of Nerva as emperor
98–117	Reign of Trajan as emperor, taking the Empire to its greatest extent
117–138	Reign of Hadrian as emperor
138–161	Reign of Antoninus Pius as emperor
161–180	Reign of Marcus Aurelius as emperor
167	Commodus becomes co-emperor to Marcus Aurelius
193–208	Reign of Septimius Severus as emperor
208–111	Reign of Caracalla and Geta as co-emperors
212	Caracalla murders Geta
217	Caracalla murdered, and Opellius Macrinus proclaimed emperor
218	Macrinus defeated by Elagabalus. Severus Alexander succeeds as emperor
235	Severus Alexander murdered. Maximinus proclaimed emperor, and is first Roman emperor to fight in battle

Chapter 9
THE ROMANS

Background

An emperor's power relied on his military force and strength, and many foreign wars at this time were attempts either to prove this strength, or protect weaknesses from exploitation. After Trajan expanded the Empire to its largest geographical size, the priority shifted from adding new lands to the Empire, to protecting existing ones from attack. Inside Rome, the corruption of emperors and their governments meant the priority was often personal gain, and survival.

Augustus and the Senate

Military power lay behind the Augustan regime, but attention was rarely drawn to this. Most of the Republic's institutions persisted. The Senate was reformed and reduced in size to remove many of the less suitable men who had been enrolled in reward for dubious favours to the various sides in the civil wars. More Italians were included, and in time senators would come from the aristocratic families of many of the provinces. Augustus attended the Senate as simply another member, if a highly distinguished one, and encouraged the members to debate freely and to vote with their conscience. Augustus may have genuinely desired them to do this, but in practice this was a sham. Every senator knew that his future career depended on the emperor's favour, and so the vast majority said what they felt he wanted them to say. Both the senators and emperor wished publicly to pretend that Rome had not become a monarchy, politely ignoring the obvious reality. From early in his reign Augustus began to groom a successor, although the appallingly high mortality rate within the imperial family meant that quite a few individuals filled this role. When Augustus finally died in AD14 at the age of 76, his successor, Tiberius, then aged 56, had his powers formally voted to him by the Senate and at first feigned reluctance to take on the role. By this time scarcely anyone could conceive of, or remember, life without an emperor.

Foreign fighting

The wars fought with foreign enemies during this period were not as aggressively expansionist as those of earlier years, since there remained little of the Mediterranean and immediate regions that had not already been consumed by the Roman Empire. Augustus did attempt to push the Empire borders back beyond the Rhine, but an entire Roman force of three legions was wiped out in AD9 in the Teutoburg forest, resulting in Augustus

bringing his troops back behind the Rhine, and suggesting to Tiberius not to attempt to push the boundaries further. Threats to the Empire's stability caused constant concern, and saw the emperors taking their armies on hard-fought campaigns for security and stability.

Julius Caesar. This relief from 161 AD shows the apotheosis of Caesar. Suetonius says this about Caesar becoming a god:

> He was 55 years old when he died and his immediate deification, formally decreed by the loyalists in the Senate, convinced the city as a whole; if only because, on the first day of the Games given by his successor Augustus in honor of this apotheosis, a comet appeared about an hour before sunset and shone for several days running. This was held to be Caesar's soul, elevated to Heaven; hence the star, now placed above the forehead of his divine image.
> (© R. Sheridan/AAA Collection Ltd)

Claudius' invasion of Britain

Claudius unexpectedly became emperor in AD41 when his nephew Caligula was assassinated. Needing military success to consolidate his position, he embarked on the conquest of southern Britain in AD43, an enterprise originally planned by his predecessor. The invasion force was composed of four legions and auxiliary forces under the command of Aulus Plautius. Advancing rapidly, the Roman forces won a major victory outside Camulodunum (Colchester) and the emperor entered the tribal capital in triumph on an elephant. Claudius quickly accepted the surrender of 11 tribal kings, before returning to Rome, and leaving Plautius behind as governor of Britain. Although the conquest had begun well, the complete submission of Britain to Rome was to take much more time and effort. One by one, each of the native British Celtic tribes were either crushed, or became client kingdoms. Caractacus, son of the Catuvellaunian king Cunobelinus, attempted to lead a revolt among a number of tribes, but was eventually captured after being betrayed by another tribal leader, Cartimandua, leader of the Brigantes. Another serious uprising under Boudicca, queen of the Iceni tribe, in 60AD was eventually suppressed, but not before the sacking of many major Roman towns, including Colchester, St Albans and London.

In AD77, the new governor of Britain, Agricola, decided to bring the tribes of Wales and Scotland under his command. He oversaw a dreadful massacre of the Druids on the island of Anglesey, and campaigned further and further north until he reached Perthshire. He was unable to subdue the tribes north of there, and they remained free from the yoke of Roman rule for the duration of the Empire. In AD122, Hadrian decided to set the British boundary of Roman lands at the Tyne–Solway line, and for the next 17 years he oversaw the construction of a wall, Hadrian's Wall, to attempt to keep the northern tribes from making incursions on Roman territory. Britain, now the Roman province of Britannia, enjoyed a couple of centuries of relative peace, until around 300AD, when the barbarian threat to Roman lands in Europe saw the withdrawal of some of the troops in Britain to help in central Europe. In the absence of as much protection from Rome, the Romano-Britons started to receive more attacks from the neighbouring British Picts and Celts. Eventually, in AD410 the Emperor Constantine removed the whole of the Roman garrison in Britain back to the Rhine frontier to attempt to defend it from the Goths. The Romans never returned to Britain.

Wars with the Germanics and Dacians

Throughout the history of the Roman Empire, its northern frontier with the lands of Germanic and Dacian tribes had always been vulnerable, due, largely, to the ferocity of these tribes as fighters, and their constant need to migrate to cope with their mounting population problems. Stability along this frontier required active defence, and there were major

A Roman relief showing senators. The Senate was reformed by Augustus, and attempts were made to suggest that the political system of Republican Rome had not changed since she became an Empire, but the reality was inevitably different. (© R. Sheridan/AAA Collection Ltd)

campaigns commanded by an emperor in the 90s (Domitian), 170s (Marcus Aurelius) and 230s (Severus Alexander). The Rhine provided a partial barrier to tribal movement, which the Roman could control through naval squadrons and by supervising recognised crossing-points. Beyond the Rhine were numerous tribal groups whose relationship with the Romans was not always hostile: tribesmen served in Roman armies, Roman garrisons had considerable wealth (by local standards) to spend on slaves, furs or basic foodstuffs, while the Romans were a source of luxury goods such as wine or spices. A symbiotic relationship could emerge, and a cyclical pattern to relations on the frontier can be seen: the Romans bolstered the authority of compliant leaders whose expanding following generated greater demands; when these became excessive, conflict ensued between Rome and a major tribal grouping; thereafter the cycle would begin again.

The second major European river frontier, along the Danube, was joined to the Rhine frontier by linear defences. In the first century AD a process of consolidation similar to that on the Rhine got under way, and the need to dominate the Dacian tribes of the lower Danube led to major campaigns across the river under the Emperor Trajan (98–117) in the early second century. After the murder of Severus Alexander in 235 the Roman Empire experienced 50 years of instability, commonly termed the Third-century Crisis, a period which marks the transition to the later Empire.

These problems were compounded by events on the Danube, where the Romans had to face a new enemy. Here change had been slow, the result of the gradual movement of Gothic peoples from northern Poland. The first attested Gothic incursion came in 238, when they sacked Istria near the Danube mouth; a decade later they swept across the north-eastern Balkans, and Emperor Decius was killed and his army annihilated while trying to force the Goths back across the Danube in 251.

This great movement of Goths naturally displaced other peoples who might find themselves squeezed against the Roman frontier; this process could trigger the formation of substantial federations as different tribes steeled themselves for the ultimate challenge of attacking the Romans. On the upper Danube the Vandals, Quadi and Marcomanni breached the frontier, and on the upper Rhine the Alamanni increased their strength to the extent that they twice invaded Italy in the 260s. On the lower Rhine the Franks gradually came to dominate another large federation that threatened frontier defences during the latter half of the century.

Of the Roman world, only Africa, the Iberian peninsula and, to a lesser extent, Britain, were spared invasion. The cumulative nature of the frontier pressure is evident, with emperors unable to divert troops from one sector to another and instead constrained to confront invaders in conditions that led to defeat. The consequences for imperial prestige are obvious,

Augustus was Caesar's adopted heir, had risen to power as his father's avenger, and copied some of Caesar's innovations to create the Principate, although in other respects he learned from the dictator's mistakes and did things very differently. (© R. Sheridan/AAA Collection Ltd)

ROMAN ROADS IN BRITAIN

Apart from Julius Caesar's expeditions in 55–54BC, the Roman presence in Britain began with their invasion in AD43. Presumably making use of existing trackways where possible, a system of military roads was a priority. London (Londinium) was the lowest point at which the river Thames could be bridged and from there a road ran east to Colchester, the capital of the province. At what time additional roads were built or rebuilt by the Romans is not clear. It seems likely that routes from so important a place as Colchester would soon be properly paved, but by the time of Boudicca's rising only 17 years had elapsed since the invasion and there must have been a limit to what even the Romans, free of planning permissions and compulsory purchase legislation, could achieve. The state of the roads described is thus unclear and some may have been primitive tracks. Stane Street ran west from Colchester to Great Dunmow, where another road set off towards Cambridge and thence on to Godmanchester, where it joined Ermine Street to Peterborough and on to Lincoln. As today, London was the centre from which many roads radiated and Watling Street, the road to Wroxeter (Viroconium), Chester and Anglesey (Mona) struck off north-west while the major road to the west ran by way of Silchester (Calleva), halfway between Reading and Basingstoke, and on north-west to Cirencester (Corinium).

The south-east had succumbed swiftly to Roman domination, but the north-west was a tougher proposition so a military zone was created along an axis running up from Cirencester to Lincoln (Lindum) with lateral movement along it aided by the road known as the Foss Way. This crossed Watling Street at High Cross (Venonis), near Lutterworth. The Foss Way was later developed all the way down to Exeter but David Johnston has it that that town was supplied mainly by sea at this time and that the roads were not yet fully engineered or Romanised. A forward position at Gloucester (Glevum) was reached by a spur from Cirencester called Ermin Way, and at some time, maybe later, a road north went to Worcester, across what is now Birmingham, and joined Watling Street at Wall (Letocetum). Between Wall and High Cross there was at least a camp, maybe not yet a fort, at Mancetter (Manduessedum). On a west to east axis only one other route existed, Akeman Street, from Cirencester to Alchester just south of Bicester where it forked. To the right, via Aylesbury, it went to St Albans. To the left it ran north-east to Towcester (Lactodorum).

Movement was, of course, possible off the Roman roads but it was along these roads that camps, forts and towns were built in which troops could rest and acquire supplies. Swift marches could more easily be made along these routes as food and fresh horses, for example, might be had.

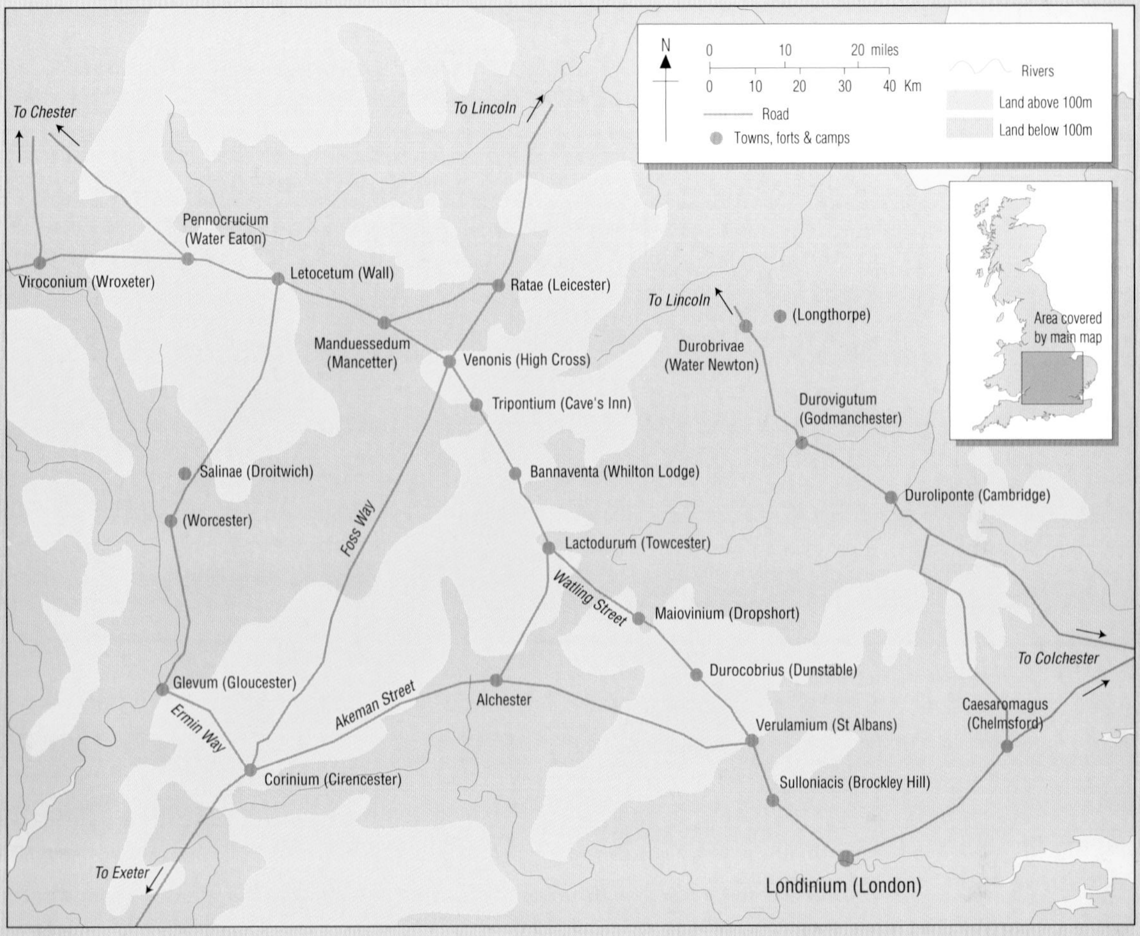

Roman roads in Britain.

and in the late 260s the Empire was virtually split into three units, which attended separately to their own security. The Empire was only reunited by Aurelian in a series of energetic campaigns, which were helped by instability in Gaul. Also, Aurelian was prepared to abandon the exposed province of Dacia, and redeploy Roman troops along the lower Danube.

Prolonged warfare inside the frontiers, regular defeat and the rapid turnover of emperors cumulatively had a major impact on the strength of the Empire, and were to play a key part in subsequent events that led to the Empire's collapse.

The Parthian Wars

Only in the east did the Romans face an enemy with a sophistication comparable to their own. In the eastern Empire the Romans encountered the Parthians during the first century BC, experiencing one of their worst defeats in 53BC when three legions were annihilated at Carrhae (Harran) in Mesopotamia. Until the mid-first century AD, small client kingdoms

This section of Hadrian's Wall passes Housesteads Fort near Hexham in Northumberland. Although the remains of the wall are only a few courses high, the original wall was 4.5m (15ft) high with 1.8m (6ft) battlements on top of it. (© G Tortoli/AAA Collection Ltd)

constituted buffer states for Roman territory in Anatolia and the Levant. Thereafter the upper and middle Euphrates provided a suitable line on which to base legionary positions – though, as along the Rhine and the Danube, the Romans maintained a key interest in events beyond. Between the river Euphrates and the Arabian Gulf, desert offered a reliable buffer zone, although tribes who knew how to operate in this inhospitable terrain troubled Roman lands to the west intermittently. For the Romans the east was the prestigious area for conflict, ideally for expansion, with the renown of Alexander the Great's achievements luring successive western rulers to emulation: in AD20, Augustus Caesar regained the Armenian and Transcaucasian lands lost the year before Carrhae, and the Parthians returned the Roman standards lost at Carrhae. However, when a new Armenian ruler was appointed by the Parthian king Vologases I in the 60s, the Romans felt their power was being threatened, and their commander Cnaeus Domitius Corbulo invaded Armenia. It was finally decided that the Parthians could have their own prince, but that he must be approved and controlled by Rome.

This arrangement worked for a while, until 114 when the Parthian king Vologases III dethroned an Armenian leader, and Trajan invaded Parthia. Roman success was decisive, and Trajan campaigned to the head of the Persian Gulf, briefly establishing a province in Mesopotamia; in the 160s Lucius Verus (161–69) fought energetically in Lower Mesopotamia, and in the 190s Septimius Severus (193–211) again defeated the Parthians and annexed new territory. In 226 the Parthian monarchy was overthrown by the Sassanid Persians, who in 260 captured the Roman emperor Valerian, and successively reduced Roman fortresses in Mesopotamia.

A Roman mosaic from Carthage showing a Vandal horseman. Procopius had this to say about the Vandals, describing their defeat by the Moors in North Africa:

> [They] were no good with javelin and bow, nor did they know how to fight on foot...and their horses, upset by the sight of the camels, totally refused to be urged against the enemy.

(© AAA Collection Ltd)

Roman military reform

Augustus and the army

Before he became emperor, Octavian remodelled the army into a permanent force of 28 legions. The support of the army was crucial to him because as emperor, Augustus' powers rested on military force. For the first time Rome received a permanent garrison. The emperor had his Praetorian Guard, and also formed a police force (the Urban Cohorts) and fire brigade (the Vigiles). All of these troops were kept directly under his personal control. He also took great care to ensure the loyalty of the army. Service conditions were fixed, as were the soldiers' legal status and rights. On honourable discharge each soldier was entitled either to a plot of land or a lump sum of money. This, along with the soldiers' pay, was funded by a special Military Treasury *(aerarium militare)* which was supervised, and often subsidised, by Augustus. The problem of veterans looking to their commanders to provide them with some form of livelihood was at long last averted, and Augustus also took care that the legionaries' loyalty was focused on him and no one else. The men were paid by the emperor, swore an oath of loyalty to him, and, when they performed any feat of gallantry, received medals awarded by him.

The Roman Empire depended on the power of its armies, which had always been composed of a combination of citizen and non-citizen troops. Before the universal extension of citizenship in AD212, citizens were recruited into the legions, while non-citizens traditionally entered the auxiliary units. Remarkably little is known about the process of recruitment: conscription was probably always a feature, with manpower needs being apportioned in line with census records of citizens, but there was also some element of hereditary service as units drew on veteran settlements. At times, perhaps often, military service offered a reasonably good and quite safe career for the young provincials, especially if they served close to home. More and more newly created citizens were employed in the Roman army, a situation which was to later highlight the weaknesses inherent in training your enemies to your fighting technique.

A snapshot of the Praetorian Guard at the time of the Julio-Claudians

The Praetorian Guard has become a byword for military force that is used to prop up a ruthless regime. There is no doubt that they performed this function in the Roman Empire. As the main body of troops in Rome they were the emperor's instrument to discourage plotting and rebellion and to crush unrest. They were the emperor's most immediate line of defence; they could also, on occasion, be his most deadly enemies.

Comfortable and relatively safe in their barracks in Rome, enjoying shorter service and better pay and bonuses than any other unit in the Empire, and often involved in nothing more arduous than sentry-duty at the palace, the Praetorians were the envy of the legionaries stationed at the frontiers. All this might seem an unlikely background for an elite fighting unit, yet when the Guard did take the field, they appear to have been well enough trained and officered to acquit themselves well. Indeed, in the late first and second centuries, when emperors frequently campaigned in person and took the Guard with them, they proved efficient and loyal.

Organisation

The great majority of the Praetorian Guard were infantry but, as with the legions, the Guard did include an attachment of cavalry. Inscriptions suggest that men could become cavalry (*equites*) after about five years' service as infantry. The Guard also had a special elite cavalry section, known as the *speculatores Augusti,* who formed the emperor's cavalry bodyguard. These men were apparently distinguished by a special form of boot of unknown form, the *caliga speculatoria,* and they received specific honorific bronze diplomas on discharge. The strength of this body of men is uncertain, but they had their own riding instructor and were commanded by a *centurio speculatorum*.

For the first century of the Principate, the Julio-Claudian emperors had a personal bodyguard of German troops operating alongside the Praetorians. Their origin lay in the period of the civil wars, when foreign mercenaries seem to have been regarded as more reliable than a guard of Roman citizens whose loyalties might be divided. Unlike the Praetorians the Germans (*Germani Corporis Custodes*) were in effect a private force. Recruitment was direct from Germany and Gaul, and inscriptions show that the individuals did not become Roman citizens. The use of Germans, with their shaggy beards, immense size and renowned ferocity, was intended to discourage assassins.

The Germans acted as infantry when on guard at the palace but as cavalry in the field, and were always closely associated with the Praetorians. They were, however, paramilitary rather than a genuine part of the Roman army.

Uniform and equipment

The appearance of the Praetorians undoubtedly changed somewhat throughout the course of their history, but some types of equipment have always been regarded as characteristic of the Guard, in particular the so-called 'Attic' helmet with bushy crest, and the oval shield. These appear in a famous relief now in the Louvre, Paris, which was once dated to the early second century, but is now recognised as coming from the Arch of Claudius erected in AD51. The combination of Attic helmet and oval shield has been thought of as imparting a conscious archaic look to the Praetorians – something akin to the red tunics and bearskins of the modern British Foot Guards – but recent research suggests that the Praetorians were simply equipped in a manner similar to their contemporaries in the legions. The *tunica* was the basic Roman male garment, worn by soldiers and civilians alike, although soldiers wore it short above the knee. It is frequently assumed that the soldier's tunic was usually red, but the available evidence suggests that the normal colour was white or off-white, the colour of undyed wool.

There is nothing to suggest that the rest of the Praetorians' arms and equipment differed from that of the legions. Trajan's Column, which depicts the story of Trajan's two Dacian wars, seems to make no distinction between Praetorian and legionary equipment, ascribing segmented armour to both, whilst following a convention of distinguishing auxiliaries by their use of mail shirts. Praetorians and legionaries are armed identically with javelin and a sword worn on the right side.

There were, nevertheless, certain items of dress and insignia which were peculiar to the Guard. Most distinctive of all, perhaps, was the civilian toga worn whilst on duty at the palace and in the Capitol in the first two centuries AD. The symbolism and political significance of this impractical form of dress is a feature apparently unique to the Praetorians. Less out-of-the-ordinary is the special form of standard used by the Praetorians. Literary sources suggest that Praetorian standards had imperial portraits (*imagines*) attached to them, whereas the legions and auxiliaries seem for the most part to have had such *imagines* carried separately by special portrait-bearers (*imaginiferi*). Praetorian standards have therefore been identified on Trajan's Column and other reliefs from their display of such portraits along with military decorations – mainly different types of crowns. Praetorian standard-bearers, whilst they carry the small round shield and are otherwise equipped like legionary standard-bearers on the monuments, are nevertheless distinguished from them by wearing lion masks and pelts, as opposed to bearskins, over their helmets and down their backs.

Duties

Until 2BC each Praetorian cohort was an independent unit under the separate command of a tribune of equestrian rank (i.e. a Roman knight). At that point Augustus appointed two

THE GUARD AND THE JULIO-CLAUDIAN EMPERORS

Augustus (27BC–AD14)

After his victory over Antony, Octavian amalgamated his own force with those of his opponent in a symbolic reunification of Julius Caesar's army. With his own Praetorians and those of Antony, Octavian already had the administrative basis for a permanent Praetorian Guard. We know from Suetonius that Augustus, as he was then, was careful to have only three cohorts based in Rome itself, and these were not in a camp but billeted around the city; the others were scattered round the towns of Italy. It is clear that Augustus was extremely wary of flaunting too blatantly the basis of his power.

Tiberius (14–37)

The Guard took the field in earnest for the first time in AD14, as Augustus' successor Tiberius faced mutinies amongst both the Rhine and the Pannonian armies who were complaining about their conditions of service, especially in comparison with those of the Praetorians.

The Pannonian forces were dealt with by Tiberius' young brother Drusus, accompanied by two Praetorian Cohorts, Praetorian cavalry and the German bodyguard. The Rhine mutiny was put down by Tiberius' nephew and intended heir Germanicus, who then led the legions and detachments of the Guard in an invasion of Germany which continued over the next two years.

Caligula (37–41)

Tiberius' successor was Gaius Caligula, who came to the throne with the aid of the Praetorian Prefect Quintus Sutorius Marco. Caligula's follies supposedly included leading the Guard in triumph on a bridge of boats spanning the Bay of Naples, and taking the Praetorian cavalry on a farcical raid across the Rhine. In 41 it was the sheer disgust and hostility that he had engendered in a tough Praetorian tribune by the name of Cassius Charea – whom Caligula teased mercilessly about his squeaky voice – which led to Caligula's assassination by officers of the Guard. The German bodyguard went on the rampage searching for the murderers, whilst the Senate deliberated on the restoration of a Republic.

Claudius (41–54)

While the Praetorians were looting the palace in the confusion after Caligula's death, they came across Caligula's uncle Claudius hiding behind a curtain. In need of an emperor to justify their own existence, they took Claudius off to the Praetorian camp and proclaimed his accession. The Senate were forced to accede to this coup: the Praetorians' first attempt at king-making had succeeded. Claudius rewarded the Guard with an unsurprising but generous bonus of five years' salary. According to Dio, auxiliaries were also granted the rights of married men *(conubium)*. Inscriptions reveal that Claudius also took the Guard with him to witness the conclusion of his invasion of Britain in AD43.

Nero (54–68)

When Claudius was poisoned by his wife Agrippina and stepson Nero, the Guard were not slow to transfer their allegiance and ensure the latter's accession. Once again a Praetorian Prefect, Sextus Afranius Burrus, wielded enormous influence, this time to the good. After Burrus' death, however, the mounting catalogue of Nero's crimes, which included matricide, again provoked revulsion among the conservative officers of the Guard, and a number of them, including one of Burrus' successors, were involved in the dangerous Pisonian conspiracy of AD65. Another Praetorian Prefect took the lead in the suppression of the conspiracy, and the Guard was rewarded with a bonus of 500 *denarii* per man.

Under the Julio-Claudian emperors the Guard continued to develop its political role in the most dangerous way possible, but saw little action in the field. However, all this changed following the death of Nero. In the 'Year of Four Emperors' which followed, the Praetorians were engaged in major campaigning for the first time in a century of their existence.

The Louvre relief, now thought to be from the Arch of Claudius erected in AD51, has been the most influential of all images of the Praetorian Guard. The lower half of the right-hand figure, portions of the middle two, and the heads of all three figures in the foreground are modern restorations. The Attic-style helmets are almost certainly an artistic convention, but the eagle in the background may be a form of Praetorian standard. (© R Sheridan/AAA Collection Ltd)

senior Roman knights to take overall command as Praetorian Prefects. Whilst in Rome their principal duty was to mount guard at Augustus' home on the Palatine. Each afternoon, at the eighth hour, the tribune of the cohort on duty would receive the watchword from the emperor in person. After the construction of the Praetorian camp in AD23 there was a tribune on duty there, too. Other duties included escorting the emperor and other members of the imperial family and, if necessary, acting as a form of riot police. Again, to avoid antagonising the population of Rome and in accordance with Republican custom, the Praetorians did not wear armour when performing such duties within the city. Instead, they wore the rather formal toga, which would still make them conspicuous in a crowd but was a civilian garment and the mark of a Roman citizen. Even military displays were infrequent, and the troops appeared in armour in Rome only on very special occasions.

On the left, a flag-bearer (*vexillarius*) of the Praetorian cavalry (*Equites Praetoriani*) waits as a squadron commander (*optio*, in the middle) prepares to lead his 30-man *turma* in a charge during the First Dacian War. The shields and flag (*vexillum*) mark these men as Praetorian cavalry. (Painting by Richard Hook © Osprey Publishing Ltd)

The Praetorian camp (*Castra Praetoria*)

The walls of the camp built for the Praetorians in AD23 can still be seen in Rome today. The remaining northern, eastern and southern walls stand on the Viminal Hill, where they house the modern-day garrison of Rome. They enclose an area of just over 17 hectares, about two-thirds the size of the average legionary fortress on the frontiers. This suggests a capacity of something like 4,000 men, but the few internal buildings which can be traced include extra rooms ranged around the inside of the walls and traces of two-storey barracks, so a true capacity of 12,000 men or more may therefore not be fanciful.

Service in the Praetorian cohorts

Recruitment

Service in the Praetorian Guard was in many ways an attractive proposition, offering a shorter period of service and better pay than the legions, together with the perks and advantages of living in Rome, and less frequent exposure to danger and discomfort. We know from inscriptions that men were recruited between the ages of 15 and 32, a rather broader spread than for legionary recruitment, which was usually between 17 and 23.

Most Praetorian Guards were recruited from central and northern Italy, and also from Spain and Macedonia in the first two centuries AD. This means the Guard was drawn from the most prosperous and Romanised parts of the Empire. When Septimius Severus came to power, however, he dismissed the unruly Praetorians who had tried to buy and sell the Empire in 193, and replaced them with men from his own Danubian legions. After this, Italians were no longer recruited at all; instead it was mostly men from the less Romanised Danube region who served in the Guard, after four to nine years' service in the legions.

Remuneration

From 5BC onwards, Praetorians signed up for 16 years' service, compared to the 25 years demanded in the legions. In 27BC, Augustus established the pay of Praetorians as double that of legionaries. By AD14 they were receiving 720 *denarii* per year, three times the 225 of the legionaries; this differential is likely to have remained constant throughout the history of the Guard. Claudius gave the Guard five years' salary at his accession, becoming the first emperor to buy their loyalty in this way, according to Suetonius. Most emperors followed suit to a greater or lesser extent while at the same time the legions often got nothing. Such slender evidence as exists also suggests that Praetorians were more likely to be decorated for courage in battle than legionaries. On retirement they received proportionally larger discharge bonuses, 5,000 as opposed to 3,000 *denarii* and, unlike legionaries, they were presented with honorific diplomas on bronze which made legitimate their first marriages and the children born of them. The huge discrepancy in the treatment of Praetorians and of legionaries was obviously the result of their constant presence in Rome, and their ability to create and destroy emperors.

Career path

In order to be accepted into the Guard and reap these rewards, a man would need to be physically fit, of good character and respectable family. He would also have to make use of all the patronage available, by obtaining letters of recommendation from any men of

This scene depicts a Praetorian centurion speaking with a young Praetorian guardsman inside the turf rampart and palisade of a temporary camp. The setting is the campaigns of Germanicus Caesar in Germany (AD14–16), and their equipment closely conforms to that of the figures on the late first century BC Altar of Domitius Ahenobarbus and to that found in the archaeological record for the early part of the first century AD. (Painting by Richard Hook © Osprey Publishing Ltd)

importance he knew. If he passed the induction procedure and became *probates*, he would be assigned as a *miles* to one of the centuries of a cohort. After a few years, providing he could gain the attention of his officers by influence or merit, he might obtain a post as an *immunis*, perhaps as a headquarters clerk or a technician, any of which would free him from normal fatigues. A few more years' service might advance him to *principalis*, with double pay, in charge of passing on the watchword (*tesserarius)* or as a centurion's deputy (*optio*) or standard-bearer (*signifer)* in the century; or, if highly literate and numerate, he might be appointed to the Prefect's staff.

Only a small number of soldiers would achieve the grade of *principalis* but those who did might, on completion of their service, be appointed *evocati Augusti* by the emperor. This appointment enabled them to take up administrative, technical or instructor posts in Rome, or a centurionate in a legion, and so extend their careers. Alternatively, some *principales* might before the end of their service be advanced to the rank of centurion in the Guard. The centurionate was enormously prestigious and well paid and we know that some Roman knights gave up their equestrian status in order to obtain a direct commission to this rank. For the man who had risen to this position it would probably be the culmination of his career, and although there was no restriction on the length of service, he would probably retire in it. Anyone who wished to climb further up the ladder would have to transfer to a legion, and very few would be able to do this.

THE AUCTION OF THE EMPIRE

In AD193 the Praetorian Guard murdered the emperor Pertinax when he tried to discipline them following a small mutiny. There was no formally agreed successor to replace Pertinax, which led to one of the most unusual events in the history of Rome. The father-in-law of Pertinax, Flavius Sulpicianus, was a prefect of the city, and he went to the camp to try to persuade the guard to accept him as a successor. He was an unpopular choice amongst the Praetorian Guard, but they could not find a suitable alternative, even after they had searched the streets of Rome for a contender. It was then that Didius Julianus, a rich senator in the midst of a late-night drinking session, heard of what was taking place, and went to the walls of the camp. Once there he shouted to the Guard that he would offer them as much money, gold and silver as they wanted in return for the emperorship. An impromptu 'auction' began between Didius Julianus and Flavius Sulpicianus, which was eventually won by Didius Julianus for a price of 25,000 *sesterces* per guard. The empire was sold and Didius Julianus was proclaimed emperor. Inevitably, Didius Julianus was not a popular choice amongst the citizens of Rome, who saw his climb to power as risible. Didius Julianus did not get much for his money, since he was emperor for only two months – his reign reached an untimely end when he was beheaded during Septimius Severus' conquest of Rome.

Chapter 10
THE BRITISH CELTS

Celtic campaigns against Rome

Background

Nearly 90 years after the assassination of Julius Caesar, Tiberius Claudius Drusus – the emperor Claudius of Rome and her Empire – succeeded his nephew Caligula unexpectedly, and at the sword-points of the mutinous Praetorian Guard. Shy, handicapped and stammering, the new emperor was advised that an exploit to provide a pretext for the award of triumphal honours would be in order. The conquest of Britain offered an opportunity to accept such honours without undue risk.

Claudius invades Britain

In AD43, a convenient appeal for Roman help against the powerful Catuvellauni tribe was received from Verica, king of the Atrebates of southern Hampshire. Claudius assembled four legions and strong auxiliary forces in Gaul, under the command of Aulus Plautius. This army was shipped across Oceanus Britannicus (the Channel), landing at Rutupiae (Richborough) and other points on the Kent coast, and establishing their supply base with, apparently, no significant interference from the Celts. Moving inland, they made a contested crossing of the river Medway, and the Celts fell back before them to the Thames. This, too, was crossed against spirited opposition; as at the Medway, the Romans committed specialist Batavian troops first, who swam their horses across under fire and established a bridgehead. On the northern bank the Romans built a fort, and awaited the arrival of the emperor.

Claudius was kept in seclusion as a child, because he was thought to be mentally and physically unfit. He had a stammer and a limp, and was a very sickly child. During this time alone, Claudius read voraciously, equipping himself with an extensive knowledge, which would become extremely useful in his role as emperor. (© R. Sheridan/AAA Collection Ltd)

Claudius arrived in August, bringing with him a detachment of the Praetorian Guard, and probably reinforcements in the form of vexillations from the Rhine legions (and, according to Dio Cassius, elephants!). The army advanced on the Catuvellaunian capital of Camulodunum (Colchester) and here Claudius received the formal submission of a number of tribes, then returned to Rome after a stay of only two weeks, and well before the onset of the miserable northern winter. Rome celebrated Claudius' triumph, and the army left in Britain set about crushing the inland Celtic tribes.

The major tribes of mainland Britain in about AD44.

Conquering the Celtic tribes

By 47 Rome had a British province up to a line running from the Bristol Channel in the south-west to the Humber in the north-east. Between 47 and 60 the Roman forces were intermittently but heavily engaged in Wales, against the Silures of the south-east and the Ordovices of the central highlands – the latter apparently led by Caractacus, a son of the

THE CELTIC FEAST AND THE RAID

Celtic feasts were important social gatherings, usually wild and drunken, sometimes even deadly, and often with ritual significance. A strict ceremonial was observed with regard to precedence and hospitality. Seating was arranged according to rank and prowess. Poseidonius lived among the Gauls, and his work survives in that of Diodorus and Strabo. Poseidonius noted:

> ...they sit in a circle with the most influential man in the centre, whether he be the greatest in warlike skill, nobility of family, or wealth. Beside him sits the host and on either side of them the others in order of distinction. Their shield bearers stand behind them while their spearmen are seated on the opposite side and feast in common like their lords.

Also in attendance were bards who would celebrate the lineage, bravery and wealth of their patrons. Strangers were allowed to join a meal before being asked their name and business. Everyone had a joint of meat according to their status. Traditionally, the greatest warrior received the choicest cut, the champion's portion of the thigh piece. It was a moment when any other warrior had the right to dispute his position and challenge him. Others sought to reinforce their status in a rough-and-tumble that often escalated into more serious violence. Poseidonius again:

> The Celts sometimes engage in single combat at dinner. Assembling in arms they engage in mock battle drill and mutual thrust and parry. Sometimes wounds are inflicted, and the irritation caused by this may even lead to the killing of the opponent unless they are held back by their friends...When the hindquarters were served up, the bravest hero took the thigh piece; if another man claimed it they stood up and fought in single combat to the death.

Amidst the drinking, boasting and singing, a warrior might propose to lead a raid and would encourage others to join him, tempting them with the prospect of loot and glory. The number of warriors who agreed to follow was determined by the leader's status. The more volunteers he could recruit, the greater chance he had of a successful outcome. A raid that brought spoils for him to distribute among his retinue would enhance his status as a leader. On a future occasion he would be able to attract a larger following, which in turn would have higher expectations of success and loot to be gained. Initially, younger warriors competed with each other but, once they had experienced initial success, they would dare to challenge their elders too. Small-scale raids on neighbouring clans to reive a few head of cattle would grow into inter-tribal conflicts and wider raiding over longer distances.

Catuvellaunian king, Cunobelinus. In 59–60, Suetonius Paulinus, the Roman military governor of Britain, led two legions into north-west Wales. The climax of the campaign was an attack on the island of Mona (Anglesey), a Druidic cult centre that was fiercely defended. He swam his cavalry across the Menai Strait, accompanied by the infantry in flat-bottomed boats. In bloody fighting embittered by the evidence of hideous atrocities and by the presence of shrieking Druids whipping up the Celtic warriors, the sanctuary was wiped out. While the army paused in Wales, ready to crush any remaining resistance, there came news of a disaster to the east.

Boudicca

The Iceni were a Belgic tribe occupying areas in Suffolk, Norfolk and Cambridgeshire. At the time of the Roman invasion their king Antedios diplomatically allied the tribe to Rome, thus avoiding conquest and slavery for his people, and preserving his personal wealth. Antedios was soon succeeded by Prasutagus who renewed the treaty with Rome. When he, too, died in 60, the Romans decided to annexe the kingdom outright. Roman soldiers plundered the tribal territory, causing widespread hardship and outrage. Even the king's widow, Boudicca, was flogged and her daughters raped. The exact sequence of events is unknown, but soon afterwards the whole region boiled over into rebellion, with previously pacified tribes such as the Trinovantes joining the Iceni under Boudicca's leadership.

Writing a century after her death, the historian Dio Cassius in his history of Rome says that Boudicca was:

> ...tall, terrible to look on, and gifted with a powerful voice. A flood of bright red hair ran down to her knees; she wore a golden necklet made up of ornate pieces; a multi-coloured robe; and over it, a thick cloak held together with a brooch. She took up a long spear to cause dread in all who set eyes on her.

Boudicca's name was derived from the British word *boud* meaning 'victory'. There is also a Celtic goddess named Boudiga. It is possible that Boudicca was not her name at all, but a title that she was given by her followers, to bring them victory. (© R. Sheridan/AAA Collection Ltd)

This gravestone of a cavalryman from Colchester shows fairly complete scale armour which would also have been worn throughout the later Empire. Gravestones from the third century onwards tended, however, to depict soldiers without their armour, even though cavalry armour became more complete in the later Empire. (© R. Sheridan/AAA Collection Ltd)

The combined host of rebel warriors swept south. Camulodunum (Colchester), former capital of Cunobelinus and the site of the Britons' formal surrender to the emperor, was now a Romanised town occupied largely by Roman veterans and their families. Although built within what had been the wall of a legionary fort, its defences had been neglected. The last defenders took refuge in the partly built temple of Claudius, probably the most substantial building available; it was burned down and the defenders massacred. A relief force of about 2,000 men and some 500 auxiliary troopers, hurrying over open country, was wiped out somewhere north-east of Colchester.

Next, Verulamium (St Albans) and Londinium (London) were overwhelmed by Boudicca's forces and put to the sack. The procurator and many of the richer citizens escaped to Gaul – those who could not escape (by far the majority) were massacred, many suffering atrocious torture.

Forced marches eventually brought Suetonius Paulinus and his troops back from their Welsh campaign, to somewhere just east of where the little river Anker is crossed by Watling Street, near Lichfield. Boudicca's Britons arrived on the field in huge numbers, the warriors in an uncontrollable mass, their families camping in a huge arc of wagons behind them. After the usual display of clashing arms, trumpeting, waving swords and deep-throated bellowing, the Celts charged the waiting cohorts. They were met in the textbook manner by two volleys of javelins followed by a legionary counter-charge, and the tribesmen were pushed backwards. The lay of the ground, and the packed mass of non-combatants and wagons behind their position, combined to trap the Celts in a way that allowed the legions and the auxiliary cavalry to cut them to pieces. The fighting lasted for many hours, and the slaughter was great. Her rebellion in ruins, Boudicca, the great red lady of the Iceni, soon died herself – there are conflicting claims for natural causes and poison.

Vexillations from the Rhine legions were shipped to Britain to reinforce the weakened garrison. The army was kept in the field, in its leather tents, despite the onset of winter. A merciless punitive campaign laid waste the tribal territories. Finally, in 61, a new governor was sent out; Petronius Turpilianus replaced the terror campaign of Suetonius Paulinus with a more flexible and diplomatic policy, and conquered Britain began to be eased from tribal anarchy towards capital oligarchy.

Agricola

Even so, it was to be more than 20 years before Roman arms pushed the frontier of the province into the far north. It was AD84 when Julius Agricola (a most able military governor, whose tenure had been extended to allow him to pursue a series of campaigns of northwards expansion) finally stood face to face with Britain's last Celtic army. Under the leadership of Calgacus, some 30,000 Caledonian warriors stood at bay somewhere near Inverurie in Scotland – the exact site of 'Mons Graupius' is subject to much scholarly debate. Agricola inflicted defeat on the Celts, with great loss of life, without even committing his legionary infantry.

Archaeology suggests that at one time Rome intended to occupy at least part of the Scottish Highlands; whatever the reason, the forts were abandoned uncompleted, and the consolidation of the pacified province took place behind the barrier of Hadrian's Wall, that extraordinary feat of engineering which lies across the country from sea to sea just south of the modern English–Scottish border. Rome briefly occupied the more northerly Antonine

When the Romans were busy foraging, scattered and with their weapons laid aside, the Britons suddenly attacked; they swarmed around with cavalry and chariots, killing a few and throwing the rest into confusion before they could form up.

There was a fierce engagement as the British cavalry and chariots clashed with our cavalry on the march. However, our men prevailed and drove the enemy into the woods and hills, killing a good many of them, though suffering a number of casualties themselves through pressing the pursuit too far. Then, after a while, when our men were off their guard and busy fortifying the camp, the Britons suddenly rushed out of the woods, charged down on the outposts on picket duty and started a fierce battle there.

These two passages from Caesar provide a good illustration of the combined tactics used by Celtic horsemen and chariot warriors to harass and snipe at the Roman forces feeling their way in unfamiliar territory. Native British horses were smaller than those in Gaul, where cross-breeding had improved the stock. The scene here portrays an attack by Cassivelaunus' forces on a Roman foraging party. (Painting by Wayne Reynolds © Osprey Publishing Ltd)

Wall between the Firths of Clyde and Forth during the second century AD; and later emperors made forays into Caledonia in response to pressure on the northern frontier. But in general, the highland fastness of Scotland remained the last free refuge of the Celtic people of Britain.

British Celtic troops

The warrior's role and status

To his Roman adversaries the Celtic warrior was the archetypal barbarian: huge in stature, immensely strong and bloodthirsty beyond description. Charging into battle without armour, impervious to wounds and wielding a terrible sword with which to take the heads of his enemies, he was the antithesis of the drilled and disciplined soldiers of the Roman cohort.

Celtic society, both before and after the Roman period, has often been described as 'heroic', dominated by a warrior elite whose lives were spent in an environment of perpetual conflict. Rich grave goods, including weapons and armour, together with later myths and legends, have reinforced this image. Indeed, warfare and conflict played an essential part in the maintenance of the very structure of Celtic society itself.

At the lowest level, Celtic society was made up of extended families or clans that were grouped together to form territorially based tribes. These were usually governed by a king or high chief, often in pairs. Most decisions were taken, or at least endorsed, by a popular assembly of all the free men of the tribe. Real power lay with a smaller council of leading nobles from among whom kings and chieftains were chosen.

The Druids formed part of the privileged class known in Ireland as 'men of art', which also included bards, who extolled the warrior hero in song. Artisans, especially blacksmiths and other metalworkers, who manufactured not only everyday tools but also much of the finery – weapons and jewellery – worn by the Celtic nobles to emphasise their wealth and rank, were also regarded as men of art.

The role of the Celtic warrior was to wage war and in doing so increase his personal reputation in the eyes of his peers. Caesar wrote:

> Whenever war breaks out and their services are required...they all take the field, surrounded by their retainers and dependants of whom each noble has a greater or smaller number according to his birth and fortune. The possession of such a following is the only criterion of influence and power that they recognise.

Cattle-reiving, slave-raiding and vendetta between clans and tribes formed the basis of a low-intensity warfare that permeated Celtic society. Such conflicts provided a starting point for the young warrior, giving him the opportunity to demonstrate his bravery and skill at weapons-handling.

THE CELTIC OTHERWORLD

Ritual and spiritual belief pervaded all aspects of the warrior's life. The supernatural was all around him: every tree and river, mountain and spring was imbued with its own particular spirit. Trees and watercourses were held to be especially sacred. The most important ceremonies took place within sacred groves of oak trees called *drunemeton*, while rivers, lakes and bogs across Europe have revealed ritual objects ranging from weapons and jewellery to animal and human sacrifices. Birds and animals held special significance too. Certain creatures were revered by the warrior for specific qualities, such as valour, speed, ferocity and fidelity. Most commonly regarded as revered were the horse, the bull, the wild boar, the raven and the dog. By adopting the symbol, on clothing or on armour, and also in appearance, and by invoking the spirit of a particular animal, the warrior believed that he would be granted the same qualities as the revered beast.

The everyday world of men and the Otherworld of the gods and the dead existed side by side. The line dividing one from the other was often blurred and ill defined. Neither was there any firm boundary between human and animal form. The story of the warrior hero who strays unwittingly into the Otherworld while pursuing some enchanted beast is a common theme in Welsh and Irish legend. Linking the two worlds stood the Druids, whose name is cognate with the Celtic word for oak. Known definitely only in Britain and Gaul, it is nevertheless more than likely that an equivalent class existed throughout the Celtic world. The Galatians, for example, had judges who assisted the tribal leaders. Druids enjoyed high status as the guardians of tribal tradition, as administrators of tribal law, and as mediators with the gods. Their main role was to interpret and control supernatural forces by means of divination. Caesar wrote:

> The Druids officiate at the worship of the gods, regulate public and private sacrifice, and rule on all religious questions.

Druid authority was both spiritual and civil, and extended from individuals to whole tribes. Anyone foolhardy enough to defy or disregard a Druid's ruling was excommunicated, debarred from taking part in sacrifice: according to Caesar the heaviest punishment that could be inflicted on a Gaul. Such individuals were shunned by others as unclean.

Appearance and dress

Appearance

Both on the field of battle and away from it, the Celtic warrior sought to demonstrate his wealth and status in his appearance and by the quality of his dress and equipment. To the Romans, more used to darker hair and complexions, fair-haired Celts seemed strange and outlandish. Diodorus Siculus describes them at some length:

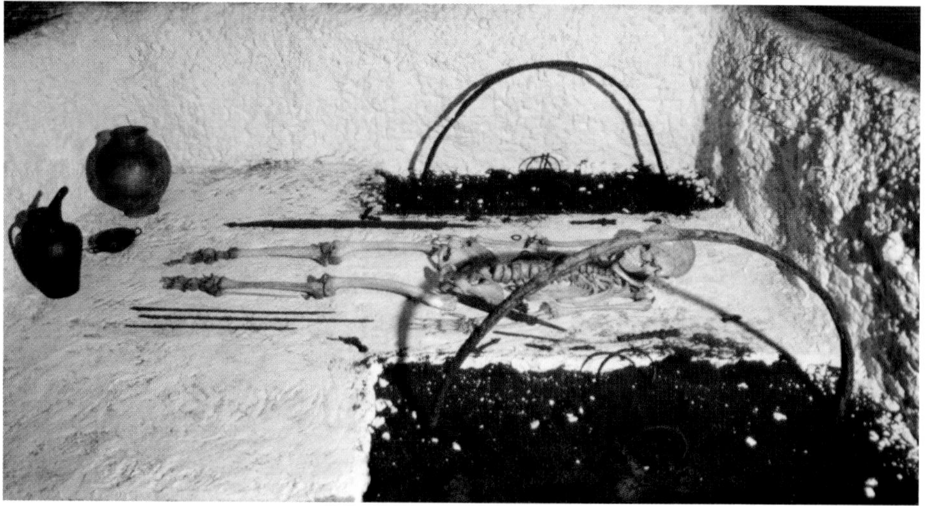

Chariot or cart burials such as this one from Somme-Bionne provide an indication of the status of the deceased. (© R. Sheridan/AAA Collection Ltd)

> …tall of body, with rippling muscles, and white of skin. Their hair is fair, not only by nature but also because of their custom of accentuating it by artificial means. They wash their hair in lime-water then pull it back so that it differs little from a horse's mane. Some of them shave their beard, others let it grow. The nobles shave their cheeks but let their moustache grow until it covers their mouth.

Despite their reputation for being tall, archaeological remains seem to indicate that the average height for a man was 1.7m (5ft 7ins). The average height for Romans, however, was several centimetres shorter. The reference to lime-washed hair is interesting in the light of the spiritual symbolism of the horse, and such hair was probably worn by warriors who had adopted this animal as their totem, thus invoking the protection of Epona, the horse goddess. Lime-washing had a practical benefit as well, since the process coarsened and stiffened the hair, providing a degree of protection from blows to the head. The disadvantage was that repeated application caused burning to the scalp and the hair to fall out. It was also difficult for the warrior to wear a helmet with lime-washed hair, although it is unlikely a Celt would have desired or felt the need to do so, believing himself to be adequately protected by his totem.

British Celts presented an even stranger spectacle due to their habit of painting or tattooing their bodies with woad, a plant from which a deep blue dye was extracted. This was, once again, believed to protect the individual, and his strength would be enhanced by the sacred symbolism of the swirling forms on his face, arms and torso.

Dress

Diodorus Siculus had this to say about how the Celts dressed:

> The clothing they wear is striking – tunics which have been dyed and embroidered in various colours and breeches; they also wear striped cloaks

> fastened by a brooch on the shoulder, heavy for winter and light for summer, in which are set checks, close together and of various hues.

From contemporary descriptions and from the fragments of textiles recovered from graves a fair idea may be gained of the clothes worn by the Celtic warrior. Most items were colourful, well made and of wool or linen. The highest-status nobles, whose clothes were often embroidered with gold thread, also wore some silk. Colours, however bright when new, would fade quickly because of the vegetable dyes used.

Celtic love of display and ornament was emphasised by the jewellery worn by the warrior to announce his wealth and status. Diodorus Siculus again:

> They amass a great quantity of gold which is used for ornament not only by the women but also by the men. They wear bracelets on their wrists and arms, and heavy necklaces of solid gold, rings of great value, and even gold corselets.

Of all the Celtic jewellery, the most impressive in the eyes of the Roman commentators was the neck-ring or 'torc'. To the Romans it characterised the Celtic warrior although it was not unique to the Celts. The torc could be of gold, bronze or iron according to the wealth of the wearer. It was almost certainly an indication of rank, with perhaps in some cases ritual or religious overtones.

The cavalry

Tacitus wrote that the main strength of the Celts lay in their infantry. However, they were also experienced in rearing and using horses, which were regarded as prestige animals and revered for their courage, speed and sexual vigour. Each horseman had two attendants, also skilled riders. When the horseman was engaged with the enemy, these attendants remained behind the ranks, but if the horseman was killed, one of the attendants would replace him. If the first horseman was injured, the second attendant would help him back to camp. If the horse was injured, one of the attendants would bring the horseman a new mount. These made maximum use of both horse and rider, ensuring that should one fall, full benefit was still made of the other, be it rider or horse. The combination of light-armed infantry with skirmishing cavalry was a common enough practice, although for the Celts it was probably employed more in specific circumstances such as the ambush of an unsuspecting enemy rather than in open battle.

Despite the fact that Julius Caesar did not mention the Catuvellauni tribe on his expedition to Britain, the tribe were the most dominant in Britain by the time of Claudius' invasion. The Catuvellauni seized control of most of south-east England by force, under their leader Cunobelinus. This is a Catuvellaunian coin showing the horse motif. (© R. Sheridan/ AAA Collection Ltd)

The chariot warrior

Before the development of an effective cavalry arm, the Celtic warrior would often fight from a chariot. From the end of the third century BC

The slinger (back right) represents the defenders of hill forts among the western British tribes, such as Maiden Castle, Dorset, and Danebury, Hertfordshire. His stone-bag would be full of 'pebbles' – actually cobble-sized and water-smoothed stones of uniform weight, gathered from beaches and rivers. Caledonian warriors like the one in front are said to have shown skill and courage in knocking aside Roman missiles with their long swords and small shields. Young men, like the one on the ground, not yet strong enough to trade sword blows in the ranks of the 'assault infantry', could still give vent to their aggressive spirit as javelineers, using skills learned in their foster-fathers' homes. (Painting by Angus McBride © Osprey Publishing Ltd)

onwards chariots had fallen from use in continental Europe, so the Roman invaders of Britain were surprised to find that they were still a major component of Celtic warfare in Britain. Panic would be caused by chariots being driven at speed towards the Roman line, in which many were trampled underfoot. The chariot was also used to 'drop off' warriors on the battlefield, who would step down to fight hand-to-hand after an exchange of missiles, while the chariot withdrew ready to pick him up again. This is a style of combat better suited to the constant low-intensity warfare between clans or tribes than the 'total war' struggles against the Romans.

Arms, armour and equipment

The bearing of arms was the right and duty of every free man in Celtic society and served to differentiate him, immediately and clearly, from the unfree majority. The basic equipment of the Celtic warrior was the spear and shield. To this he could add the sword and, for the nobility or as wealth and status permitted, a helmet and possibly a mail shirt. Diodorus Siculus provides a detailed description:

> Their arms include man-sized shields decorated according to individual taste. Some of these have projecting figures in bronze skilfully made not only for decoration but also for protection. They wear bronze helmets with large figures, which give the wearer the appearance of enormous size. In some cases horns are attached, in others the foreparts of birds or beasts...Some of them have iron breastplates or chainmail while others fight naked. They carry long swords held by a chain of bronze or iron hanging on their right side...They brandish spears which have iron heads a cubit or more in length and a little less than two palms in breadth. Some are forged straight, others are twisted so that the blow does not merely cut the flesh but in withdrawing will lacerate the wound.

Whilst the spear was the primary weapon and symbol of the common warrior, the sword was the weapon of the high-status warrior. To carry one was to display a symbol of status and prestige. For this reason, many swords and scabbards were elaborately decorated with precious metals and stones. Traditional Irish tales speak of gold- and ivory-hilted swords. Archaeological evidence has proved that Celtic swords were of high quality, flexible and with a sharp, strong cutting edge, contradicting Polybius' comments that in battle the blade quickly became so bent that the warrior had to straighten it with his foot. Confusion probably arose over the practice of ritually 'killing' a sword by deliberately bending it as part of a burial ceremony or sacrifice to the gods.

Helmets were a rare sight among Celtic warriors, worn only by those whose wealth and prestige permitted them to flaunt their status. Mail shirts were an even rarer sight on the battlefield than helmets. They were worn only by noble warriors of the very highest status. Remnants of iron mail appear for the first time in graves dating from the early third century BC, and it is believed that it was first invented by Celtic blacksmiths sometime before 300BC.

Neither the bow or the sling featured greatly among the weapons of the Celtic warrior, though both were used to some extent in Celtic warfare. Vast stockpiles of sling stones have been unearthed within several of the hill forts in southern Britain, a clear indication that their use was a major factor in the defence of these sites. The conclusion has to be that the Celtic warrior did not often use the sling or bow because they were not considered to be a

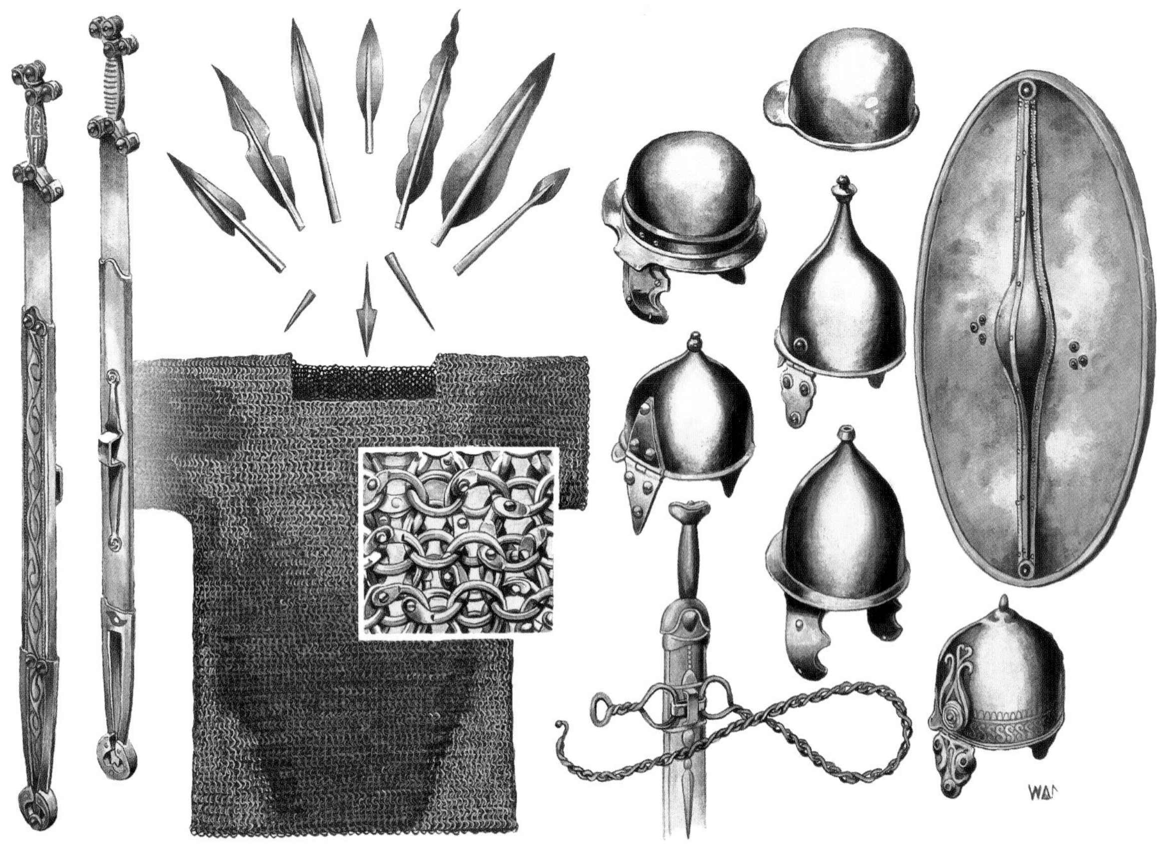

Smiths formed part of the privileged class in Celtic society and were regarded as 'men of art'. Their specialist skills were highly valued by the warriors who patronised them for the arms, equipment and fine metalwork. This illustration shows arms and equipment based on archaeological remains. (Painting by Wayne Reynolds © Osprey Publishing Ltd)

warrior's weapons. His goal on the battlefield was to engage the enemy at close quarters with spear and sword, and to measure his prowess against that of his opponent in single combat. To stand off and shoot at him from a distance went against Celtic principles – not to know who had vanquished whom, where was the honour in that?

Fighting style

Deployment

Polybius' description of the deployment of a Celtic army on the field of battle was no mere 'column of mob'. Deployment was by tribal contingents. Within tribes, clans would deploy as separate entities, doubtless according to an acknowledged or perhaps traditional pecking order. The retinues would group themselves around the highest status warriors standing in the front line. The warriors' sense of pride and honour, which was easily offended, probably precluded any other option. Even an exceptionally gifted commander had to operate within the accepted hierarchy. To identify each grouping in the battle line and to act as rallying points, the guardian deities of tribe and clan were carried into battle as standards topped with carved or cast figures of their animal forms. As with eagles of Rome, these standards were religious symbols.

Noise

As the Celtic host deployed for battle and caught sight of the enemy they set up a dreadful din. Each and every warrior gave full voice to his war cry or battle chant, doubtless mingled with taunts, insults and obscenities aimed at his opponent. To the cacophony of warriors themselves was added the sound of the carnyx (war horn). The carnyx was a long horn with a head and mouth in the form of an animal, often that of a wild boar. A particularly fine example in bronze was found at Deskford in Scotland in the early 19th century. It has been dated to the mid-first century BC. When first excavated the Deskford carnyx was found to have a wooden tongue or clapper in the mouth, which probably increased the vibration of the braying, strident sound. The fear and dread that these yells and horn-noises were supposed to create within their enemy were also felt by Paulinus' army when it faced the British force, supported by the Druids and 'banshee women' shouting and screaming awful curses while defending their Druids' 'holy of holies' on Anglesey in AD59.

Single combat

As the opposing armies faced each other, prominent warriors would step forward and throw down a challenge. Diodorus Siculus says:

> When the armies are drawn up they are wont to advance in front of the line of battle and challenge the bravest of their opponents in single combat...when someone accepts the challenge, they recite the heroic deeds of their ancestors and proclaim their own valour, at the same time abusing and belittling their opponent in an attempt to rob him of his fighting spirit.

Livy wrote of an incident where a Celtic warrior goaded a Roman into accepting his challenge by the simple expedient of poking his tongue out at him. The Roman had the last laugh, however, and killed his tormentor. On the point of robbing an enemy of his fighting spirit, in a similar confrontation, the extent of the warrior's faith in the power and favour of the gods is revealed by the utter collapse of the Celt's morale when a raven appeared to land on the Roman's helmet before flying threateningly towards the warrior. The will of the battle gods had clearly been demonstrated; resistance was useless and he was promptly despatched. In Irish myth, Badbh (the goddess of battle) and Morrigan (the queen of Darkness) both manifested themselves as a raven or crow.

Battle frenzy and hand-to-hand combat

As the respective champions fought and either conquered or died in full view of their armies, tension rose to new heights. The warrior needed no further encouragement. The

This Romano-British relief from the second century shows combat between Romans and Celts. (© R. Sheridan/AAA Collection Ltd)

frenzy of battle was upon him. The *Táin* (an epic Irish heroic tale from the eighth century) contains a graphic description of the battle frenzy of the hero Cúchulainn:

> Then the frenzy of battle came upon him. You would have thought that every hair was being driven into his head, that every hair was tipped with a spark of fire. He closed one eye until it was no wider than the eye of a needle; he opened the other until it was as big as a wooden bowl. He bared his teeth from jaw to ear and opened his mouth until his gullet could be seen.

The ferocity of the Celtic charge was legendary. They would dash out in full force, and swoop down on the enemy. Despite the mad rush of the warrior and his desire to close with his opponent, Tacitus, in his account of the battle of Mons Graupius, tells us that:

> The fighting began with an exchange of missiles. The Britons showed both steadiness and skill in parrying our spears with their huge swords or catching them on their little shields, while they themselves rained volleys on us.

Having hurled his javelin at close range, the Celtic warrior battered his way into the enemy's ranks, punching with his shield, thrusting with his spear or slashing with his sword. Against other Celts the battle was quickly transformed into a series of individual combats. Against the disciplined close-order units of the armies of Rome, however, Celtic tactics were less successful. By its very nature, the frenzied assault lacked all control. If the first mad rush failed to cause the enemy to fall or was unable to break his line, desperation soon began to set in. There was no way that hard-pressed troops could be withdrawn from the fight, and no reserve to bolster them. The warrior's code of honour made it impossible for him to stand back and watch others gain glory. For him, it was all or nothing. The fragility of Celtic armies and their lack of cohesion made for a fine line between success and failure. If one section of the battle-line began to waiver it could cause uncertainty and even panic to spread quickly. Tacitus' account of the battle of Mons Graupius noted:

> On the British side each man now behaved according to his character. Whole groups, though they had weapons in their hands, fled before inferior numbers; elsewhere unarmed men deliberately charged to certain death...and even the vanquished now and then recovered their fury and their courage. When they reached the woods they rallied and profited by their knowledge of the terrain to ambush their pursuers.

The convictions that led the warrior to fight on and, seemingly, to embrace death are difficult for us to understand and appreciate. In the end it comes to a question of personal honour, explicable in part by the mutual obligation between client and patron, and the obsessive desire of the warrior to gain prestige and stand well with his fellows, and perhaps also his foes.

Chapter 11
THE GERMANICS AND DACIANS

Germanic and Dacian campaigns against Rome

Background

Germanic homelands comprised modern Denmark, southern and central Norway, the north German coastal strip from the mouth of the Elbe to the Baltic shore, and the islands of Gotland and Bornholm. It was from these breeding grounds that warlike tribes, driven by pressures brought about by overpopulation, began their wanderings. Some lost their names, being quickly absorbed into bigger Germanic groupings during the ensuing chaos. Populating the dank and gloomy forests of northern Europe, the German 'barbarians' who overran the western Empire were descendants of peasants who had taken up arms; at the time Tacitus wrote his *Germania* in the late first century AD, a large proportion of the male population were warriors, and their society was moving towards a crisis. Successful war leaders, normally elected only for the duration of a single campaign, were becoming accepted in a permanent capacity as chieftains. The success of many leaders attracted other tribal warbands and, in an era of constant warfare, the transition from tribe to supertribe, grouped under cunning warlords, was well under way.

Germanic victory at Teutoburgwald

In the early years of the first century AD Rome decided to rationalise the northern frontier of her empire by annexing Germany up to the Elbe. The closing move, against the Marcomanni tribe, was frustrated when the new provinces in north Germany flared into revolt. The three legions stationed in the area, the XVII, XVIII and XIX, were annihilated in a series of ambushes in the Teutoburger forest in AD9. The German leader, Hermann (Arminius), chief of the Cherusci, had served in the Roman army, and used his knowledge of its operational limitations in boggy, heavily wooded areas. (Hermann aspired to more permanent power than that afforded to a war leader, and was subsequently destroyed by political enemies at home.) The indisputable outcome of this disaster was that Roman plans for the eventual control of all of Germania were permanently abandoned. Germanicus, the nephew of the Emperor Tiberius, conducted a series of short campaigns in Lower Germany, making some amends for the destruction of the three-legion garrison of the area by paying honour to them in their place of death.

The Empire was kept within its frontiers and stood on the defensive in the north. During the civil wars of 68–69, Gallic tribes of the north-east, with German allies, destroyed Roman forces on the Rhine and announced an 'Empire of the Gauls'. Roman forces moved swiftly to eradicate this Gallic empire. Vespasian and his sons then closed the dangerous gap between the Danube and the Rhine with a deep defence system. After Domitian had halted the migrating Chatti on the middle Rhine, during a series of bitterly fought campaigns in 83 and 88, Upper and Lower Germany settled down to a period of quiet, ably administered by Trajan. Legions could now be transferred from the Rhine to the Danube.

THE BATTLE OF TEUTOBURGWALD

Quinctilius Varus, acting on the information of Hermann, the trusted Chersuci war chief and former auxiliary officer, led a Roman army in autumn AD9 to contain a rebellion in partially subdued territory. Expecting to rendezvous with levies from the Chersuci, Varus was himself led into an ambush prepared by Hermann in the Teutoburg forest. Constrained by wooded hills to the left, marshes to the right, and turf walls to the front, the Roman army sustained the initial attack, but having been marching through 'friendly' territory it was strung out and disorderly and ultimately unable to extricate itself. The continual hit-and-run tactics of the Chersuci increased disorder and panic, and only a few soldiers survived to return across the river Rhine.

Velleius Paterculus, who served as a legionary legate during the Illyrian Revolt of AD6–9, witnessed the battle of Teutoburgwald first hand. His account emphasises that the disintegration and destruction of Quinctilius Varus' army was caused by the poor leadership and cowardice of Varus and his senior officers:

> An army unexcelled in bravery, the first of the Roman armies in discipline, energy and experience on the field, through negligence of its general, the treachery of the enemy and the unkindness of Fortune was surrounded, nor was as much opportunity as they had wished given to the soldiers either of fighting or of extricating themselves, except against heavy odds; indeed, some were even chastised for using their weapons and showing the spirit of the Romans. Hemmed in by forest, marshes and ambuscades, it was destroyed almost to a man by the very enemy it had always slaughtered like cattle...the general had more courage to die than to fight...*[and]* ran himself through with his sword. The two camp prefects...after most of the army had been destroyed, proposed its surrender, preferring to die by torture...than in battle. *[The legate]* Vala Numonius...previously an honourable man, set a fearful example by leaving the infantry unprotected by the cavalry, attempting to flee to the Rhine. Fortune avenged his act...he died in the act of desertion. Varus' body, partially burned, was mutilated by the enemy; his head cut off. (Velleius Paterculus, 2.119)

Dacians

The Dacians were a Thracian people, but Dacia was occupied also by Daco-Germans, and in the north-east by Celto-Dacians. In 85, Dacian forces attacked Roman defences in Moesia, harrying the countryside and killing the governor. The Emperor Domitian commanded initial operations to clear Moesia of invaders, but later passed control of the operations to Cornelius Fuscus. The campaign was carried into eastern Dacia, but the weight of Dacian numbers gradually drove the Roman forces back, and, in a final battle, they were wiped out, Fuscus suffering the fate of his army. Roman military honour was restored to some degree by the battle of Tapae, in 89, where the Dacians were thoroughly beaten. Decabalus, the king of Dacia, was forced to pay an annual tribute to Rome and to allow Roman armies passage through Dacian territory. That the emperor did not recognise the victory as conclusive is borne out by the fact that he refused the title of 'Dacius' at this juncture.

In 98, the Emperor Trajan came to power. The situation he inherited was one of increasing unease about the northern frontiers. Rome faced constant threat from German tribes in the west; and the Dacians were expanding their strongholds, it was believed, in readiness for another attack. Dacian culture at this time was far in advance of that of their fellow European barbarians. It was, in all recognisable aspects, an embryo civilisation. Towns were beginning to develop from the great defended strongholds called *oppida*, such as the capital at Sarmizegethusa. Trade was well organised and encouraged; silver and gold work, pottery, iron implements and weapons, of extremely high quality, were produced for home consumption and export to the sophisticated Roman world in the south. It was this nascent civilisation which now attracted increased Roman military interest.

In the winter of 100–101, Trajan massed ten legions and huge numbers of auxiliary troops of all kinds at Viminacium, a military base on the south bank of the Danube. The Roman army of conquest crossed the Danube on pontoon bridges, into Dacian territory, in the spring of 101. No opposition was offered until the army reached the general area of Tapae, where a large Dacian force confronted them. The ensuing battle was indecisive. The Dacians retreated to the mountains, killing livestock and burning crops to delay the Roman advance. After a further advance the Roman forces settled into winter quarters. The Dacians, together with their Sarmatian allies, mounted an attack in Lower Moesia, which was repulsed by the Romans. During the winter the Roman occupied themselves with carrying out marvels of engineering.

In the spring of 102 the Romans attacked Sarmizegethusa through the Red Tower Pass. During the whole of this period, Dacian emissaries were sent to Trajan, who constantly refused them audience. Finally receiving a deputation of prominent nobles, he sent them back with terms that the Dacian king, Decabalus, refused. After a further major battle Decabalus surrendered and Roman forces occupied the Dacian capital, Sarmizegethusa.

By 105 the Dacians had re-armed, taking the Roman garrison commander of Sarmizegethusa hostage; he, in turn, took the initiative away from the Dacians by swallowing poison. Once again the Dacians ravaged the Roman province of Moesia. With great effort the Romans relieved the province before winter closed in. In the spring of 106 the Roman

The Romans made temporary pontoon bridges by lining up many boats on the water, then laying wooden planks over them, as shown in this image from Trajan's Column. (© R. Sheridan/AAA Collection Ltd)

mounted a two-pronged assault on Sarmizegethusa, which they put to siege. When all seemed lost, some nobles took poison, others – including Decabalus – escaped. Those who fled were pursued ruthlessly; Decabalus was surrounded, but before capture he took his own life by cutting his throat. After the reduction of remaining pockets of resistance, large parts of Dacian territory were annexed as a Roman province.

The Marcomannic Wars

By the middle of the second century, pressure on Rome's northern frontier was mounting as the numerical increase among German tribes impelled their leaders to look for new ground. Goths and other German tribesmen began to move south-east in a steady stream. This movement blossomed into the Gothic nation of southern Russia and the Gepid nation of the Carpathians; the Astingi Vandals moved into territory west of the Roman province of Dacia. The Roman military command must have followed these developments with foreboding. To the north-west, the Rhine tribes were entering into the super-tribe status of permanent federation. Pressure was building on the middle Danube frontier; Roman strongholds had existed with Dacian agreement in the area since the first conquest of Dacia in 106, on the left banks of the rivers Danube, March and Thaya. During the winter of 166–7, the Lombards, a west German group, crossed the frozen Rhine, carrying with them the Lacringi, Victofali and Ubii tribes. They were immediately followed by a breakthrough

Trajan's Column records in relief the appearance of the heavy Sarmatian cataphracts. (© R. Sheridan/AAA Collection Ltd)

of Marcomanni, Quadi and Sarmatian tribes in the central Danube area.

From then on a kind of 'blitzkrieg', launched by a barbarian conspiracy, sucked in ever-increasing numbers of barbarians, in spite of a Roman offensive in 170, directed against the Quadi in particular. Roman armies were by-passed on the left and right flanks, and Greece was invaded. Early in 171, Italy, too, was subject to brief invasion, which was quickly nullified by Roman forces rushed from the frontier areas. Later in the year Marcus Aurelius rid the Empire of invaders, and peace was negotiated with the Quadi and Sarmatians. In 172 the Marcomanni were attacked by Roman forces on the Danube. The Quadi, breaking their treaty with Rome, assisted their kinsmen. After defeating the Marcomanni, Marcus turned to the Quadi who were attacked and defeated in 173. The Quadi then made peace. In 174, Roman troops attacked the Sarmatians, whereupon the Quadi broke their treaty once more. The war continued into 175, until an armistice was declared in the summer of that year.

During these vicious wars, serious weaknesses in the defences of the north were exposed. The Empire had been invaded and devastated. The constant fighting had made extremely heavy demands on the army at all levels, and, at one point, the gladiatorial schools were emptied in a desperate experiment. The struggle with Rome during the Marcomannic Wars had brought far-reaching changes to the Germanic peoples, and created in them an eagerness to launch more assaults on the colossus in the south. Sixteen of Rome's 33 legions manned the northern frontier, together with large numbers of auxiliary troops, at the end of the Marcomannic Wars – an end that proved to be only a beginning for the Germans.

The tribes most closely involved in these wars, the Marcomanni and the Quadi, were Germans belonging to the Suebian group of tribes. The Germans had become relatively civilised after a long period of contact with Noricum and Pannonia. Their close knowledge of the operational system and eager acquisition of the technology of the Roman army made these tribes formidable opponents.

The Goths

From their geographical position the Goths, the most powerful Germanic group, seem to have been the last of that family to settle in Europe. They occupied territory in Scandinavia and what is now northern Prussia, under various names given them by classical writers, such as Gothones and Guttones, Gothini and Getae. Their own name for themselves appears to have been the Gutthinda. From the latter years of the second century AD, the Goths were in possession of large tracts of country north of the Danube, on the coast of

Marcus Aurelius (Emperor 161–180AD) was one of the so-called 'Five Good Emperors', and combined great leadership and military excellence with high intelligence and a fundamental desire for peace. (© R. Sheridan/AAA Collection Ltd)

the Euxine, as far east as the Tauric Chersonese or Crimea, deep in territory once belonging to the Sarmatians, from whom they learned the use of heavy cavalry, the *kontos* (a large, heavy lance) and the stirrup.

These shock troops, heavy cataphract cavalry, were not completely new. Cataphracts had been in existence among Iranian nomads for centuries. The Sarmatians had perfected their use, but the Goths seem to have overthrown the Sarmatians by their ferocity in battle, probably hamstringing the horses (a German tactic). Thus, equipped with a heavy cavalry force to support the masses of traditional infantry, they faced the Roman army of the third century, which was now composed largely of Germans, Illyrians and North Africans. In the mid-third century Goths broke into the Balkans, killing the Emperor Decius (Hostilianus). This was followed, in 256, by a cave-in of the Rhine frontier. Gaul was overrun by Franks and Alamanni, some of them reaching Spain and Italy. The Goths, after exhausting the Balkans, also spread into Anatolia. Their stay in the Balkans was marked by constant defeats by Roman forces led by the Illyrian emperors.

In 275 Rome formally abandoned Dacia, which was promptly occupied by the Gepids and the western branch of the numerous Goths, known as the Visigoths. On the Rhine, the angle formed by the Danube in the Black Forest region was also vacated by Rome and occupied by the Alemanni.

Germanic and Dacian troops

Appearance and status

> Drinking bouts, lasting a day and night, are not considered in any way disgraceful...No one in Germany finds vice amusing, or calls it 'up-to-date' to debauch and be debauched...If they approve, they clash spears. No form, of approval can carry more honour than praise expressed by arms.

This excerpt from Tacitus' *Germania* describes a world in which the warrior's status was dependent on his battle prowess. For this reason, Germanic warriors pursued battle above all else, and won the respect of the peers through their behaviour on the battlefield. Tacitus continues:

> You will find it harder to persuade a German to plough the land and await its annual produce with patience than to challenge a foe and earn the prize of wounds. He thinks it spiritless and slack to gain slowly by the sweat of his brow what can be got quickly by the loss of a little blood...When not engaged in warfare they spend a certain amount of time hunting, but much more in idleness, thinking of nothing else but sleeping and eating. For the boldest and most warlike men have no regular employment, the care of the house, home and fields being left to the women, old men and weaklings of the family.

An essential factor in Germanic warfare was the warrior's own large, powerful frame. The German proper was a variant of the earlier Nordic type introduced by the Indo-European invasion. He was, in general, larger, due to racial mixture with the great northern hunters still surviving in northern Europe from the last Ice Age. The body was heavier and thicker than the pure Nordic type, with a large skull. He was characteristically blond or red-headed, as seen in his modern descendants and commented on by numerous early historians. The diet was heavy and rich in protein, broadly including pork, beef and fish (fresh and salted), mutton, venison, game, bread, beer and dairy produce.

Everyday dress varied from group to group. The overall costume, however, was the same throughout the north – a simple tunic, long trousers and cloak, which was usually of a blackish or dark brown wool. The tunic reached the knees and had either long or short sleeves. Several tunics could be worn at once, supplemented with fur and pelts of different kinds in cold weather. In summer, of course, upper garments were often left off altogether. Linen was known but was an expensive import from the south and was, for that reason, only worn by the wealthier or far-travelled tribesmen. Trousers were held up by rawhide thonging, and sometimes cross-thonging held them into the lower legs or ankles. Trousers were made from wool, as well as fur and skins. Knee-length breeches, when worn, were combined with a tight leg covering. The rough woollen cloth used by the Germans was woven in plain colours, of striped or other geometric design. Vegetable extracts were used for dyeing the cloth, a skill that had existed in the north since the Bronze Age, if not before. Red was obtained from madder root, yellow from saffron flowers, and the stalks or leaves of weld, blue from woad, and green from what is now known as 'dyers' greenweed'. Many garments were also left in their natural hue – wool has a number of natural shades, ranging from almost white, through fawn, brown and grey to black.

The early German rider on the left is mounted on a tough but probably poor-quality pony; we may infer this from the fact that the Romans, who used horsemen like this extensively, gave them better horses before training them to operate in formation. The other two warriors belong to one of the extensive group of Suebic tribes; their hair is dressed in the style called the 'Suebian knot', which involved either drawing it up into a top-knot, or drawing it over to the right and knotting it above the temple. (Painting by Gerry Embleton © Osprey Publishing Ltd)

Belts of varied thickness were worn at the waist or across the shoulder, sometimes both, and such straps could be used for carrying the warrior's shield. The warrior's cloak was secured with *fibulae* or brooches of differing kinds, some types being more popular among some tribes than others. Shoes were of a very simple design, in some ways similar to the moccasins of the North American Indian, turned up over the foot from the sole and tied at the ankle.

The Germanic warrior's hair was often left long, being sometimes plaited, gathered into a top-knot, or twisted into the curious knot peculiar to the Suebian tribes such as the Marcomanni or the Quadi. Beards were usually but not always worn, and tribesmen normally went bare-headed, but a woollen or fur cap might be worn in cold weather.

Bracelets, earrings, armlets, necklets, beads and rings were worn by both sexes, to a greater or lesser degree according to taste and status.

Germanic arms, armour and equipment

Germanic weapons

After the Roman conquest of Gaul, Roman weapons played an increasing part in the arming of Germanic war bands until, in the late Empire, a steady flow of arms northwards was sustained by illicit arms deals, loot from Roman arsenals and armies, and equipment brought home by the large numbers of Germans who had served in the Roman army.

Swordsmen numbered about one in ten among Germanic warriors at this time. In the early first century AD, a new process, called pattern-welding, was invented by European sword-smiths. The process was complicated, but not so long and drawn out as many earlier tempering methods. The central section of the blade was prepared by forging narrow billets of high-quality carburised iron, twisting them together in pairs, laying the twists side by side, welding them, and finally adding further strips of carburised iron to the sides and welding them to form the cutting edges. At this stage the blade was a long, flat, oblong billet which had to be filed and ground down to the desired form. It was then burnished and etched with an acid such as tannin, urine, sour beer or vinegar. When the central section and fuller were polished, a pattern having the appearance of a snake's back emerged, a result of the twisting carried out at an earlier stage in the sword-making process. Many variations of pattern were possible, according to the method used in the twisting phase.

On the pommels of some of these swords, rings, mostly decorated, are attached. These are believed to be special gifts from a grateful chieftain. Some scabbards have large beads attached to them, either of pottery, glass, meerschaum, crystal or, rarely, gold set with stones and occasionally gold or silver mounts. These are amulets – charms to bring good luck – and were believed to have the magical property to heal wounds made by the sword to which they were attached.

There was an increase at this time in the use of axes in battle, especially the throwing-axe. Germanic warriors also used bows, made of yew wood or fir wood. They were recognisable long bows of deep 'D' section. It is probable that, like the English longbow of later ages, these were 'compound' bows – a combination of sapwood, which resists stretching, for the back, and heat-wood, resistant to compression, for the belly or inside of the bow. Some of the arrow points used by the German archers were designed to puncture armour.

Germanic armour

> The Germans wear no breast-plates or helmets. Even their shields are not reinforced with iron or leather, but are merely plaited wickerwork or painted boards. Spears, of a sort, are limited to their front rank. The rest have clubs, burnt at the ends or with short metal points. Physically, they are formidable and good for a short rush. But they cannot stand being hurt... (Part of an eve-of-battle speech to his troops by Germanicus, 16.)

There is not much evidence of armour or helmets at this time, except in the case of a very few chieftains. During the second century AD more Roman-style mail garments were used, although they were still rare. The shield was either round, rectangular or sexagonal, and it was dish-shaped with a prominent projecting boss and iron or bronze edging.

Dacian arms, armour and equipment

Trajan's Column

The column erected in the Forum of Rome and dedicated to the Emperor Trajan in 113 illustrates in a spiral ribbon of reliefs the phases and main incidents of Trajan's conquest of Dacia. The square pedestal at the base of the column carried examples of arms and armour in confused abundance. On confronting the highly decorated, carved sides of the pedestal, it becomes obvious that the formal abbreviations of costume and weapons used on the column are absent: the column shows the narrative of the wars, and the pedestal shows graphic examples of the masses of equipment captured by Roman forces from their opponents in Dacia, sculpted from actual examples of the trophies. In their original condition, these bas-reliefs would have been painted in realistic colours, with details of armour and weapons added in metal. This was repainted and touched up periodically throughout the life of the Empire.

Dacian weapons

There are many representations of Dacian swords on the pedestal of Trajan's Column, including the Celtic La Tène type, and longer swords, which hang from plated belts around the warrior's waist. The murderous *falx* was also used by the Dacian warrior – a two-handed iron battle-scythe with the cutting edge on the inside of the curve. It is believed that these scythe-like weapons were so effective in early actions between Roman and Dacian infantry that special Roman armour, based on unique patterns, was devised to attempt to withstand its cut, and shields were reinforced.

Spears and javelins appear on the pedestal, as do bows. Celtic-style carnyx battle trumpets are also shown, in the shape of monster serpents.

This warrior, from the beginning of the German Migrations, is representative of those men who were among the first to settle on the Roman side of the Upper Rhine. His dress and equipment are mostly of native manufacture, showing little Roman influence. After campaigning in Gaul, and with initial successes against Roman troops, he would have gradually changed his appearance, adding weapons, armour and clothing of Roman manufacture. By the time of the battle of Strasbourg, he would have been barely distinguishable from his Roman opponents. His arms and equipment are typical of a well-equipped warrior in a chieftain's band along the Rhine frontier. (Painting by Angus McBride © Osprey Publishing Ltd)

Dacian armour

The dominant articles on the pedestal reliefs of Trajan's Column are the large, richly decorated, oval shields. They are the only type of body shield shown, and all are of the

The Dacian chieftain in the middle wears a bronze helmet, a corselet of iron 'leaf'-scale armour, and a black wool tunic and trousers decorated with red and white embroidery. The dismounted Dacian warrior on the right carries a seven-foot spear, and a long bronze sword hangs at his belt. The Dacian tribal warrior on the left carries a two-handed murderous *falx*, an iron battle-scythe with the cutting edge on the inside of the curve. The *falx* was an ethnic weapon of the Thracian people in general, and was used by part of the infantry in all Thracian groups. (Painting by Gerry Embleton © Osprey Publishing Ltd)

same shape and style of decoration, with the exception being those covered in a scale pattern. Dacian shields, as shown on the pedestal, were heavily decorated with floriate, braided, geometric designs. The helmets on the pedestal fall into two categories: one with a neat, rounded cone-shaped shell, the other with its apex curved forward into the characteristic 'Phrygian' peak. Both are highly decorated in the same fashion as the shields. The body armour of the Dacians is represented in three ways on the pedestal – mail, leaf-scale and banded construction – and the Dacian costume is the ubiquitous tunic and cloak combination of this time. Armour was probably not widely worn, and indeed the figures on the column show no signs of body armour, their only defence being the shield.

Roman influence on Germanic warfare

The kind of warfare that fuelled and maintained Germanic society was different from that which a Roman might have understood. There were no equivalents to the life and death struggles between Rome and Carthage, where the aim became the total destruction of an enemy society. Early Germanic warfare, like that of most warrior societies, was almost a ritual part of life. Struggles between families or clans were to accumulate wealth and prestige, or exact revenge for previous successes by an opponent, rather than the total defeat and destruction of the enemy. Weapons and tactics were relatively simple, and although their battles would cause casualties, they were unlikely to be massive.

Contact with the advancing Romans had many effects on Germanic society: warfare certainly became more deadly, and weapons and equipment improved. The usual tactic adopted at this time was to attack at a headlong rush, in wedge formation, so as to close in quickly, thus nullifying the murderous volley of legionary *pila*: the 'Furore Teutonicus' or 'German fury' of legend. Warriors preferred single combat, but knew the benefits of moving in rank, and took commands from appointed leaders. Tactics were uncomplicated, however, and relied on the ferocity of the charge, and the bloodthirstiness of the individual warrior. It would be wrong to try and differentiate too much between infantry and cavalry in Germanic warriors of this time, as most were all-rounders, able to fight on horseback if one was available, but equally able to dismount and fight on the ground. For this reason it has been suggested that mounted Germanic warriors were not so much cavalry, as simply warriors on horseback. As discussed above, however, the Gothic tribes of Germans developed a heavy cavalry shock force in the latter years of the second century, which they learned from the Sarmatians.

Those Germans living close to the Rhine found themselves having to fight for survival. As a result, small tribes and clans began to coalesce into loose confederacies such as the Franks and Alamanni and were thus able to draw on a much larger pool of manpower. Many Germans saw service in Roman armies, and although relatively few of them eventually returned to Germania at the end of their service, some did. Such men would have accumulated wealth beyond the wildest dreams of those who stayed behind, thus elevating them to positions of prominence.

Although Roman ideas of command and control could never be completely imposed on a heroic warrior society, contact with Rome saw the erosion of a tribal system and its gradual replacement by men of wealth and power who gathered followers from across tribal lines and maintained them through success in war. These great men and their followers evolved into the kings and nobles of early medieval society.

Chapter 12
THE PARTHIANS

Parthian campaigns against Rome

Background

The Parthians were a Parni people, a branch of Scythians, and their Empire was established in 247BC, by their own tradition, around the former Persian province of the same name. In the mid-second century BC the Parthian Empire had grown large and powerful under its king, Mithridates I (160–140BC), who made the Empire encompass modern-day Iran, Iraq, Afghanistan Armenia, Azerbaijan, Georgia, parts of Turkey, Tajikistan and Turkmenistan. However, the Empire suffered constant internal strife, which was exploited by Rome, anxious to keep the Parthians out of western Asian politics. The Romans sought neutrality treaties in buffer states between the Parthian and Roman empires, and within the Parthian kingdom

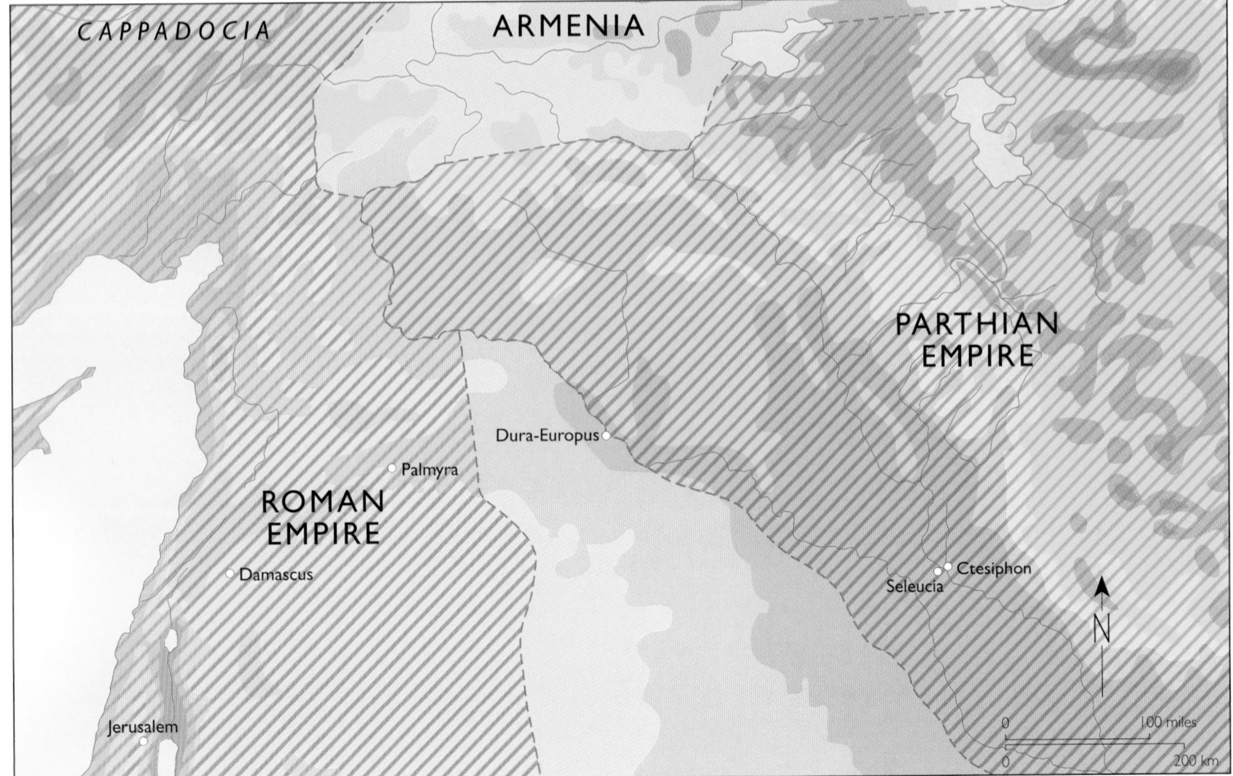

The traditional border between Rome and Parthia, lasting until Trajan's invasion.

itself. Rome even attempted to aid the vassal-states of Parthia to assassinate the Parthian kings, but with no success.

The enthusiasm of Rome for the removal of the Parthian threat was well demonstrated when, in 53BC at the age of 60, Marcus Licinius Crassus took up his proconsular duties in Syria. Excited by his new acquisition and hot from the power politics of Rome, this ambitious aristocrat accepted the command of the Roman army in the east, and prepared for a series of conquests that would equal those of Alexander the Great. No war with Parthia was contemplated by the Senate, but any objections they made to Crassus' plans were brushed aside. The Senate argued that the Parthians were protected by valid neutrality treaties with Rome, and could therefore expect to be safe from Roman attack. Undeterred, Crassus crossed the Euphrates and marched into Parthia with his army. Crassus met the Parthian army on the battlefield at Carrhae, and the result was a massive disaster for the Romans. Carrhae was a traumatic shock for Rome and her army. Having experienced the full weight and ferociousness of the famous Parthian cataphracts at first hand, the very few survivors of the battle would never forget it. It became apparent that the Parthians were not the sort of enemy who would easily roll over in defeat.

Roman invasion of Parthia

When 36-year-old Octavian Caesar, emperor of the west, became Augustus, total hegemon of the Roman world in 27BC, his summary of Parthian military capabilities was that they were capable of no sustained offensive warfare, probably due to their inability to sustain internal stability. Augustus resolved to compromise and reach some kind of *modus vivendi* with the great Asian nation. Strategic perimeters around the Roman and Parthian empires were strengthened by re-asserting Roman control over Transcaucasia and Armenia, and a Romanisation programme was set in motion. Augustus even negotiated with the king of Parthia, then Phraates IV, for the return of the Roman standards that were lost to the Parthians on three occasions, 53BC, 41BC and 36BC. These were duly returned in AD20.

This early depiction of a Persian or Parthian warrior comes from the sixth century and is part of the Oxus treasure – a unique collection of Achaemenid Persian metalwork. The warrior's short sword, or knife, can clearly be seen hanging from his belt, and he appears to be carrying some kind of fasces. (© R. Sheridan/AAA Collection Ltd)

During the first century AD Parthia started to experience a gradual Persian cultural resurgence. Relations with Rome at this time were fairly stable, despite hostilities in the middle of the century when Vologases I made his brother Tiridates king of Armenia without seeking Roman consent or approval. Nero, then emperor of Rome, ordered an invasion of Armenia to show his anger at this move, and in 63, an agreement was reached, whereby Tiridates was crowned prince of Armenia by Nero himself, thus agreeing to be under overall control of Rome. This agreement kept the situation stable and relatively peaceful between the two armies until Trajan's invasion in the second century.

Trajan's conquest of Armenia and Transcaucasia in 114 brought him to the Euphrates, which he crossed the next year. Adiabene and Mesopotamia were conquered, and the Parthian capital of Ctesiphon was taken; the king and his daughter were captured. Trajan decided to end his conquests on reaching Charax, and in 117 he died. His successor, the Emperor Hadrian, pulled the Roman troops back to the line of the Euphrates, and there was a period of relative peace between Rome and Parthia until 162.

Phraates IV, king of Parthia 37–32 BC. Phraates IV secured the throne through extremely ruthless methods, involving killing his father and his 30 brothers and their families. Phraates IV married an Italian slave-girl called Musa who was a gift from Augutsus. She, and their son Phraaktes, later killed Phraates IV. (© R. Sheridan/AAA Collection Ltd)

Parthian victory over Rome

A vacated Armenian throne in 162 led the Parthian king, then Vologases IV, to invade Armenia and Syria and defeat Sohaemus, who had been the Roman choice for the Armenian throne. Rome retaliated under the command of Lucius Verus, co-emperor to Marcus Aurelius, inflicting a heavy defeat on the Parthians, and capturing Ctesiphon once more. The palace was burnt down, but Roman troops retired when an outbreak of plague began to rage throughout Iran. A Mesopotamian revolt against the Roman leaders in 195 was seized upon and supported by Vologases V, and Parthia took back the province for a short while, provoking Septimius Severus to once more invade Parthia, once more capture Ctesiphon, and once more burn down the royal residence. However, internal struggles within the Parthian Empire were difficult distractions, and significantly weakened Vologases' ability to fight back against the Romans. Vologases did eventually beat Severus in 199, whilst Severus was trying to capture the pro-Parthian Mesopotamian state of Hatra, marking the end of that period of campaigning.

Civil war in Parthia in 208 was seized upon by the Roman emperor – then Caracalla – as a good time to once more invade Parthia in search of triumph and glory. The war started in 216, and was promptly taken up by Caracalla's successor, the Emperor Macrinus, after the early assassination of Caracalla. The Parthian king, Atrabanus V, inflicted a decisive defeat on the Romans at Nisibis in 217, and Atrabanus was able to impose a heavy tribute on the Emperor Macrinus.

THE BATTLE OF CARRHAE, 53BC

Having been abandoned by the promised reinforcements from Armenia and by the Arab recruits within the legion, Crassus marched his army at infantry pace across desert, towards the ancient town of Carrhae (now known as Harran). As they approached Carrhae, Roman vedettes began to return from their posts in advance of the column, reporting that some of the Roman cavalry screen had been killed by Parthians, whose main force was now deploying ahead for an immediate engagement. According to Plutarch, Crassus seems to have been caught completely unawares and began to show signs of panic, giving hasty and unconsidered orders. Cassius, a staff officer, stepped in to advise him to extend the infantry in its line of battle across the plain, dividing the cavalry between the wings. These manoeuvres were underway when Crassus changed his mind and gave orders for the legions to go into hollow square with 12 cohorts on each side, each with cavalry and light infantry support. Crassus took his position inside the huge square together with his guard and the Gallic cavalry commanded by his son Publius, and the baggage train.

In this formation Crassus gave the order to advance. After some time the little Ballisur stream was reached. Crassus was advised to stop here for the night, engaging the enemy the next day after assessing their strength; but Publius and his Gauls were impatient for action, and Crassus was persuaded to press on. He gave orders for the men to be fed and watered as they stood in the gigantic square, but most had not finished their meal when Crassus gave the order to advance without rest until the enemy were sighted.

When the Parthian army came into full view they seemed to the Romans neither impressive nor numerous. Plutarch says that Surena had hidden his main force behind the front ranks. It seems that the Roman troops had expected to see Parthian cataphracts in complete armour, and were pleasantly surprised when none seemed to be present. Surena had evidently told his cataphracts to cover themselves with coats and hides so as to hide their glittering armour. As the Roman troops reached the battleground and stood ready for action Surena gave a signal, and the air was filled with the loud throbbing of large drums, with attached bronze bells, from positions all over the battlefield. At this moment the cataphracts dropped the covers from their armour. Plutarch says:

> Now they could be seen clearly, their helmets and breastplates blazing like fire… their horses armoured with plates of bronze and steel.

Surena seems to have planned to break the Roman square with a charge by his 1,000 cataphracts, so that horse-archers could attack a disordered enemy. This plan was quickly changed when he discovered the depth of the Roman lines: the cataphracts withdrew, and the horse-archers began to envelop the square.

A charge by some Roman light infantry achieved nothing: the horse-archers merely withdrew, peppering the auxiliary infantry with arrows and driving them back into the square. The Romans became aware that Parthian arrows could punch through their armour and shields as the arrow-storm began to fall among the packed ranks of the square. The Romans clung to the hope that this phase of the battle would peter out as Parthian quivers emptied. Hope was shattered when it was seen that some horse-archers were returning from an ammunition train of camels with replenished quivers.

Seeing his rear about to be attacked, Crassus put together an assault force of Gallic cavalry, 300 light troopers, 500 foot archers and eight cohorts of the legions under the command of his son Publius, with orders to attack the gathering Parthian bowmen. As the Roman force advanced the horse-archers turned and galloped away. Publius was taken in, and followed in pursuit, losing sight of the Roman main body. After some time the Parthians wheeled about, now joined by a larger Parthian force including cataphracts. The Romans halted, and were promptly attacked by horse-archers darting in and out. Publius led the Gauls in an attack on the cataphracts. Although the Gallic spears failed to penetrate Parthian armour, the Gauls bravely pressed home their attack, grabbing the enemy's long lances, pulling the riders to the ground and scrambling under the horses' bellies to stab them. They even drove their own mounts on to the long Parthian lances. The Gauls were eventually forced to retire with the wounded Publius to a small hillock, where they were surrounded and attacked. About 500 of them were taken prisoner. Publius was killed, and his head was cut off. The Parthian troops rode back to Surena's main force.

Crassus, noticing that pressure on his square had slackened, and unaware of the disaster overtaking Publius and his force, relocated his army on sloping ground in conventional battle order. After several of Publius' messengers had been killed, others got through to tell Crassus of his son's predicament. Crassus sent no support, but began ad advance. Again, Parthian drums began to throb, and Surena had Publius' head paraded in front of Roman lines on a spear. The advance was stopped by the bowmen and cataphracts. When night fell the Parthians offered Crassus his life if he would surrender, giving him the right to mourn the death of his son.

During the night Crassus lost self-control, and it fell to his subordinates to call a staff meeting. The agreed action was to leave the wounded and retreat under cover of night. The cavalry, on hearing the decision, decided to leave forthwith to avoid the chaos of a night retreat. As they passed the town of Carrhae they told the sentries on the wall of the disaster, and rode on to Zeugma.

The Parthians quietly watched the Roman retreat without interfering. They slaughtered the wounded left in the Roman camp. Crassus and the remains of the Roman army reached Carrhae, and were taken into safety. Some time later, four legionary cohorts commanded by Vargontius, who had strayed from the main Roman column during the retreat, were surrounded and destroyed; 20 survivors were allowed to march to Carrhae, in compliment to the boldness they had shown in attempting to hack their way to freedom through the Parthian ranks.

The attempts to bring Parthia under Roman control had failed, and a Parthian invasion of Asia Minor was imminent; but in 224, at Susiana, Atrabanus was killed in battle against the army of the Sassanid Persians. Within two years the Sassanians had completely overthrown the Parthians. The Parthians had ruled Persia for nearly 400 years. During their paramountcy Rome – apart from a few fleeting successes – had been held at bay for three centuries.

Parthian troops

The Parthians had seen how the use of heavily armed, well-trained cavalry could devastate infantry-based armies in the conquests of Alexander the Great. Skilled in horsemanship and archery from an early age, it made sense for the Parthians to rely on their cavalry in battle,

These figures represent Parthian horse-archers from the fourth century BC (right), the second century BC (middle) and the third century AD (left). (Painting by Angus McBride © Osprey Publishing Ltd)

and only use infantry soldiers in small numbers. Lacking a standing army, Parthia could never hope to arm and train an infantry to rival the disciplined phalanxes and cohorts of Rome, so this approach made most use of what the Parthians had available to them. This quote from Justinus, writing about the Parthians in the second century AD, shows how they were natural horsemen:

> On horses they go to war, to banquets, to public and private tasks, and on them they travel, stay still, do business and chat.

There is evidence that the Parthian archers also used camels on occasion, which had great stamina and gave a good advantage point from which to fire, but their effectiveness was limited due to their soft feet, which would quickly become injured walking on the debris of a battlefield.

Appearance and status

The feudal system of the Parthians roughly resembled feudalism as developed in Europe during the 'Dark Ages'. Society was headed by seven powerful clans. This upper level of society supported a petty aristocracy who, together with their retainers, enjoyed status well above the peasants and serfs, who were native Persians. Loyalty was strongest between the great clan leaders and their small vassals. The king, as a member of one of the clans, could usually command complete loyalty from his own clan and its vassals, less from other Parthians.

The crown did not pass from father to son as of right. Worthiness to lead was weighed and opinion expressed by the aristocratic clan leaders in council. While the monarchy was new the great lords were its strength. During most of the Parthian history, however, the nobles were allowed to dominate the monarchy to such a degree that internecine warfare was endemic. Kings were made and unmade, sometimes with outside help from either Rome or the nomads.

The Parthians were a warrior people. Though possessing no regular army they were superb horsemen and archers, and in time of war the nobility provided heavily armoured knights mounted on weight-carrying chargers. The mass of lesser nobles and their retainers were traditional horse-archers, mounted on tough steppe ponies and armed with the reflex bow. The infantry was composed of good quality hillmen, and of peasants who were of indifferent military worth.

Armour

Heavy cavalry

The increasing use of body armour by cavalrymen was brought about by a number of factors, the most important of which was the breeding of a weight-carrying horse, using the Nisaean breed of Persia. The breed was designed to carry super-heavy cavalrymen, or *cataphractarii,* throughout Asia in the centuries to come. The nearest living example is

Delli de nation
Parthique qui signifie
fol hardy ou enfant perdu

thought to be the Akal-Teke, a sub-breed of the Turkoman standing between 15 and 16 hands. This horse, although tall, does not compare well with those depicted on Persian reliefs, which appear much bulkier. Soon, armour for the new type of heavy cavalry was being constructed from rawhide, horn, iron and bronze cut into scales. Some horse-trappers were of thick felt, which was possibly dyed in colours somewhat similar to those shown in Persian graphic art. In his *Anabasis*, Xenophon describes Persian cavalry armour of the fourth century BC. He says that the troopers had a helmet, cuirass and thigh armour, and that the horses had frontlets for the head and chest defences. The panoply of the *cataphractarii* was very expensive, and varied between individuals. Any degree of standardisation may only have been present among the royal guard and retainers of some of the greater nobles. Broadly speaking, more easily obtainable materials were used for armour by early Parthian knights, as well as those throughout the period who could not afford the more expensive metal armours.

The standard turn-out would have included helmets of bronze or iron, sometimes with a neck guard and/or an aventail of lamellar, scale or mail, sometimes sporting a small plume of horsehair, either dyed or left natural; and a corselet of lamellar, mail or scale for the torso. Arm guards were also worn, and some wore gauntlets too. The feet were often protected by armour over mail 'socks', and mail was often used to bridge defences at limb joints. A small fabric tabard and/or cloak might be worn, and this was very likely to be made of a rich material such as silk brocade.

Horse-archers

Parthian horse-archers were dressed in a variation of Scythian costume consisting of a leather or felt kaftan neatly finished off with a plain or ornate embroidered border; this was of wrap-over design, held by a waist belt. Richly decorated trousers were tucked into ankle boots, which were also decorated in some cases. Wide chap-like over-trousers were attached by two suspenders at the back; they were very baggy, and hung to form tightly draped folds around the legs. These may have been worn as protection for the patterned trousers. Later Parthians, from about the first century AD, seem to have preferred to show off their carefully tonsured hair, usually only wearing a fillet of thick ribbon; before then the Scythian cap was worn more frequently. The bow was slung from the waist belt on the left side in a case, together with a supply of arrows.

Horse armour

The panoply could be completed by horse defences such as a chamfron to protect the animal's head and peytrals to protect the chest, both of thick felt embroidered for reinforcement. Bronze scale armour was also sometimes used for horses, especially those of the *cataphractarii*, who would be engaged in fighting at the closest quarters. Such scale armour sometimes covered the horse from its neck back, and sometimes it fully covered the horse, including the head. It should be stressed, however, that horse armour was not always used by these heavy troopers.

OPPOSITE This engraving from 1662 shows a highly stylised portrayal of a Parthian chief wearing a feathered headdress and carrying a sword and a sceptre. The royal bird or falcon was a Parthian symbol of royal investiture, so it may be that this engraving is a Parthian king, wearing the symbolic feathers of his position. (© C. Hellier/AAA Collection Ltd)

These heavy Parthian and Armenian cataphracts show the near-total armour used by horse and rider. (Painting by Angus McBride © Osprey Publishing Ltd)

Weapons

Heavy cavalry

The primary weapon of the Parthian warrior was the 12-foot lance known as the *kontos*. It had a large leaf-shaped blade and a butt spike. The *kontos* was used in a downwards stabbing overarm motion, or forwards as in bayonet fighting, and was always wielded with two hands. Secondary weapons included a long sword, axe, mace and dagger.

Horse-archers

The primary weapon of the light cavalrymen was the powerful, recurved, composite bow constructed of layers of horn, wood and sinew. The wooden core formed the frame and was relatively 'neutral'. The strips of buffalo horn were laid along the belly to resist compression. The sinew – dried, broken into fibres, saturated in glue and layered on the back – resisted tension. In this way tremendous energy was stored during the draw and

This Parthian dish depicting a scene from a lion hunt shows clearly the 'Parthian shot', where the horse archer fires backwards while retreating. (© R. Sheridan/AAA Collection Ltd)

unleashed at the release. The ears of Parthian and Sassanian bows were extended and stiffened with horn, which increased tension and controlled the release.

Arrows were about 75cm (30in) long and were stowed in a combined quiver and bowcase of careful design. To facilitate the smooth loosing of the arrow, a horned thumb ring was used, which allowed the string to ride smoothly over the polished surface during the release without chafing the skin. These rings were made of various hard materials, and many later examples are minor works of art in their own right. Axes, short swords, daggers and sometimes long swords were secondary weapons worn at the belt.

Islamic art of a later period shows drums carried by asses and camels, which may have followed Parthian tradition. Although elephants seem to play no part in the Parthian army, they were often used by the Parthians' conquerors – the Sassanids. Standards were of a wide variety of shapes and sizes, and Parthian examples probably included the dragon standard, shaped like a wind sock. Others, produced for Persia's 2,500-year anniversary celebrations during the reign of the late Shah included horses, moon and star, a large ear of corn, a Mithras and a sun standard.

Fighting style

Horse-archers

Of the two great divisions of Parthian armies, the horse-archers were the most spectacular and traditional. These formations were manned by the less well-off petty nobility and their followers. Varying numbers of mounted bowmen from the Iranian tribes of the steppes were

This head of a Parthian is the detail of a capital from the Doge's Palace, Venice. (© R. Ashworth/AAA Collection Ltd)

also used from time to time. Light horse-archers could attack in various ways: arrows were carried in the left or bow hand, and one was nocked ready for release. At a signal, the assault would begin at a walk, later breaking into a canter and gallop. The arrows were released at the gallop when within range. At about 45m from the enemy front the archers swerved to the right and galloped out to the flank, shooting into the enemy lines. A more spectacular tactic was performed by bringing the mount to a skidding half-turn: as the bowman galloped away arrows were shot over the horse's rump. Firing from this position became known as a 'Parthian' shot, which is believed to be the root of the phrase 'a parting shot'. If circumstances were such that the enemy could be surrounded, as at Carrhae, horse-archers were able to kill at leisure, if well-led. Islamic archery manuals give quite a number of firing directions and positions possible for mounted bowmen, and it is reasonable to suppose that earlier bowmen used the same methods prior to the Arab conquests.

Horse-archers were almost impossible to destroy; however, they could be dispersed by good light cavalry, who might in turn be open to eventual counter attack. Enemy cavalry could be attacked while the bowmen's own cataphracts threatened any enemy counterattacking. Concentrated fire directed at a given point of the enemy line could produce an opening for cataphracts to break into. The effect on heavy infantry was more demoralising than destructive. At Carrhae it is believed that 20,000 Roman troops out of a force of about 36,000 died at the hands of the Parthians. Whatever the proportion actually killed by horse-archers, the lion's share was credited to them by the Greek historian Oligarch.

Heavy cavalry

The enemy having been softened up by the horse-archers, the Parthians would next charge in their heavy cavalry. The Parthian army usually took the field with its heavy assault cavalry, protected by fast, light, hit-and-run mounted bowmen. The proportional balance of an army at a given engagement varied widely, Large numbers of cataphracts, or *clibanarii*, might be accompanied by equal numbers of horse-archers; or relatively few troopers might appear with masses of horse-archers. Cataphracts were heavy enough to break any other type of cavalry which opposed them; they were reasonably immune from hand-propelled missiles and arrows, less so from sling pellets or machine weapons. Their attack would be carried out at an ambling trot in close order, and was often only a feint to

Terracotta Parthian head from the first century BC to the second century AD. The figure appears to be wearing a turban-like cap or hood. The rank or position that this cap conveys is unknown, as it was worn by many classes of society, including servants and maids. (© B. Wilson/AAA Collection Ltd)

cause infantry to regroup into close formation, to enable the mounted bowmen to create havoc, thus producing a close-order/open-order dilemma in the ranks. If the charge was pressed home against infantry who had been subjected to prolonged missile attack, who were suffering from lack of food, water or rest, or who were already disordered, the chance of success was high. Good, fresh, well-prepared infantry in dense formation were difficult, if not impossible, to break, and could prove lethal.

LATE EMPIRE AD235–500

The Empire of Rome must, for a while, have seemed immortal, its armies conquering and defending ever-increasing swathes of land.

But small cracks had become serious flaws in Rome's foundations, and the emergence of stronger warriors pushing at her frontiers was about to topple this once-mighty tower of strength...

BRITAIN
GERMANY
BELGICA
GAUL
DACIA
CISALPINE GAUL
ILLYRICUM
THRACE
ITALY
MACEDONIA
SPAIN
MEDITERRANEAN
SICILY
MAURETANIA
NUMIDIA
NORTH AFRICA
N
0 250 miles
0 500 km
The Roman Empire in the time of Hadrian (including green shaded area)
The Roman Empire c.500 after the fall of Rome and the West

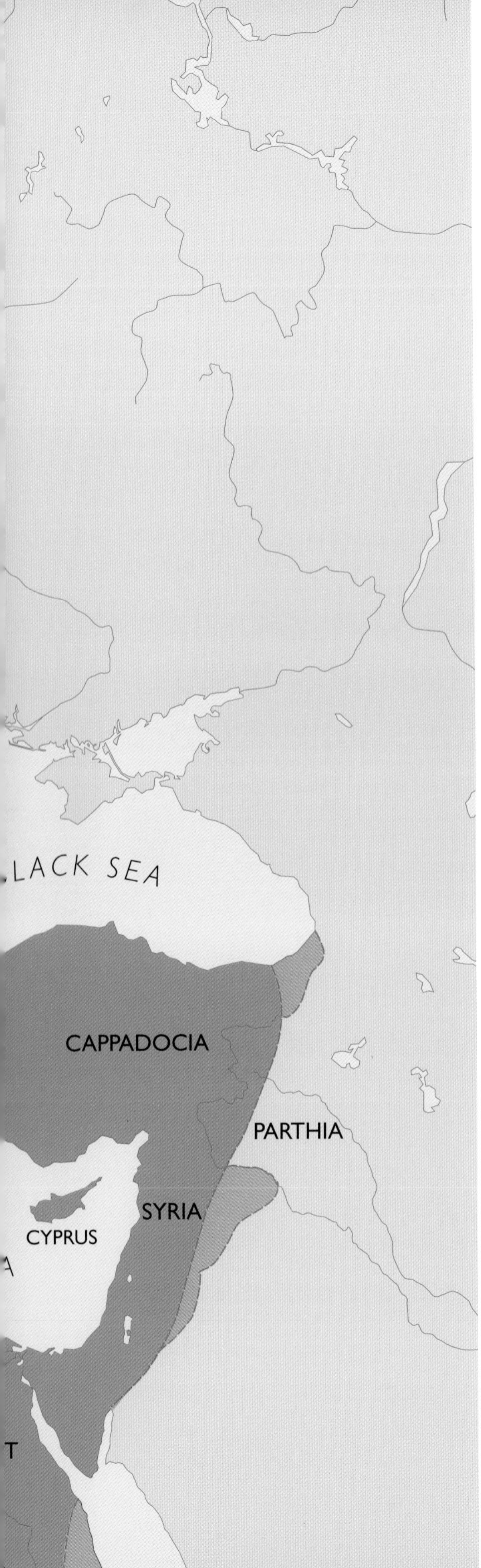

CHRONOLOGY

235	Murder of Severus Alexander by troops
243/4	Gordian defeated by Shapur I of Persia
251	Death of Decius in battle against Goths
260	Defeat and capture of Valerian by Persians Franks invade Gaul; Alamanni invade Italy; revolts in Balkans
261–68	Odaenathus of Palmyra takes control of eastern provinces
275	Murder of Aurelian
284	Accession of Diocletian
293	Tetrarchy with Maximian as co-Augustus and Constantius and Galerius as Caesars
305	Abdication of Diocletian and Maximian
324	Constantine defeats Licinius and becomes sole emperor
337	Death of Constantine at start of campaign against Persia
353	Constantius II defeats usurper Magnentius and reunifies Empire
355	Julian co-opted by Constantius as Caesar
378	Defeat and death of Valens at Adrianople
394	Theodosius defeats usurper Eugenius and reunifies Empire
395	Death of Theodosius; Empire divided between Arcadius and Honorius
408	Stilicho executed
410	Sack of Rome by Alaric and Visigoths
455	Vandals sack Rome
476	Odoacer deposes Romulus Augustulus, the last western emperor

Chapter 13
THE ROMANS

Background

Inside the Empire

In the early third century AD the Roman Empire stretched from Scotland to the Sahara and the northern river Tigris – an enormous imperial enterprise and the most powerful state in the world. Four centuries later the Empire had shrunk to consist of Anatolia, the Aegean fringes of the Balkans, and limited territories in Italy around Rome and Ravenna. An accumulation of diminishing imperial authority, undermining the fiscal and military structures that permitted the imperial machine to function, had fatally weakened the Roman Empire, making it unable to effectively resist the pressure on its western frontiers, eventually leading to the emergence and conquests of stronger peoples.

Imperial crisis and consequences

Overall, the Empire was prosperous during the first two centuries AD, as can be seen from the archaeological remains of provincial cities where local elites competed to beautify their home towns. On the other hand, there were already ominous signs of strain in the second century, the golden age of imperial prosperity. Prolonged warfare was expensive, especially along the European river frontiers where booty was unlikely to offset costs: troops had to be moved to the area of conflict, imposing demands on communities along their lines of march, and extra resources were demanded to make good losses. The cumulative nature of the frontier pressure on the Empire is evident, with emperors unable to divert troops from one sector to another, and instead constrained to confront invaders in conditions that led to defeat. Between 235 and 284, the Empire saw at least 23 different emperors attempting to impose rule. Each new emperor meant another donation to the troops; each civil war meant more loss of life, physical destruction and distraction from the frontiers. Prolonged warfare inside the frontiers, regular defeat, and the rapid turnover of emperors had major economic consequences.

Diocletian's stabilisation

Diocletian came to power in 284, and during his 20-year reign he re-established imperial stability, before his planned retirement. The secret of his success was an imperial college, since one factor promoting earlier disunity had been the desire of major armies to have their own emperor. Diocletian elevated a long-standing colleague, Maximian, to the rank of Caesar in

285, and despatched him to Gaul to quell an uprising. In 286 Maximian was promoted to Augustus. After six years of joint reign, rebellion in Egypt prompted Diocletian to increase his imperial resources by appointing two junior colleagues as Caesars, Galerius for the east and Constantius for the west. Marriage between the Caesars and daughters of the Augusti united the Tetrarchy. Diocletian's administrative overhaul doubled the number of provinces, and reformed the tax system to distribute the burden of land and poll tax more fairly.

Constantine and conversion

Diocletian retired in 305, to a specially prepared palace at Spalato (Split), but his succession arrangements faltered because they disregarded the soldiers' strong dynastic loyalties: when Constantius, the new Augustus of the west, died at York in 306, his troops promptly acclaimed his son, Constantine. Over the next six years Constantine schemed and fought his way to mastery of the whole western empire, a process which culminated outside Rome at the battle of the Milvian Bridge in 312: his opponent, Maxentius, son of Diocletian's partner Maximian, deployed his troops on the north bank of the Tiber, but they were routed and during the confused flight back to the city the wooden bridge collapsed. The most significant aspect of Constantine's victory was that his men fought under the sign of Christ, whose inspiration Constantine proclaimed. Lactantius and Eusebius, writing in the fourth century AD, claim that Constantine prayed the night before the battle, but that he was unsure of the god to whom his prayers were directed until a sign was sent to him in the sky. This sign was the chi rho (see p234), under which symbol Constantine's troops went into battle the next day. After the battle he set about rewarding his new God. Constantine's conversion eventually led to the Christianisation of the Empire and so of Europe.

The colonnaded streets of Palmyra were evidence of the wealth derived by the city from its trading activities. (© G. Tortoli/AAA Collection Ltd)

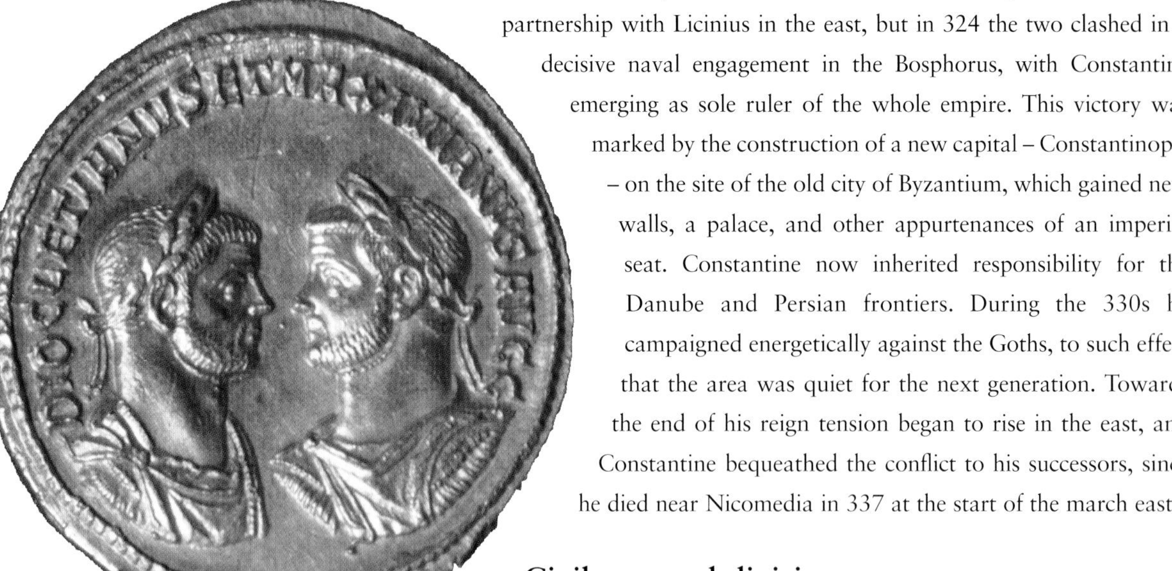

This coin marks the joint reign of Diocletian and Maximian from 286 to 305. (© R. Sheridan/AAA Collection Ltd)

For the next 12 years Constantine shared the Empire in an uneasy partnership with Licinius in the east, but in 324 the two clashed in a decisive naval engagement in the Bosphorus, with Constantine emerging as sole ruler of the whole empire. This victory was marked by the construction of a new capital – Constantinople – on the site of the old city of Byzantium, which gained new walls, a palace, and other appurtenances of an imperial seat. Constantine now inherited responsibility for the Danube and Persian frontiers. During the 330s he campaigned energetically against the Goths, to such effect that the area was quiet for the next generation. Towards the end of his reign tension began to rise in the east, and Constantine bequeathed the conflict to his successors, since he died near Nicomedia in 337 at the start of the march east.

Civil war and division

The Empire was divided between Constantine's three surviving sons, Constantine II in Gaul, Constans in Rome, and Constantius II in the east inheriting the war against the Sassanid Persian Shapur. Civil war erupted, and once again legion fought legion until Julian (who had been sent to Gaul in 355 because internal conflict had permitted Franks and Alamanni to breach the frontier) was acclaimed Augustus at Paris in February 360. After his death in Persia, Julian was succeeded by his general Jovian, and

The chi rho was the Christian symbol used by Constantine after his conversion. From then on it appeared on increasingly more Roman artefacts. The symbol is formed by superimposing the Greek letters *chi* (X) and *rho* (P), which are the first two letters of the Greek word Christos. This chi rho is from the fresco from Lullingstone, from around 360. (© R. Sheridan/AAA Collection Ltd)

then the brothers Valentinian and Valens shared the Empire, with the senior Valentinian taking charge of the Rhine and Upper Danube, and Valens responsible for the Lower Danube and east. Valens was killed by Goths in the massive Roman defeat at Adrianople, and succeeded by Theodosius, who in 382 settled the Goths in the Balkans as federates.

In 395 Theodosius defeated his usurpers to reunify the Empire, and become the sole leader of Rome, but he was to be the last to do so. In 395 he was succeeded by the young Honorius, but the west was controlled by Stilicho, a general of Vandal descent. Under Stilicho, Alaric the Goth built up an army which, in 410, sacked Rome, and brought fatal weakness to the western Empire.

Fighting at the frontiers

This late imperial period saw the Romans pitted against enemies in three main sectors: along the Rhine against the Alamanni, Franks and other Germanic tribes; on the Danube against the Sarmatians and Goths, then the Hunnic tribes; in Armenia and Mesopotamia against the Sassanid Persians.

The eastern frontier

In 226, beyond the eastern frontier, the Sassanid Ardashir was crowned in Ctesiphon, the old Parthian capital, the Sassanids having finally defeated and overrun the Parthians. The change was significant since the Romans had generally dominated the Parthians, and indeed repeated Roman successes had contributed to undermining royal prestige, but the Sassanids propagated a dynamic nationalism, including links with the Achaemenids who ruled Persia before Alexander the Great's conquests. Embassies demanded the return of their ancestral property, with war as the consequence of the inevitable refusal. Ardashir's son, Shapur, invaded the eastern provinces of the Empire in 253 and 260, capturing the major city of Antioch. The Emperor Valerian was captured in battle at Edessa (Urfa) in 260 and taken back to Persia. For the next decade, imperial authority in the east was limited. The east had become an expensive military arena for the Romans, and the substantial tax revenues of its provinces were jeopardised.

Constantine was an extremely important emperor in terms of the history of the Roman Empire, introducing, as he did, Christianity to the Empire, and establishing a second capital, or 'New Rome' at Byzantium. This 'New Rome' was to survive when the original Rome fell. (© N. Greaves/AAA Collection Ltd)

Constantius II pursued a dogged 24 years of war against the Sassanid Persians, managing to preserve the eastern frontier with only limited losses in the face of one of the most dynamic Persian rulers, Shapur. Constantius' strategy was to build new forts and rely on the major cities of the frontier to hold up Persian incursions.

Julian inherited the empire of the east after the death of Constantius in 361, with a reputation as a successful general and a need to demonstrate that he could surpass Constantius. A major factor in this was religion: Julian espoused the old gods and had renounced formal adherence to Christianity. Persia offered the greatest testing ground, where Julian could prove the rectitude of his beliefs and the pusillanimity of Constantius' policies. A planned grand invasion in 363 began well, with Julian

Valens' last stand at Adrianople. As his army fled, Valens sought refuge amongst his troops who stood firm despite the carnage around them. The situation, however, was hopeless and Valens perished along with most of the men from these two veteran units. After the slaughter at Adrianople the Roman army would never be the same again. (Painting by Howard Gerrard © Osprey Publishing Ltd)

overrunning Persian forts along the Euphrates and reaching the vicinity of the capital Ctesiphon; however, treacherous guides led Julian astray, and then Shapur, whose army had not been tied down effectively in the north, began to harass. Julian was mortally wounded in a skirmish and his successor, the officer Jovian, could only extract his armies by surrendering territories to the east of the Tigris, plus Nisibis and Singara. Although the loss of Nisibis rankled, Jovian's agreement of 363 ushered in the most prolonged period of peace which the Roman eastern frontier had ever experienced, a fact crucial to the eastern Empire's survival in the fifth century. There were moments of tension, and two brief conflicts, but no prolonged warfare until 502. Hunnic activity in the Balkans, and Persian distractions on the north-eastern frontier, kept the two sides away from prolonged and costly war with each other.

The western frontier

The Danube

Slow change came about along the Danube frontier throughout the third century, as the Gothic peoples began gradually to migrate from northern Poland. The first attested Gothic incursion came in 238, when they sacked Istria near the Danube mouth; a decade later they swept across the north-east Balkans, and Emperor Decius was killed and his army annihilated while trying to force them back across the Danube in 251.

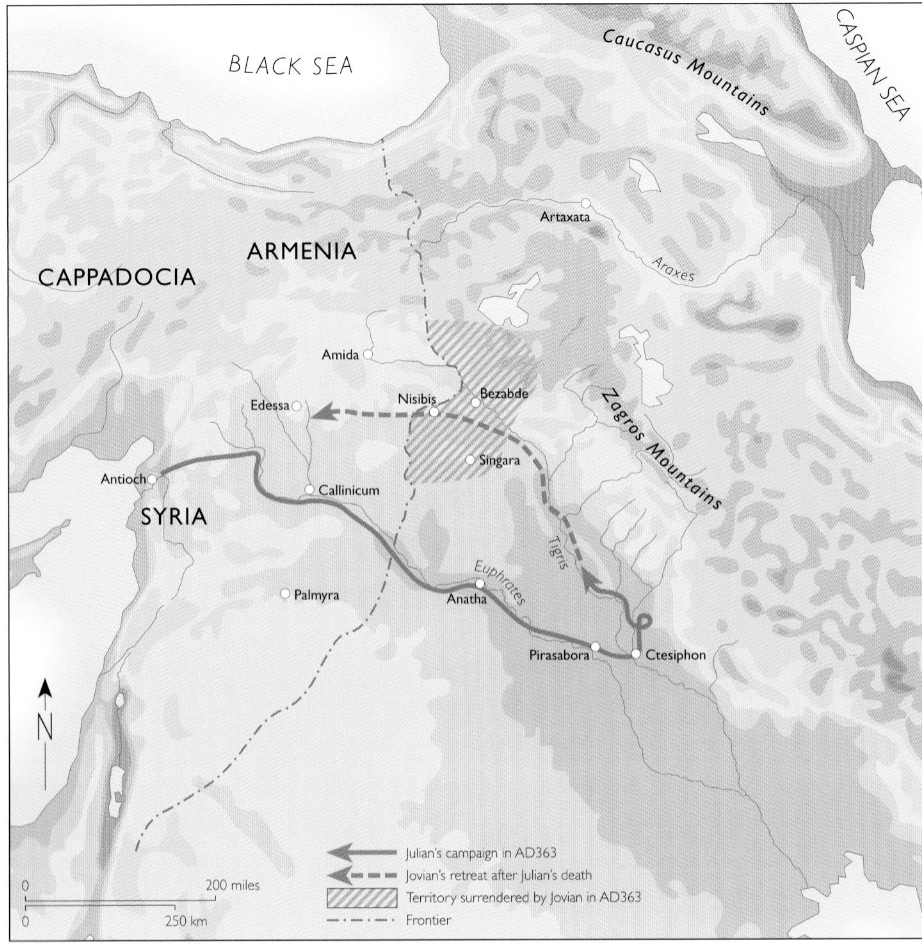

The eastern frontier in the fourth century.

This great movement of Goths naturally displaced other peoples who might find themselves squeezed against the Roman frontier; this process could trigger the formation of substantial federations as different tribes steeled themselves for the ultimate challenge of attacking the Romans. On the upper Danube, the Vandals, Quadi and Marcomanni breached the frontier.

Stability was brought briefly to the frontier under Constantine, which held under Julian and for a while under Valens, but when Gratian, of limited military experience, succeeded Valentinian in 367, masses of Goths arrived on the lower Danube frontier, to pester Roman officials for the right to cross and settle peacefully.

Their desperation was caused by the westward movement of the Huns, who had been displaced from further east and were now approaching the Black Sea with a consequent domino effect on the tribes there. After initial failure, the Romans managed to contain the Gothic threat by exploiting control of food and by harassing the Goths as soon as they dispersed to seek supplies. In 378, two-thirds of the Roman army, including the emperor of the east, Valens, were killed by Goths at the battle of Adrianople. The rise of the Goths was to blur the division between the frontiers of the Danube and Rhine, as both were decisively and fatally breached.

THE REASONS FOR ROMAN DEFEAT AT ADRIANOPLE

How was it that the best organised, equipped and disciplined army in the world could have been so thoroughly defeated by what amounted to an ad hoc force of refugees and deserters? Various explanations have been offered over the years to explain away the improbable. Some claim that the Goths had a huge numerical superiority, quoting numbers as high as 200,000 when in fact they would have been lucky to have a tenth of that number. Others put it down to a tactical superiority of cavalry over infantry, when in fact the battle was a classic infantry versus infantry clash with a timely cavalry charge swinging the balance. Some modern historians claim in all seriousness that the Gothic cavalry were successful because they rode with stirrups, which were not introduced in the west until the arrival of the Avars several centuries later.

The Romans lost the Adrianople campaign for a number of fairly mundane strategic as well as tactical reasons. At the strategic level, because of the constant threats along the frontiers, the Romans were simply unable to draw together enough high-quality troops to deal quickly and decisively with the Gothic threat. Furthermore, all the Roman commanders, with the possible exception of Sebastian, acted with the typical arrogance of a well-equipped 'civilised' army dealing with what they saw as a rabble. They allowed themselves to be drawn into battle without proper preparation or reconnaissance and without ensuring that the odds were stacked in their favour before committing to a fight.

Finally, it is quite probable that the quality and morale of the east Roman army was low before the campaign even began. Only 13 years earlier they had suffered a humiliating defeat at the hands of the Persians and the army had probably not fully recovered. Furthermore, like society, the army was torn apart by religious controversy as pagans, Avrian Christians and Catholic Christians fought and persecuted each other. It has been speculated that some of the cavalry, under the influence of Victor, the Catholic *magister equitum*, may have deliberately deserted Valens, who was an Arian. The Roman failings must also be matched against the strategic skill shown by Fritigern, who despite horrendous logistical problems, managed to dictate the terms and tempo of the campaign throughout.

At the tactical level the Gothic victory was won by relatively fresh troops fighting hot, tired and thirsty men who were surprised by the unexpected appearance of enemy reinforcements. The Roman cavalry performed poorly and showed an alarming lack of discipline. They were easily driven off, some deserting without a fight. Without cavalry support, the Roman infantry were hit in the flank while engaged to their front and despite some stubborn resistance by several units, the result was inevitable.

The Rhine

The Rhine provided a partial barrier to tribal movement that the Romans could control through naval squadrons and by supervising recognised crossing-points. On the upper Rhine the Alamanni increased their strength to the extent that they twice

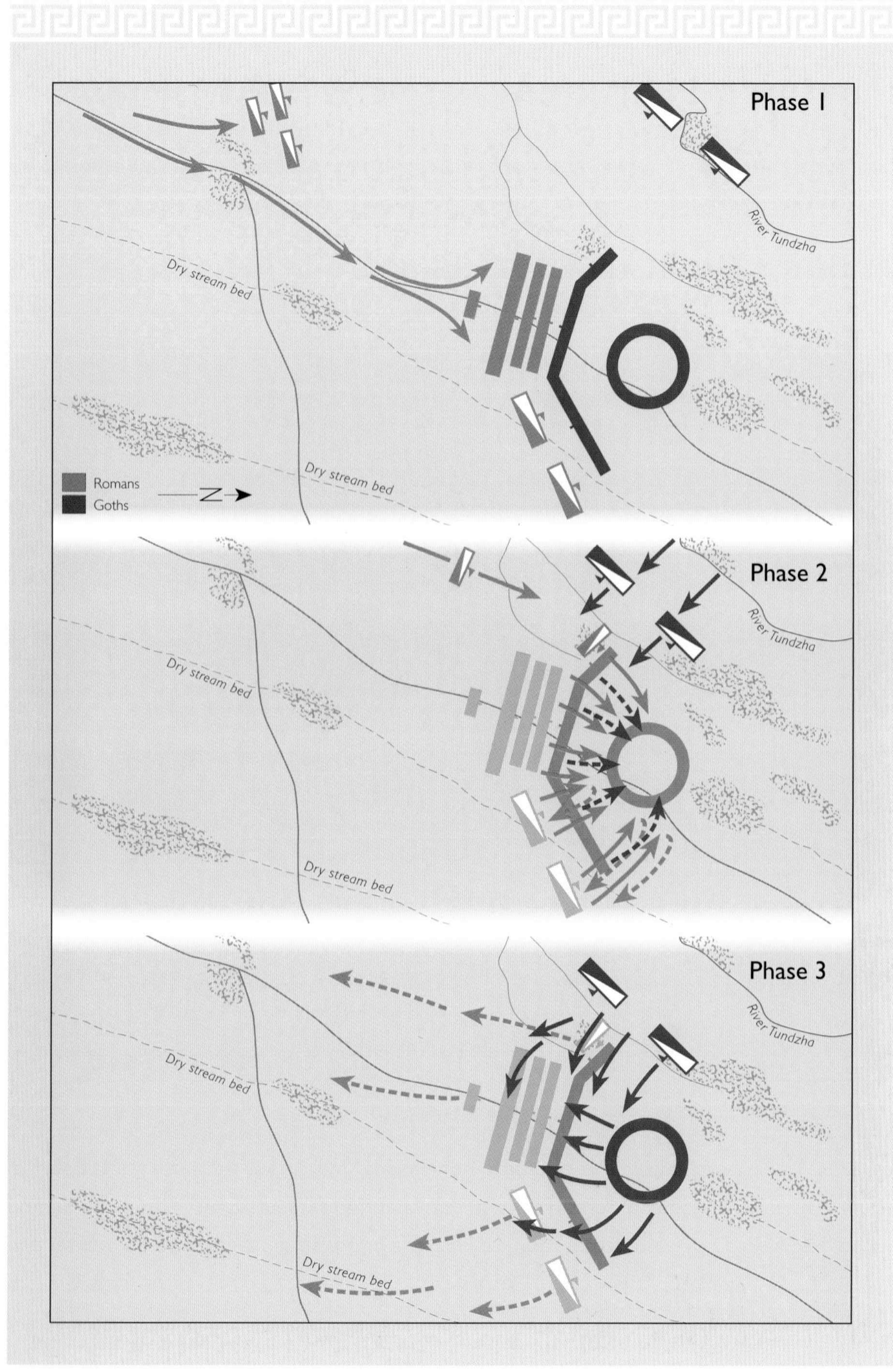

The battle of Adrianople.

invaded Italy in the 260s. On the lower Rhine the Franks gradually came to dominate another large federation that threatened frontier defences during the latter half of the century, and Saxon pirates began to raid across the North Sea and down the channel.

During 356 Julian campaigned energetically and re-established Roman authority along the Rhine, but in August 357, Julian confronted the Alamanni on the right bank of the Rhine near Argentoratum (Strasbourg): it was a hard-fought struggle. Superior Roman discipline and training overcame the Alamanni's advantage in physical size, and the battle was won by the Roman infantry, whereas their cavalry was forced to flee. The Goths were weakened by casualties during the reign of Theodosius, but when control of the western Empire was assumed by Stilicho, the Goths seized upon the Empire being split again to demand a better deal.

Alaric, a Gothic commander under the Emperor Theodosius, emerged as leader of a force capable of withstanding an imperial army, but still struggled to secure lasting benefits for the Goths. His success only came after other tribal groups breached the western defences. On 31 December 406, Vandals, Alans and Suevi swarmed across the Rhine, triggering the proclamation of local commanders as emperors. Stilicho's authority crumbled and his family was eliminated; with it disappeared the main Roman army in northern Italy, since many of Stilicho's Gothic troops chose to join Alaric. Alaric failed to obtain concessions from Honorius, established his own emperor, and on 24 August 410 captured Rome. This brief sack of Rome was of symbolic significance; of greater importance were Honorius' imperial rivals in Gaul and Spain, whose ambitions permitted the invading tribes to exploit Roman divisions. Inevitably local protectors appeared who had to exploit the available military manpower, which was often roaming tribal bands; incompatible objectives emerged, with the policy of crushing invaders at odds with a desire to preserve their manpower for future use.

This sketch of a tomb relief from the fourth century shows the consul Jovinus with his dog. Dogs played many roles in the Roman world, some being used as guard dogs, some as hunting dogs, and others as vicious fighting dogs which fought against slaves and wild animals. The Romans also used dogs in warfare, and had a breed called the Molossians, not unlike giant Rottweilers, which could tear the enemy apart. (© R. Sheridan/AAA Collection Ltd)

Alaric died whilst trying to reach Africa, and his followers, whom it is now convenient to call Visigoths (west Goths) moved to Spain where they helped to subdue the Suevi and Vandals. One consequence of Visigothic involvement in Spain was the Vandal crossing to Africa, although the precise cause was, naturally, internal Roman conflict. The Vandals' arrival in Africa in 429 condemned the western Empire: within a decade they had taken over the north African provinces, captured Carthage (in 439) and withstood eastern Empire attempts to repulse them. The loss of North Africa decisively reduced the resources on which emperors could call, and to compound the problem the Vandals used Roman ships at Carthage to dominate Sicily and Sardinia and to ravage Italy.

They sacked Rome in 455, a much more destructive event than Alaric's entry in 410. From the Roman perspective the priorities now were to restore battered

Ivory Relief of Stilicho, 400. Stilicho was born of a Vandal mother and a Roman father, and became the chief general of Theodosius I. whose niece he married. Stilicho went on to assume control of the western Empire on Theodosius' death. (© R.Sheridan/AAA Collection Ltd)

imperial authority, stabilise the tribal groups, and gradually weaken their independence. However, continuing conflict between emperors within the empire meant that Roman strength could not be secured enough to allow any of this to happen, and a Roman dispute in 425 brought the Huns into western Empire affairs. Attila the Hun's attempted invasion in 451 was repulsed by the Roman Aetius at the battle of the Catalaunian Plains, but when Attila turned to northern Italy in 452, Aetius could not prevent the loss of many northern cities. Eventually Pope Leo had to be deployed to encourage Attila to leave. In September 454, Valentinian assassinated Aetius, only for Aetius' bodyguards to take revenge in March 455. For the next two decades control was contested between the different power blocks with interests in the western state: the Visigoths, Vandals, the eastern Empire and the Italian army under the patrician Ricimer, backed by a rapid succession of rulers.

One final attempt to crush the Vandals and restore western resources was made in 468 when a massive naval expedition was sent from Constantinople, but this was thwarted by Vandal fireships. Failure was ruinous for the eastern state – which spent 64,000 pounds of gold (more than a year's revenue) – and fatal for the western state: in 476, after a rapid turnover of rulers, the army of Italy under Odoacer deposed the young Romulus and returned the imperial insignia to Constantinople. Odoacer controlled Italy until Theodoric

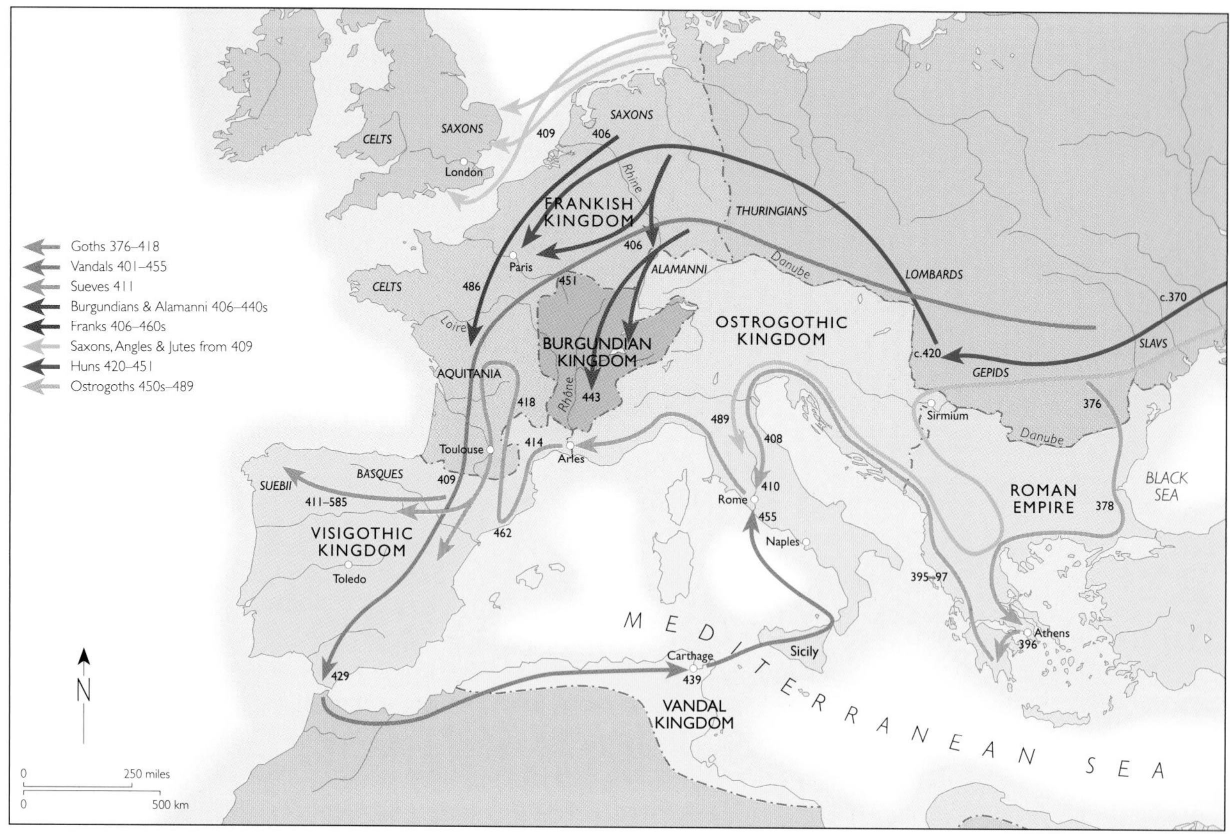

The disintegration of the western Empire.

the Amal took Ravenna in 491 and established the Ostrogothic (east Goth) kingdom. Theodoric in his long reign (493–526) created a successful Romano-Gothic realm during which Italy prospered, and a ruler at Ravenna secured considerable power in southern Gaul and Spain and intermittent influence in Vandal Africa.

A snapshot of the late Roman army

Roman military reform – the *comitatenses* and *limitanei*

During the third century the Roman army made and unmade emperors at the drop of a hat. The rapid turnover of emperors meant many changes within the army, and the Empire itself would probably have collapsed far earlier than it did, had it not been for a series of soldier-emperors from Illyria. These men, commanding soldiers raised in the same region, managed to secure the frontiers and bring about a degree of stability. In terms of military organisation, Diocletian's major concern was for frontiers, reflected in the strengthening of defensive constructions, the construction of new roads, and the deployment of troops near the frontiers.

Diocletian's successor, Constantine, spent half of his reign involved in civil conflicts which actively diverted attention from the frontiers: he reorganised the central forces which accompanied the emperor, the *comitatus*, and created two prestigious commands for cavalry and infantry, the *magister equitum* and *magister peditum*. At provincial level military command was also separated from civilian duties. The new army that emerged from this reorganisation bore little resemblance to that which had preceded it. It was designed to provide a defence in depth; static troops of reduced status manned the frontiers, while field armies of new, smaller, more flexible units were held in reserve, ready to respond to sudden threats. At the core of the new army were the *comitatenses* – regional field armies based in central locations. They were formed partly by withdrawing some detachments from the frontier and partly by raising new units. Frontier forces, descendents of the old legions and auxiliaries, dropped in status and became stationary garrison troops known as *limitanei* (guarding the frontier zones – *limes*) or *ripenei* (based along the river frontiers). Eventually these troops became little more than a part-time militia, and they were rarely called on to take part in major campaigns. The new units created for the field armies were markedly smaller than the old 6,000-men legions: probably no more than 1,000–1,200 men. The majority of the army's foot soldiers, however, were provided by new-style units called *auxilia*.

Recruitment and service

By the time of the late Empire, soldiering was no longer considered to be an honourable or desirable profession, and it became increasingly difficult to find recruits to fill the ranks of the army. The obligation to serve in the army passed from generation to generation. Sons of soldiers, including officers, were expected to serve unless physically unfit. Volunteers were used, and at times bounties were offered to attract them. Slaves were normally not allowed to join, but exceptions were made in crises. Senators and municipal officials were also barred from the army. Hereditary and voluntary enlistment were not enough to fill the ranks, however, making an annual conscription necessary. The levy of conscripts was conducted in much the same way as the gathering of tax, with each village or estate being required to provide a set number of recruits.

Military service was seemingly so unpopular that great lengths were taken to avoid it, including self-mutilation. Press gangs were occasionally employed to round up deserters and veterans' sons who were avoiding their duty. New conscripts were supposed to be between 19 and 25 years and physically fit. Sons of veterans up to the age of 35 who had evaded service could be drafted. Once accepted, the recruit was given an identity disc and certificate of recruitment. There are recorded instances of conscripts being branded on the hand or arm to identify them and make desertion more difficult. Desertion was certainly a problem, particularly amongst new recruits, and as a precaution draftees were locked up in prison each night while en route to their units.

The quality of soldiers recruited by conscription undoubtedly left a great deal to be desired, and would account for the fact that authorities looked more and more to foreigners to fill the ranks. The late Roman *pedes*, or ordinary infantryman, was probably not a Roman at all, and may even have had difficulty speaking any recognisable form of Latin. He was probably a German, but he could have been from anywhere inside or outside the borders of the Roman world. Roman armies continued to rely on substantial units of non-citizens during the years of the later Empire, especially when troops had to be recruited quickly, as in civil war or after military defeat, or for special expeditions. These 'outsiders' were often excellent troops who provided reliable bodyguards for emperors and generals.

Calculating the size of late Roman armies is a complex game for which most of the pieces are missing. In the third century army units probably numbered upwards of 350,000, with a further 40,000 in the navy. Numbers increased significantly under Diocletian and Constantine, so that the total military establishment exceeded 500,000 – perhaps even 600,000. But paper strength will always have surpassed disposable strength, and many troops were committed to particular assignments so that only a small proportion of the total establishment could be deployed for individual campaigns. In the fourth century an army of 50,000 was large, and by the sixth century mobile armies rarely exceeded 30,000.

Training

In addition to 'on the job' training, the recruit was formally instructed in weapons handling and drilled in unit manoeuvre. As in all armies, training varied considerably, not only in time and place, but also between units. Some units of *limitanei*, for instance, were little more than part-time peasant militia, with soldiers running their own farms and becoming involved in other trades. There are many examples of soldiers neglecting drill and becoming engaged in a variety of non-military activities, even cultivating the estates of powerful landowners. A variety of laws from the end of the fourth century indicate that the authorities tried to stop this – but apparently with little success.

Weapons handling was the first and most important skill to be taught to the new recruit. He was expected to become proficient with a variety of weapons and to use them in different situations. In order to increase strength and accuracy, recruits were trained with weapons that were much heavier than normal, so that the task would seem much easier when they came to use the real thing.

It is unclear how much drill, physical fitness or marching was included in the training of the late Roman soldier. Some Roman historians lamented that such exercises were being neglected, but to what degree probably varied considerably between units. Drill is described in the sixth century *Strategikon*, a military manual written to assist with the training of the late Roman army. It begins with the command:

> *Silentum. Mandata captate. Non vos turbatis. Ordinem Servate. Bando sequite. Nemo demittat bandum et inimicos seque.*

or 'Silence. Observe orders. Don't worry. Keep your position. Follow the standard. Do not leave the standard and pursue the enemy.' The soldiers had to learn to respond to commands by voice, hand signal and trumpet so as not to be confused by the din of battle. They were trained to advance in silence while maintaining their alignment.

As the infantryman came to be employed more defensively, his ability to use longer-range missile weapons became critical. Archery training was particularly important and required a constant effort for the soldiers to achieve and maintain proficiency. Vegetius says: 'A third or fourth of the recruits, those with talent, should be exercised at the post with wooden bows and training arrows...' This scene shows several new recruits from the eastern provinces of the Empire undergoing archery training. (Painting by Gerry Embleton © Osprey Publishing Ltd)

Organisation and logistics

Both legions and *auxilia* were essentially heavy infantry, performing basically the same task on the battlefield and being similarly equipped. A portion of the men in each unit, however, appear to have been trained as light infantrymen. There were also a number of specialist infantry such as *sagitarii* (archers), *exulcatores* (probably javelinmen), *funditories* (slingers) and *balistarii* who acted as skirmishers or perhaps crossbowmen.

As the cavalry increased in importance in the fifth and sixth centuries, the infantry began to decline. However, this is not to say that the Romans switched entirely to reliance on heavy-mailed cavalry, an anticipation of medieval knights. Infantry remained the basis for most armies, and Roman foot-soldiers, when properly trained and led, were capable of defying all opponents. The infantry remained the backbone of the Roman army until well into the fifth century, although the average infantryman differed from his predecessors – he may not have been as well disciplined, but in many ways he was more flexible, ready for deployment to trouble spots, and for fighting both as a skirmisher and a heavy infantryman.

This painting shows the training of a cavalryman of the fifth century AD. The *Strategikon* gives us an idea of what the individual cavalryman was supposed to do:

> On horseback at a run he should fire one or two arrows rapidly and put the strung bow in its case, then he should grab the spear which he has been carrying on his back. With the strung bow in its case he should hold the spear in his hand, then quickly replace it on his back and grab the bow.

Such exercises would have required expert horsemanship as well as proficient weapons handling, and could have been expected only of the better units. (Painting by Christa Hook © Osprey Publishing Ltd)

There had been a gradual change in the deployment of Roman armies. In the early empire legions were quartered in major bases near the frontier (e.g. Cologne), but military need dictated that units were detached for specific duties at frontier garrisons or in the interior. Later this ad hoc dispersal was consolidated so that troops were spread across provinces in numerous forts and cities. Emperors, however, also needed mobile forces for more rapid deployment. In the east there came to be two armies 'in the presence' stationed near Constantinople, and others in the Balkans and the east; in the west Gaul and Italy had their own armies until imperial authority contracted from the former.

Appearance and equipment

Uniform

By the end of the fourth century, the uniformity of Roman soldiers in appearance and dress would not have been anywhere near as regular as it had been in earlier years. Uniform issues were beginning to be replaced by a clothing allowance and by the sixth century even weapons and armour were expected to be purchased by the soldiers from an allowance. Troops of the *limitanei* probably bought their clothing from stores attached to their fort, so we can assume that a certain amount of 'local flavour' would have crept into the soldier's appearance. Field armies had no fixed base, and were nearly always on campaign, so it is likely that their clothing differed greatly as well, due to logistical problems of supplying such troops. It is easy to picture such units after a long campaign presenting a very motley appearance; clothing does not last long in the field, and the soldiers would have had to make local purchases fairly regularly.

Because of the lack of defined uniform, it would have been difficult to distinguish between a 'Roman' soldier (perhaps born a Goth) serving in the army of Stilicho, and a 'Gothic' soldier (perhaps born a Roman) in Alaric's army. To identify such units in the field, shields were often of the same colour, and helmet plumes, too, were often a uniform colour. Such simple details could provide a degree of uniformity.

Armour

The question of how much armour was worn by the late Roman soldier has been a matter of debate. Writing in the fifth century, Vegetius says:

> For though after the example of the Goths, the Alans and the Huns, we have made some improvements in the arms of the cavalry, it is plain that the infantry are completely exposed. From the foundation of the city until the reign of the Emperor Gratian the foot wore cuirasses and helmets. But negligence and sloth having by degrees introduced a total relaxation of discipline, the soldiers began to consider their armour too heavy and seldom put it on. They first requested leave from the Emperor to lay aside the cuirass, and afterwards the helmet.

Conversely, Ammianus Marcellinus, who was a soldier himself, makes frequent reference to fourth century infantry in 'gleaming armour' and describes the infantry at Adrianople in 378 as 'weighed down by the burden of their armour'.

Vegetius' claim that infantry armour was abandoned in the mid fourth century can be partially accounted for by the obvious material losses sustained in the Persian and Gothic disasters of the time. It is also consistent with the increase in use of federate troops and the introduction of allowances in place of issued equipment. If the main field armies of the fifth century were composed of barbarians and a few elite Roman cavalry units, it is quite likely that an infantryman would not have been willing to pay for expensive armour out of his allowance, not have any real need for it. A large shield would probably have been sufficient protection for troops who only had a static supporting role.

For most of the soldier's service he would have no call to wear armour. Marches were conducted with armour carried in wagons, while routine guard duty, foraging expeditions and skirmishing rarely called for armour. Only when called to fight in the line of battle did the late Roman soldier seem to need such added protection.

Deployment and tactics

Skirmishes and sieges

On any campaign, most of the action consisted of small skirmishes, which would involve only a few men in the advance, rear or flank guards. Full-scale battles were very rare, perhaps only one in an entire campaign. For the most part, a typical soldier in the rank of the main body would trudge along day after day more concerned about the weather and food than the enemy. The fitter men in each party would sometimes be selected for a foraging or reconnaissance party.

Most contact with the enemy would have occurred when a fortified town was reached. Often they could be induced to surrender or, if too strong, they would be bypassed as there was no time to settle down to a long siege. When an enemy fortification was reached that did not surrender but that could not be assaulted, the army began siege operations.

Battle formations

The most common formation was the battle-line, or phalanx. This was solely designed to repel and attack, and was used because the infantry were usually deployed defensively in this period, with cavalry providing the army's offensive capability. Arrian's *Against the Alans*, an actual battle order for a legion preparing to face cavalry, gives us a good idea of how such a formation would have looked:

> The legionaries will be formed in eight ranks and deployed in close order. The first four ranks will consist of men armed with the spear *[probably pilum]* ...The men of the first rank will present their spears at the approach of the enemy...those of the second, third and fourth ranks will be in a position to throw their spears. They will be directed to aim their strike accurately at the right time in order to knock down the horses and throw the riders...The four ranks immediately behind will consist of men armed with the lancea *[a light*

> *spear]*. Behind these there will be a ninth rank composed of archers, those of the Numidians, Kyreneans, Bosposriuans and the Itureans.

One thing that is clear in all descriptions is that the various ranks in a formation performed different tasks. The first four ranks were expected to do the real fighting and consequently were more heavily armed. The file closers in the rear rank had a supervisory role, while the men in the intervening ranks were to provide depth to the formation and throw light javelins over the heads of the front ranks. Attached archers from other units would be drawn up behind and also fire overhead.

PREPARATION FOR BATTLE

It was felt imperative that the soldier be well fed and rested prior to a battle. The *Strategikon* suggests advises that the 'foot soldiers should not be expected to march long distances in full armour' in order that they be fresh when they met the enemy. This was on Julian's mind prior to the battle of Strasbourg when he told his men,

> We are tired from our march...what are we to do when we meet the attack of the enemy hordes who will be rested and refreshed by food and drink? What strength shall we have to encounter them when we are worn out by hunger, thirst and toil?...I propose, therefore, that we set a watch and rest here, where we are protected by a rampart and ditch; then at first light, after an adequate allowance of sleep and food, let us, God willing, advance our eagles to triumph...

According to Ammianus, one of the contributing factors to the Roman defeat at Adrianople was the fact that the soldiers had to march eight miles over rough ground under a burning sun before reaching the battlefield. Once there they had to stand in formation for several hours, without food or drink.

The *Strategikon* describes the process of forming up for battle under ideal conditions,

> The divisions are drawn up in the battle line with intervals of one or two hundred feet between them, so they will not be crowded together while marching, but can still act in unison during battle and provide support for each other.

The general's standard would be posted in the centre of the battle line, and the first unit would form up there with the follow-on units forming to the left and right of it. Once in place the soldiers were expected to remain absolutely quiet. It could be many hours before they would be called upon to play their part in the engagement, particularly if their unit was second in line. In such a case the men would sit down and rest. 'If the weather is hot let them remove their helmets and get some air' advises the *Strategikon*. 'Only when the enemy gets close should the men be called to attention, and they will be fresh and in good condition.'

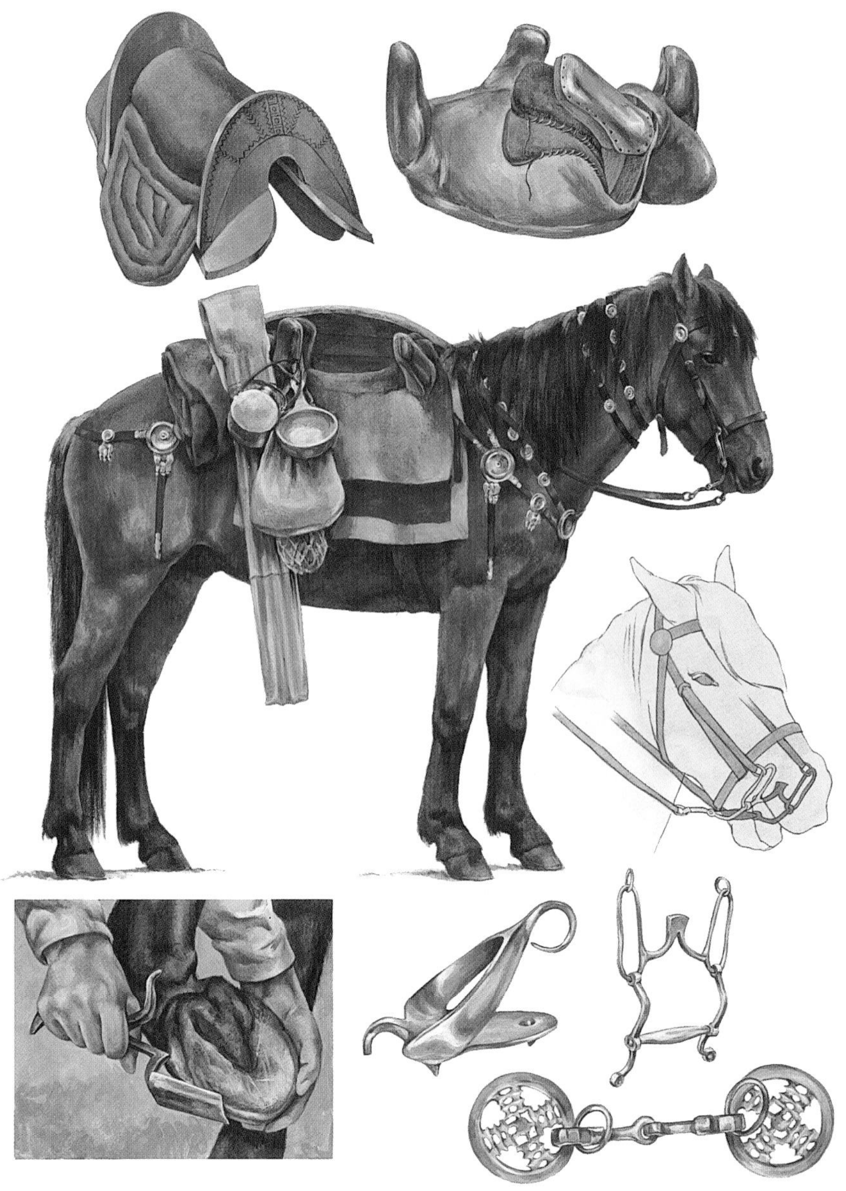

The Roman cavalryman's horse was smaller than modern horses: somewhere between 130cm and 150cm high. Even horses described by ancient writers as 'large', such as Parthian, Sarmatian and Hunnish breeds, rarely exceeded 155cm, and would be considered of medium size today. This horse is loaded up for the march with everything the cavalryman would need to be self sufficient. His shield, javelin case, water bottle, cooking utensils and rations are attached to the saddle, and his cloak is rolled up behind. The bits were extremely severe, to ensure absolute obedience from the mount. The slightest pressure on the reins would drive a plate into the roof of the horse's mouth, causing intense pain. (Painting by Christa Hook © Osprey Publishing Ltd)

Cavalry

Before the fifth century Roman commanders expected to win their battles with a decisive infantry clash. The cavalryman's job on the battlefield was to support the infantryman and to provide the circumstances that would allow the former to do his job. Most Roman cavalry fought using skirmish tactics, and although they might have worn armour, they could be considered as 'light cavalry'. When the army formed up for battle the cavalry would be called upon to screen the deployment, hamper enemy deployment, protect the flanks of the infantry, defeat enemy cavalry and pursue broken opponents. They were not expected to deliver the crushing blow that would defeat the enemy army: that was the job of the infantry.

Over the fifth and sixth centuries this situation began to change, as Roman warlords surrounded themselves with bands of mounted retainers. By the sixth century the *Strategikon* recommends:

> The general would be well advised to have more cavalry than infantry. The latter is set only for close combat, while the former is easily able to pursue or to retreat, and when dismounted the men are all set to fight on foot.

This late Roman soldier was in fact much more than a cavalryman: he had become an all-round mounted warrior. With his bow he could skirmish at a distance, but he was also heavily armoured and well equipped for close mounted combat. When a steady force was needed to hold ground, he was quite happy to dismount and fight as a heavy infantryman. By the sixth century, Roman field armies had evolved into large followings of mounted warriors who owed allegiance to powerful warlords – direct ancestors of the feudal host. The old regional field armies were reduced, as were the *limitanei*, to static garrisons, and the cavalry had become the arm of decision.

Chapter 14
THE SASSANID PERSIANS

Sassanid Persian campaigns against Rome

Background

Scholars, popular imagination and the media are all excited by the likes of Alexander, Caesar, Hannibal, Attila and Napoleon, but few know of Shapur I who defeated three Roman emperors in his lifetime or the death of Julian the Apostate in Persia, an event which ensured Christianity's survival in the west. The Sassanians were the 'other superpower', east of the Romans, and despite the bombastic and triumphant tone of certain Roman sources as well as the somewhat biased views of certain contemporary historians, modern scholarship and examination of primary sources and other evidence reveals the Sassanians to have been an adversary on a par with the Romans.

Roman defeat at the hands of Shapur I

By the early third century the Iranian peoples of the Persian Empire no longer trusted Parthian abilities in safeguarding Persia against Roman incursions. When the Sassanian Ardashir and his son Shapur overthrew the Parthians at Firuzabad in 224, Iranian highlanders (Medes, Kurds, northern Iranians), Persians and Eastern Iranians joined the Sassanian banner. Ardashir's overthrow of the Parthians signalled to Rome the rise of a new and vigorous dynasty in Persia. In response, the Roman emperor Alexander Severus attacked the new empire in 231–33, with inconclusive results. When Ardashir's son, Shapur I (241–72), became king, Rome continued the attempt to crush the new menace from Persia. Gordian III (238–44) attacked the empire of Shapur with initial success in 243, and advanced as far as Misiche (present-day Anbar) north of the capital Ctesiphon by 244. The opposing armies joined battle there and the Romans were defeated. It is

This relief of Shapur I (241–72) shows the emperor of the Aryans on horseback followed by a line of dignitaries. Sassanian rock carvings, Naqsh-e Rajab. (© AAA Collection Ltd)

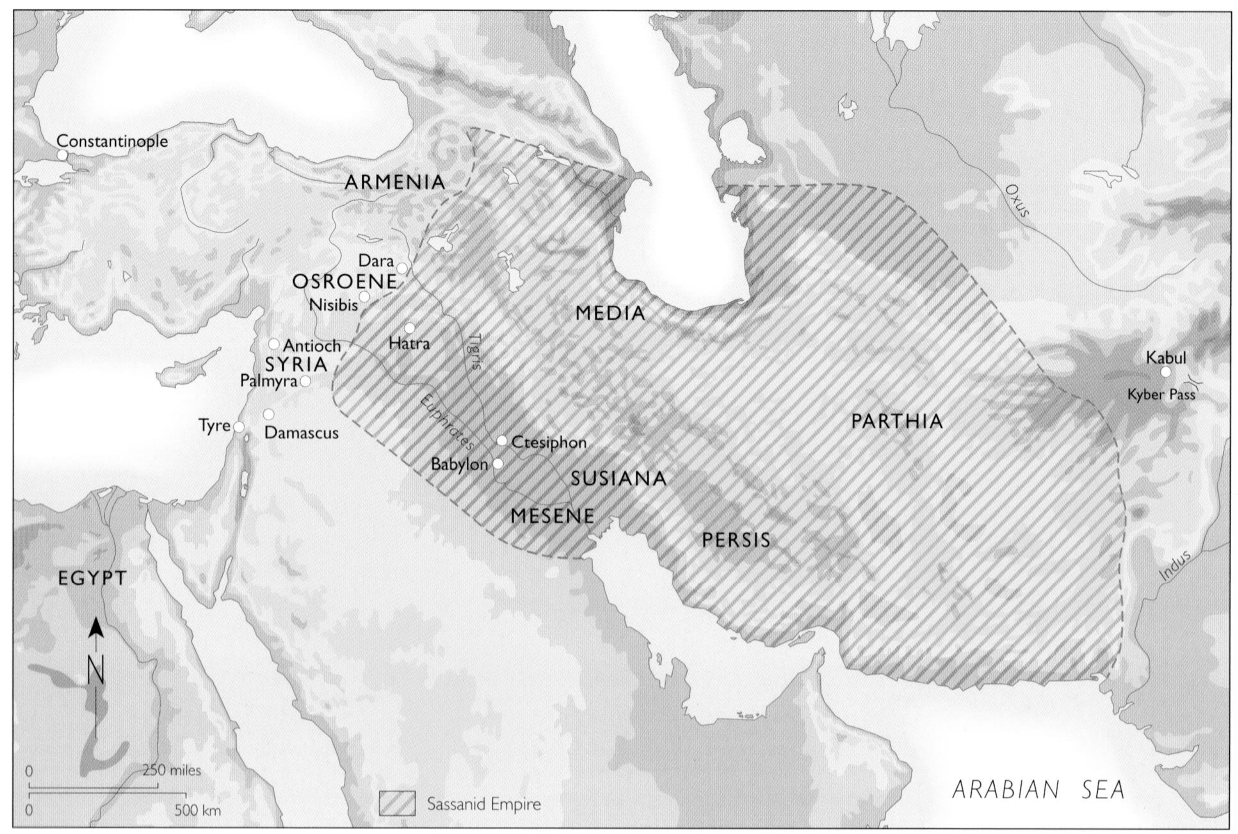

The Sassanid Empire.

unclear whether Gordian was killed in battle against Shapur, or assassinated afterwards by his own officers. Philip the Arab (244–49) was then proclaimed emperor of Rome. He quickly made peace with Shapur and agreed to pay him a large ransom. Roman incursions into Armenia provided Shapur with the pretext to resume hostilities. Shapur thrust his army deep into Roman Mesopotamia and joined battle with Philip in Barbalissos, this time destroying a large Roman army of 60,000–70,000 troops. This defeat led to the capture of Roman Antioch and Dura Europus in Syria around 256.

Rome was determined to avenge the defeat of its arms and prestige, and endeavoured to vanquish Shapur and the new Sassanian kingdom once and for all. This final campaign was led by Emperor Valerian. At first, Valerian was successful in that he drove the Sassanians out of Antioch in 256. In response, Shapur then seems to have besieged Edessa and Harran (Carrhae). This action forced Valerian to move against him there. Shapur defeated the Romans decisively in around 260 as indicated by the following inscription of Shapur I's words on a stone tower near Persepolis:

> ...Valerian Caesar came upon us having with him...a force of seventy thousands...and Valerian Caesar with our own hand we made captive. And the rest, the Praetorian prefect, senators and generals, and whatever of that force were officers, all we made captive and away to...the Aryan Empire...

This Sassanian relief at Naghsh-e-Rostam shows Shapur I defeating Philip I. In a later campaign, Shapur used the captive Roman emperor Valerian as a stool on which he stood to mount his horse. He later had Valerian's dead body stuffed and put on display in one of his temples. (© Dr S. Coyne/AAA Collection Ltd)

PERSIAN RELIGION – ZOROASTRIANISM

Sassanid Persians believed that the world was created by Ahura Mazda, the god of the religion that most Sassanid Persians favoured – Zoroastrianism. This form of religion is one of the oldest still in existence, and was believed to have been adapted from an earlier faith by Zarathushtra (Zoroaster) in Persia around 1,000BC. Adherents also believe that Zarathushtra wrote the hymns, or Gathas of the holy book of Zoroastrianism, called the *Avesta*. Zoroastrianism has the fight between good and evil at its core, like many religions, and the devil-like figure of Angra Mainyu (or Ahriman), an evil being who personifies death and violence, fights an eternal struggle with Ahura Mazda, with good overcoming evil most of the time. Many scholars believe that Zoroastrianism has influenced subsequent religions, as it has at its core the fundamentals of a Day of Judgement, Heaven and Hell, resurrection, and the reuniting of soul and body after the Last Judgement, and eternal life thereafter. According to the religion, the dead are placed in 'Towers of Silence', where the corpses are disposed of by being eaten by vultures and other birds of prey. Zoroastrianism also has only one god, who created heaven and earth, and who sits in judgement. The religion survives today, and its most famous recent adherent was Freddie Mercury from the rock band 'Queen'.

Notwithstanding the failures of Gordian III and Philip the Arab, the Valerian disaster was perhaps one of Rome's greatest military defeats. The capture of an emperor along with members of his entourage came as a powerful shock to the Roman Empire. It is a mystery why Valerian would choose to deploy his army in the open plains of Carrhae and Edessa which would maximise the advantages of the Savaran (see p255). This was almost a repeat of the mistake of Marcus Crassus at the doomed battle of Carrhae in 53 BC.

Rome paid dearly for these defeats, and lost a good proportion of its professional soldiers – troops who were needed to confront European (i.e. Gothic) threats to its western and northern borders. Shapur had forced the reluctant Romans to accept the Sassanians as monarchs of an empire very much the equal of Rome. Rome did recover, however, and learned important lessons from these defeats.

Shapur II versus Julian the Apostate

Julian became emperor in 361, and soon abjured his Christian faith in favour of pagan beliefs. He proceeded to attempt to eliminate the threat to Rome's eastern frontier: Sassanian Persia. Julian invaded Persia in 362 with 65,000 men, a combination of mobile army units and local frontier troops. He split his army in two and his campaign began with success.

In hindsight, it might have been wiser not to divide the army since Julian proved unable to maintain proper co-ordination and communication with Procopius, the general of the second army. This led to disaster for Rome. Unable to conclusively defeat the Sassanian forces at their capital of Ctesiphon, Julian decided to march east into Persia to finally defeat Shapur II. The absence of Procopius' forces was fully felt when Julian marched into the Persian heartland. Like Napoleon's forces more than 1,300 years later in Russia, Julian found his opponents devising a scorched-earth strategy.

Even as Shapur made an appearance with his army, he refused to enter into a set-piece battle. The battle in front of Ctesiphon convinced Shapur that the Roman army was too strong and well trained to defeat in a face-to-face battle. Persia's defense now rested solely on the actions of her elite cavalry, the Savaran, who would charge with their lances against the Roman columns at their most vulnerable points. Another factor that may have damaged Roman morale were Sassanian war elephants. These were also used in 'shock' charges in co-ordination with the Savaran. The Romans had seen elephants in Hannibal's time, but that was centuries ago and these beasts were a new phenomenon to Julian's generation of legionaries. Their use alongside the heavy cavalry certainly added more power to Sassanian cavalry raids.

Julian did finally have his battle on 22 June, 363 at Maranga. However, Julian's victory was a Pyrrhic one: the bulk of the Sassanian army remained intact and their troops withdrew in good order. The Romans were now running short of supplies and their casualties could not be replaced. As a result, the longer the Romans stayed in Persia, the weaker they became. Shapur's generals realised that the battles and raids were exhausting and weakening the Roman ranks, making them even more vulnerable to Savaran attacks.

Although Julian the Apostate (361–63) was the last emperor related to Constantine to rule the Empire, he was also a non-Christian – in fact, the last non-Christian emperor of Rome. After the death of Constantius when Julian became sole Augustus he set about cutting out the bureaucracy and trimming the fat from the Roman court, even down to expelling the inordinate number of cooks and barbers who had been employed during the reign of Constantius. (© R. Sheridan/AAA Collection Ltd)

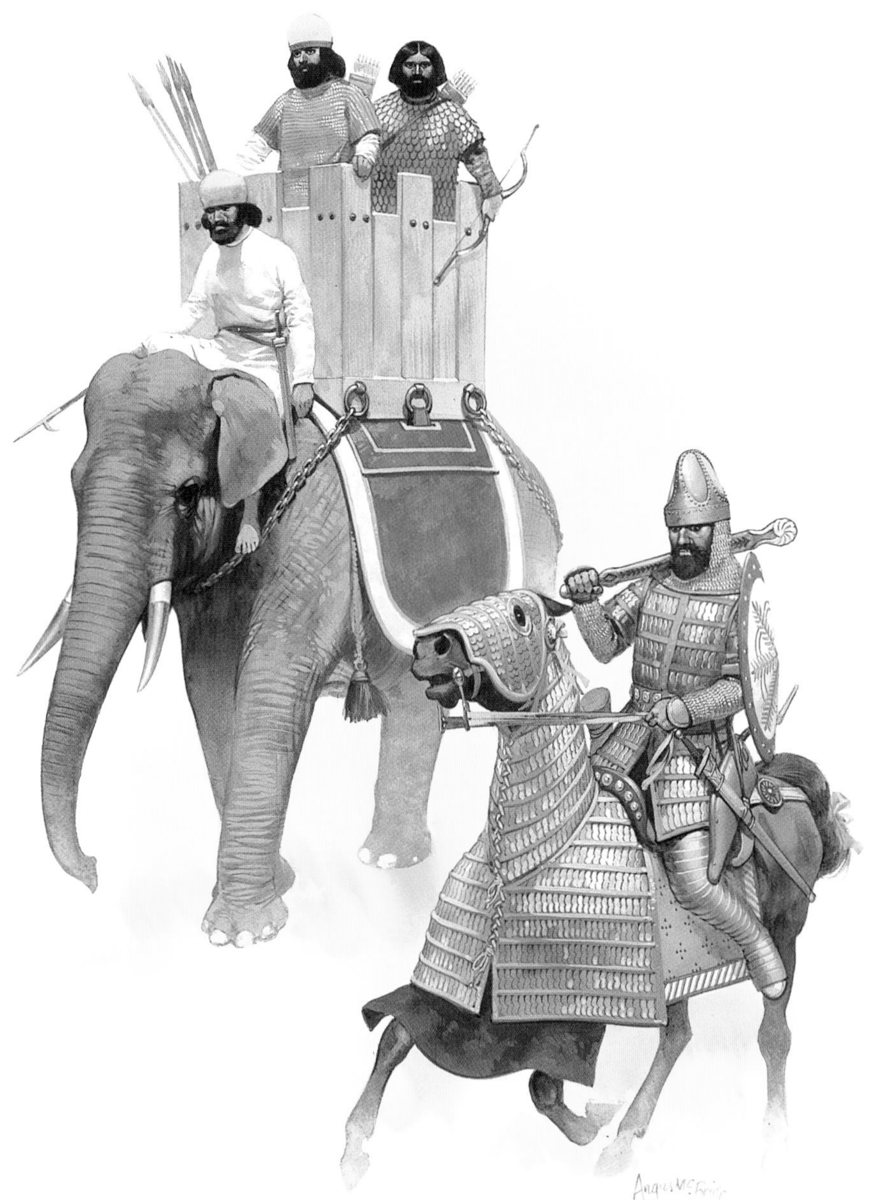

This hypothetical reconstruction is based on several relevant sources, including ancient representations. The Indian elephant bears a crenelated wooden *howdah* holding two mercenary bowmen. The tusks are sheathed with bronze. Despite their unpredictability on the battlefield, the fact that war elephants were used throughout ancient and Oriental medieval history right up until the widespread introduction of gunpowder would seem to argue for some degree of success. (Painting by Angus McBride © Osprey Publishing Ltd)

Four days after Maranga, Julian pushed further towards Samarra. The Savaran were waiting and attacked again with lances drawn. The attacks on the column were seemingly contained, except for the right wing where they were defeated. This crisis obliged Julian to foolishly appear without his armour, and as the Sassanian lance charge was being engaged, a lance struck Julian. By that evening he was dead from his wounds. It is still unclear as to who propelled the spear: a Sassanian or a disaffected Christian in Julian's camp. Shortly thereafter, the Romans under Jovian were forced by Shapur to sign a humiliating treaty and surrender strategic cities such as Nisibis in order to be granted safe passage out of Persia. Other enemies on each side's frontiers then started to assume much greater importance than further costly war between the Romans and Persians.

Sassanid Persian troops

Appearance and status

The typical Iranian riding costume of trousers, leather boots, tunic and cap has shown a remarkable continuity across time and geography. In Sassanian Persia, the traditional riding costume became almost synonymous with ceremonial attire. This meant that in addition to battlefield dress, there were possibly a variety of court costumes worn by the Savaran, noblemen and military officials. These would most likely vary according to rank and clan.

The Emperor Julian noted in his *Orationes* that Sassanian warriors

> ...imitate Persian fashions...take pride in wearing the same...raiment adorned with gold and purple...their king [Shapur II]...imitating Xerxes.

There was a great deal of continuity between Parthian and Sassanian times in terms of costume. This is because many of the noble clans of the Parthian era continued to be well represented, with many of their articles of dress continuing into Sassanian Persia. One example is the Parthian tunic, which was Scythian in style, with the right tunic breast laid over the left, a V-shaped neck line and long sleeves. Among the Parthians and early Sassanians colours of trousers had usually been blue, red and green, although colours such as brown, red, crimson and varieties of purple became increasingly common.

Each Savaran and elite unit had its own battle standard and coat of arms known as the *drafsh*. There were a very large number of *drafsh* designs with boars, tigers, gazelles, wolves as well as mythological beasts. The draco (dragon) flags were especially popular, as they were amongst northern Iranian (Sarmatian) peoples. It is also known that as an attack was to begin, a *drafsh* with the colour of fire (or flame design?) would be displayed. The Savaran would display their *drafsh* on a cross-bar or pole, however tunics and shield bosses could also display these.

Organisation and tactics

The size of a regular Sassanian army was probably 12,000 men. The army was divided into corps which were split into divisions and these in turn were divided into brigades. The military system inherited from the Parthians was based on the heavy, armoured cavalry provided by the aristocracy (the Savaran), and the light horse-archers provided by the minor nobility and nomad mercenaries. Elephants were usually placed in the rear; they would have been of Indian type, carrying armed soldiers and a driver.

Infantry

The bulk of the infantry, the *paighan*, were recruited from peasant populations. *Paighan* were to guard the baggage train, serve as pages for the Savaran, storm fortification walls, undertake entrenchment projects, and excavate mines. They were mainly armed with the spear and shield. In battle they would typically cluster close to each other for mutual protection. Their military training, combat effectiveness and morale were generally low. Their numbers actually swelled the army when siege warfare was involved.

The Medes, one of the first Iranian peoples to enter and settle the Near East, supplied high-quality slingers, javeliners and heavy infantry for the Sassanian army. The army made use of heavy infantry from the early days of the dynasty. The Roman opinion of Sassanian infantry was negative, viewing them as a mass of poorly equipped and incapable serfs. This may not be accurate since the Romans may have been confusing the *paighan* with the separate regular combat infantry. Spearman are sometimes reported as being capable of facing Roman legionaries. In battle, the heavy infantry initially stood behind the foot-archers who would fire their missiles until their supplies were exhausted. The archers would retire behind the ranks of the heavy infantry, who would then engage in hand to hand fighting.

Foot-archers

Foot-archers were highly regarded. Archery was seen as vital in winning battles and training in archery was heavily emphasised. Foot-archers were used in both siege work and set-piece battles. In siege warfare, towers were often erected against enemy forts whereby archers would ascend these and fire into enemy strongholds. Archers on the surrounding ground would pour withering fire onto the defenders, reducing their ability to repel an assault.

On the battlefield, powerful volleys of arrows would be launched until supplies of arrows were exhausted. Foot-archers had one main function: softening up the enemy before the decisive strike of the Savaran. Specifically, they were to support the Savaran by releasing, with deadly precision, as many deadly volleys of missiles as possible. The objective was to damage enemy formations of archers and infantry so that they would be unable to withstand the Savaran attack. In defence, archers were entrusted with stopping enemy infantry or cavalry attacks. Interestingly, the foot-archers could shoot backwards when retreating, resembling the Parthian shot of the horse-archers.

The Savaran

The pride of the Sassanian army were the Savaran or elite cavalry. Of all the warriors, it was the Savaran who held the position of honour. In Parthian times, the proportion of heavy lance-armed cavalry in comparison to horse archers was one to ten – this proportion was to radically shift in favour of lancers by the early Sassanian era. This meant that the importance of the lancer increased such that by the rise of the early Sassanians, the heavy armoured lancer had become the dominant feature of Iranian warfare, with horse-archery in decline.

The figure on the left is a peasant from the countryside of Iran, forced into military service at need. Hardly trained, he would be used as general duties personnel or as a baggage guard, as well as acting as a spearman in battle. The middle figure is a mercenary from northern Syria, armed with a large composite bow, an axe and a bullhide shield. The figure on the right is a tough hillman of western Asia, carrying his sling stones in a goatskin bag. Hard to detect in flight and difficult to dodge, sling pellets could stun, maim or even kill. (Painting by Angus McBride © Osprey Publishing Ltd)

It is unclear why tough and well-disciplined Roman infantry forces were unable to defeat attacks by the Savaran. Rome had had plenty of experience with Iranian cavalry methods of warfare against the Parthians and Sarmatians. In response to the threat of Iranian heavy cavalry and mounted archers, traditional Roman tactics had changed to incorporate auxiliary forces of cavalry, archers and heavy infantry familiar with Iranian tactics. This may

This vase from *c*.400BC shows a Persian cavalryman in typical dress taking on a hoplite-style warrior. (© R. Sheridan/AAA Collection Ltd)

indicate that Sassanian tactics and armaments were more sophisticated than their Parthian predecessors and that the Romans were simply unaccustomed to them at the time. This may be especially true with respect to the armour of the Sassanian cavalry elite. Roman archers were a part of the Roman battle order and were certain to fire missiles at charging Sassanian cavalry. Like the Parthians in 226, the Romans may have been unpleasantly surprised to see the minimal impact of their missiles against Sassanian armour. This meant that the lance-charging cavalry were able to maintain formation and reach the Roman lines intact.

By the time of Julian's invasion of Persia, Persian heavy infantry are described by Ammianus Marcellinus as highly disciplined and 'armed like gladiators'. By this time, it is possible that the Sassanians were trying to copy the Roman legionary or trying to revive the Achaemenean infantry tradition. Shapur II is described as endeavouring to

> ...make his cavalry invulnerable...he *[Shapur]* did not limit their armour to helmet, breastplate and greaves...nor even to place bronze plates before the brow and breast of the horse...the man was covered in chain mail from his head to the end of his feet, and the horse from its crown to the tip of its hooves...they entrusted their body to the protection of iron mail. (Libianus, LIX, 69–70).

Beneath the mail was worn a combination of laminated and lamellar armour. Heliodorus remarks that the armoured protection of the super-heavy cavalry was '...proof against any missiles, and is a sure defence against all wounds'. This may suggest that armour had become so highly developed that the super-heavy Savaran did not consider Roman archery as a threat. The range of weapons used by the Savaran increased to include weapons such as axes, maces or darts.

Having reached the Roman lines, the Savaran are described as being able to impale two men at once. In addition, mounted (and infantry) archers could also overwhelm the Romans with archery. The 'softening up' of Roman lines with repeated lance charges and archery volleys may have even allowed the regular Sassanian armoured infantry to attempt to go hand-to-hand against the excellently trained Roman infantryman, although close fighting with Roman infantry was apparently avoided as much as possible. Not only were the Romans very dangerous when faced in close-quarter combat, they had also found an ingenious way of coping with the Savaran assaults. A very effective tactic was to dive under the horses of the Savaran as soon as they approached their lines and try and injure the horses from beneath. This forced the regular Savaran to disengage and use their bows from a distance. Not only were the Savaran left without support, the tiny eye slits of their face masks restricted their ability to see the legionaries in their proximity.

Armenian elite cavalry

Armenians were accorded a status equal to the elite Savaran. In fact, the equipment and regalia of Armenian cavalry were identical to the Savaran. Pro-Sassanian Armenian cavalry units fought under Sassanian banners and were allowed to enter the royal grounds of the capital, Ctesiphon. The king would then send a royal emissary to enquire about the state of Armenia – this was repeated three times. The day after, the king would honour the Armenians by personally inspecting their troops in a military review. Armenians also supplied valuable light cavalry and excellent infantry, who were especially proficient in using slings to repel enemy cavalry as well as spears for hand-to-hand combat.

Light cavalry

Lightly armed cavalry were highly proficient with the bow; however, many foreign contingents would fight with other weapons such as javelins. Light cavalry were recruited from Iranian-speaking peoples such as the Alans of Arran (modern-day Republic of Azerbaijan), Gelanis of northern Persia, Kushans of Central Asia and the Saka settlers of Afghanistan and eastern Iran. Many non-Iranian contingents such as Chionites, Hephthalites and Turkic Khazars were also recruited. Like the Lakhmid Arabs, an important function of warlike allied troops on the frontiers was to keep an invasion force in check until the arrival of the main Savaran forces.

Fighting style

A standard battle tactic was to divide the army into five units: a main line of cavalry (Savaran), a reinforcement line of heavy infantry behind the main line, two flanks (usually cavalry), and a small reserve of the best Savaran units. The main line and the reinforcement formed the centre and was known as the 'two main parts' or the 'heart'. It was imperative for these 'parts' to hold under all circumstances, to prevent either flank from collapsing in case of heavy losses. Placing these 'parts' on a slope was meant to provide greater protection against enemy thrusts. Elevated places for the centre were always recommended.

Behind the reinforcement line were reserves, usually composed of prestige units. Savaran were usually located on the right flank; however they could be on the left flank depending on the commander's strategy. Theoretically, the Savaran were to always fight at the front; this was not always the case in practice, however.

In battle, both Sassanians and Romans tried to outflank each other by attacking their respective left wing by way of their right flanks. The left flank was to adopt a defensive posture and would enter action only in extreme circumstances. It could attack if it was in imminent danger of being attacked itself. The left flank also acted as a strategic reserve, but could attack at the commander's discretion. Even when allowed by the army commander to attack, the left flank was to then return to its original defensive position. The main reason why the left flank was not favoured for the attack was because using a shield on the left generally did not allow for the heavy infantryman to use his weapons efficiently in the left direction. As a result of this perceived weakness, the left flank was actually given stronger forces as well as left-handed archers. Left-handed bowmen were viewed as being equally capable of effectively shooting from both left and right sides.

Sassanian cavalry units were formidable, but lacked long-term endurance in battle. This partly confirms the notion that Sassanian elite cavalry forces were intended as shock units to break open and/or to disorganise enemy lines. This quality was to prove useful against Julian's invasion of Persia in 362. For the Sassanians, the battle was usually decided by the shock of a single powerful thrust by the Savaran using lances. This meant that the logical focal point and power of that thrust was at its front. It is interesting that Romans fleeing before Sassanians were recommended not to counterattack them frontally due to the high risk that they would 'suffer injury on running into their well ordered ranks'.

There were three major weaknesses in the Sassanian battle order. The first was the aversion of many auxiliary troops, especially the *paighan*, to hand-to-hand fighting. The second weakness was the result of the Savaran's greatest asset, their frontal charge. The powerful frontal focus of the charge came at a price; later Savaran were tactically vulnerable at their flanks and rear. Third (perhaps the most serious weakness), was the tendency of soldiers to flee the field when their commander was slain.

Chapter 15
THE GOTHS

Gothic campaigns against Rome

Background

The Roman Empire in the latter part of the fourth century AD was very much on the defensive, and had been for many years. In the previous century, economic collapse, barbarian raids and endemic civil war almost destroyed the Empire. Diocletian's attempts to set up a smooth system of succession had failed, which meant that fourth-century emperors had to rely on the army not only to defend the frontiers of the Empire but also to fend off usurpers and rivals.

All of the Empire's frontiers were under pressure. Britain was menaced by the Saxons, Picts and Scots, while vigorous federations of German tribes such as the Franks and Alamanni pushed against the Rhine frontier.

In the east there was a virtually permanent state of hostilities with the Sassanid Persians (as Chapter 14 has shown). The African, Egyptian and Syrian frontiers were also subject to endemic raiding by the Moors, Blemyes and Arabs.

On the Danube frontier it was the Goths who posed the greatest threat. The Goths were a Germanic people whose origin is disputed by modern historians. In their own traditions they emigrated from Scandanavia through modern Poland and Ukraine to the shores of the Black Sea. The sixth-century Gothic historian Jordanes says in his *Getica*:

> From this island of Scandza *[Scandanavia]*, as from a hive of races or a womb of nations, the Goths are said to have come forth long ago under their king, Berig by name. As soon as they disembarked from their ships and set foot on the land they straightaway gave their name to the place. And even today it is said to be called Gothiscandza. Soon they moved from here to the abodes of the Ulmerugi, who then dwelt on the shores of the Ocean, where they pitched camp, joined battle with them and drove them from their homes. They then subdued their neighbours, the Vandals, and thus added to their victories.

This Frankish gravestone is one of the very few representations of a Germanic warrior not made by the Romans. A large sax (a cross between a knife and a sword used as both a tool and a weapon) features prominently at his belt, and he is apparently combing his hair. (© R. Sheridan/AAA Collection Ltd)

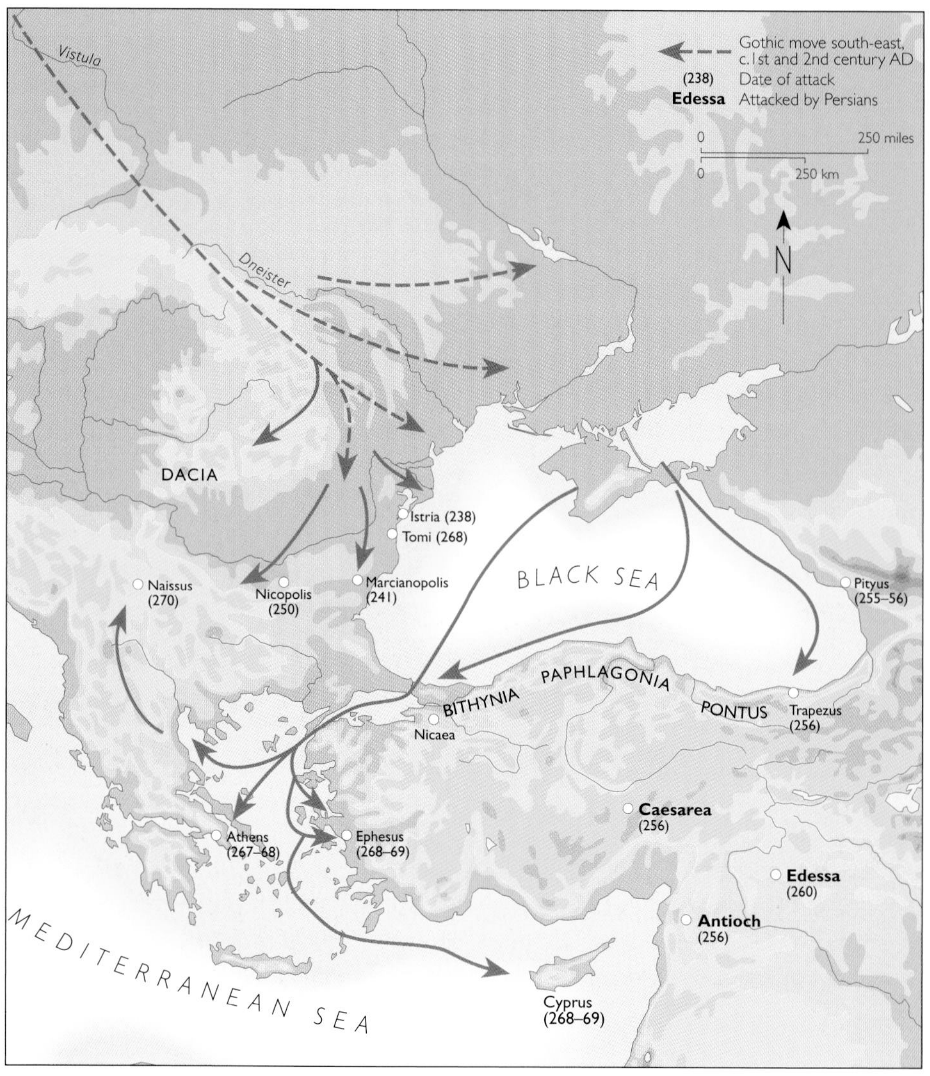

Movement of Goths across Europe.

> But when the number of people increased greatly, and Filimer, son of Gadaric, reigned as king – about the fifth since Berig – he decided that the army of Goths with their families should move from that region. In search of suitable homes and pleasant places they came to the land of Scythia.

Hostilities and stability

For much of Roman history there was little interaction between the Goths and the Empire. Tacitus, writing in the first century, mentions them in passing and they were too far from the frontier to have much of an impact. In the third century, however, the Goths expanded westward and burst on the scene with a vengeance. They sacked Histria on the mouth of the Danube in 238 then went on to ravage Moesia and Thrace (modern Bulgaria). In 251 a Gothic army led by Cniva destroyed a Roman army and killed the Emperor Decius.

Seaborne raids between 253 and 271 increasingly supplemented land attacks across the Lower Danube frontier. These at first concentrated on the coastal areas of the Black Sea, but encouraged by success they spread beyond the Bosphorus and into the Aegean. Bands of Goths and their allies ravaged the coasts of Asia Minor, Greece, Macedonia and Cyprus and then penetrated inland, sacking Ephesus and Athens. Stability was finally restored by the Emperor Claudius who won a decisive victory over a Gothic force at Naissus (Nis in modern Serbia) in 269, followed up by Aurelian who restored the Danube frontier after formally abandoning the province of Dacia (modern Romania).

For the next hundred years Goths and Romans faced each other across the Danube in a state of uneasy coexistence with relations wavering between hostility, truce and alliance. The Emperor Constantine built a 2.5km-long bridge across the Danube in 328 to enable Roman armies to more easily take offensive action against the Goths and to strike into their home territory to exact revenge for any raids against the Empire. After a successful campaign, Constantine concluded a formal peace treaty in 332 with those Goths (the Tervingi) living directly on the frontier. Under its terms the Romans paid the Goths an annual tribute while the Goths reportedly were to provide 40,000 soldiers as *foederati* (federates) to fight in the Roman army when called on. The figure of 40,000 is certainly an exaggeration and far more than the bands living along the Danube could ever hope to raise. However, after 322 Goths did fight for Rome on several occasions. The soldier-scholar Ammianus Marcellinus wrote as a contemporary of these times, and he records, for example, that 3,000 Goths went to the aid of the usurper Procopius in 365, implying that they did so under the terms of the treaty.

In summer AD251, Decius led an attack against the Goths at Abrittus. His defeat and death made him the first Roman emperor to die in battle against foreign invaders. (© R. Sheridan/AAA Collection Ltd)

The arrival of the Huns

In the early 370s the equilibrium was shattered by the arrival of the Huns on the eastern fringes of the Gothic territories. Their rapid success in battles against the Gothic clans spread terror along the frontier. Ammianus describes the Huns as 'abnormally savage' and

Merida Roman Bridge. The Romans were some of the earliest people to excel in bridge building, often using the circular arch to make their bridges strong. (© R. Sheridan/AAA Collection Ltd)

as a 'wild race, moving without encumbrances and consumed by a savage passion to pillage the property of others'. No doubt their savage reputation increased with every victory so that by 376 Ammianus records that rumour spread amongst all the German tribes that:

> ...an unknown race of men had appeared from some remote corner of the earth, uprooting and destroying everything in its path like a whirlwind descending from high mountains...

Panic ensued:

> Terrifying rumours got about of a new and unusually violent commotion among the peoples of the North. Men heard that over the whole area extending from the Marcomanni and Quadi *[Germanic tribes living along the upper Danube]* to the Black Sea, a savage horde of remote tribes, driven from their homes by unexpected pressure, were roaming with their families in the Danube region. (Ammianus Marcellinus)

Crossing the Danube

By 376 the outlook for the Goths was bleak. Driven from their homes and land and holed up in the mountain refuges or behind fortifications, they would have had little to live off. Having failed to protect his people from the Huns, Athanaric, leader of the Tervingi, began to lose authority, and a large number of the Tervingi deserted him. This breakaway group, led by Alavivus and Fritigern, applied for sanctuary within the Roman Empire.

At this time two men ruled the Empire. Flavius Valens had been ruling the east since 364, while his young nephew Flavius Gratianus (Gratian) had just been elevated as the western emperor in 375 on the death of his father Valentinian. Valens had campaigned against the Goths a few years earlier (367–369) and had concluded a formal peace treaty with Athanaric's Tervingi. It is highly probably that part of this agreement was for the Tervingi to supply troops for the Roman army. When Alavivus and Fritigern applied for asylum, Valens was campaigning against the powerful Persian Empire. A source of fresh recruits was probably welcome, and in any case with his army engaged on another front it would have been difficult for him to oppose the Goths if they tried to force the issue. Consequently the request was granted, and Roman officials were given orders to help move the Tervingi across the Danube, provide them with supplies, and give them land to settle.

> Once the Emperor's permission to cross the Danube and settle in parts of Thrace had been granted, the work of transportation went on day and night. The Goths embarked by troops on boats and rafts and canoes made from hollowed tree trunks. The crowd was such that, though the river is the most dangerous in the world and was then swollen by frequent rains, a large

> number tried to swim and were drowned in their struggle against the force of the stream. (Ammianus Marcellinus)

A sudden large influx of refuges is never easy to deal with. The situation facing Lupicinus, the *comes* (count and commander of regional troops) in charge of Thrace would have been nearly impossible to deal with for even the most competent of officials: an armed group of asylum seekers, who less than ten years ago were at war with Rome, suddenly arriving in their thousands – homeless, hungry and in desperate need of supplies and resettlement. Unfortunately, neither Lupicinus nor Maximus (the *dux* – commander of frontier troops) was up to the task. Ammianus claims that:

> ...their sinister greed was the source of all our troubles...The barbarians, after crossing the river, were distressed by want of food, and these loathsome generals devised an abominable form of barter. They collected all the dogs that their insatiable greed could find and exchanged each of them for a slave.

The Emepror Valens was a strong opponent of Nicene Christianity, and persecuted many orthodox followers. This painting shows the burning of orthodox Christian ministers in a ship by order of Emperor Valens. (© B. Wilson/AAA Collection Ltd)

Although the Tervingi were supposed to have been moved on and resettled further south, the Roman officials kept them in the area of their original crossing because, according to Ammianus, they were making a good profit by selling them poor-quality food at inflated prices. In addition, Roman authorities felt overwhelmed by the situation, while the Goths, with no means of subsistence, saw revolt as the only way out.

Meanwhile, another Gothic clan called the Greuthungi, led by Alatheus and Saphrax, had also moved to the Danube and made a similar request for asylum. Another group under Farnobius accompanied them. This time the request was refused. Presumably because the Tervingi could provide enough potential recruits for the army and since resettling them was proving difficult, there was no incentive to let any more Goths across. Athanaric, leading the remaining Tervingi who had not broken away with Alavivus and Fritigern, also moved to the Danube. However, he was persuaded, under the terms of the treaty he had signed with Valens in 369, not to set foot in Roman territory, and he withdrew back to his mountain refuge.

The Greuthungi were not prepared to take no for an answer and when Lupicinus' troops were distracted, dealing with potential trouble among the Tervingi, they made a move:

> Seeing that our men were engaged elsewhere, and that the boats which patrolled the river to prevent their crossing had ceased to operate, the Greuthungi took advantage of the opportunity to slip over on roughly made rafts, and pitched their camp a long way from Fritigern. The latter, however, whose native shrewdness served to protect him against any eventuality, found a way to both obey his orders and at the same time unite with these powerful kings. (Ammianus Marcellinus)

The Gothic revolt

The situation was now critical. Still without land or homes and desperately short of food, discontent was rising amongst the Goths. Bolstered by the new arrivals they would have had the numerical strength to stand up to the local Roman officials. At the same time their numbers would have made it nearly impossible to find enough food in the over-foraged areas of the river crossing. Although not yet in open revolt, the Goths took matters into their own hands, defied local authority, and broke out of the containment area along the Danube to strike south for the low-lying fertile region near Marcianople (Devnja in modern Bulgaria). The stage was set for conflict and it would only take a spark to set it off. That spark was a bungled assassination attempt on the Gothic leaders.

Lupicinus decided to try to bring the Goths back under control by assassinating their leaders. He invited Alavivus and Fritigern to a sumptuous dinner party letting them believe that in addition to food, drink and entertainment, they would discuss provisions for their people. He allowed only the leaders and their immediate bodyguard to enter the town and then kept the bodyguard outside his headquarters while the leaders dined. Lupicinus ordered the troops to kill the Gothic bodyguards while others manned the walls to prevent any rescue attempt. Ammianus' description of the incident is confusing but clearly things went awry. Fighting broke out and some Goths outside the town 'killed and stripped of their arms a large contingent of troops' and laid siege to the town. It is not clear whether Lupicinus intended to keep the leaders hostage or kill them, but Alavivus apparently perished while Fritigern managed to escape. Jordanes says that Fritigern managed to fight his way out, while Ammianus says he was able to convince Lupicinus that he would try to pacify his followers in order to avoid battle.

However he did it, Fritigern rejoined his people and together they began looting and burning the farms and villas surrounding the town. Lupicinus quickly gathered troops and marched out of the city to challenge the Goths. The forces engaged nine miles from the city at Marcianople, and Ammianus says:

> The Barbarians hurled themselves recklessly on our lines, dashing their shields upon the bodies of their opponents and running them through with spears and swords. In this furious and bloody assault our standards were snatched from us and our tribunes and the greater part of our men perished,

> all but their luckless commander. While the others were away fighting his one aim was to get away, and he made for the city at a gallop. After this the enemy armed themselves with Roman weapons and roamed at large unresisted.

Having defeated Lupicinus, the Goths overnight became the masters of Thrace. There was no one to oppose them. The situation worsened when Roman troops of Gothic origin joined the revolt. These men, led by Suerdias and Colias, were in winter quarters at Adrianople.

At first they remained loyal to Rome, but the situation changed when they were ordered to move east out of fear that they would join Fritigern who was moving south towards Adrianople. Denied supplies for the journey, or time to prepare properly, the Gothic Roman troops were then attacked by the 'dregs of the populace' and workers from the armaments factory in the city, incited by the chief magistrate of Adrianople. Ammianus says:

> The Goths remained immovable, but when they were finally driven desperate by curses and abuse and a few missiles were hurled at them, they broke out in open rebellion. They slew very many citizens, whom their too impudent attack had entrapped and put to flight the rest, wounding them with various kinds of weapons. Then, plundering the dead bodies and arming themselves with Roman equipment, they joined forces with Fritigern whom they saw to be near at hand. (Ammianus Marcellinus)

Defeat at Adrianople

It appeared in 378 that the Romans would crush the Goths, as Valens returned from Antioch and Gratian marched from the Rhine to co-operate against them. However, Gratian's arrival was delayed when the Alamanni heard about his plans and decided to invade. Valens still felt confident of defeating the Goths, and on 9 August 378 he led his army out of camp at Adrianople towards the Gothic position. The Romans probably outnumbered the Goths, but their deployment from the line of march was confused, and the battle was joined haphazardly, with the result that the Roman wings were driven back. At this moment the Gothic cavalry, which had been absent foraging, returned and the combination of their flank attacks, the heavy fire of Gothic archers, and the heat of the long day gradually wore down the Roman centre. Resistance was stubborn, but two-thirds of the army, including Valens, were killed.

After the battle, the Goths abandoned their attempt to besiege the city of Adrianople, and together with the Huns, Alans, and large numbers of Roman deserters, moved on to devastate the fertile Thracian lowlands. Failing an attempted siege of Constantinople, and short of food, the Goths drew back to Thrace, Illyricum and Dacia. In January 379, Gratian appointed Theodosius as eastern emperor, and responsibility for the conduct of the war passed to him. Meanwhile, in the east, Roman commanders, fearing further rebellions, massacred all Gothic soldiers serving in the Roman army.

Detail from the base of the Obelisk of Theodosius I in Istanbul. The men in the rear row are soldiers, probably Goths recruited after the treaty of 382. Their long hair sets them apart from the Romans in front.

The war dragged on for another four years, with the Goths unable to take any significant towns or cities and the Romans unable to defeat them in battle. With neither side able to make significant headway against the other, the Goths and Romans turned to negotiations to try to come to terms. Finally on 3 October 382 a treaty was signed, essentially re-affirming the original terms of 376. Fritigern's followers were given lands to settle along the southern bank of the Danube in Thrace. In return for the land, and autonomous status within the Empire they were to provide troops to serve in the Roman army and a large number did so in Theodosius' campaign in 387 against the usurper Maximus. Barbarians had long been employed in Roman armies and there was a history of settling prisoners of war as military colonists. But the treaty of 382 was different in that an entire people were settled inside the Empire, remaining under their own laws and fighting as a single entity under their own leaders.

Peace did not last long. After playing a leading role in Theodosius' victory over the usurpers Maximus and Eugenius, the Goths again revolted. Quite probably the revolt was sparked by heavy Gothic casualties in these campaigns leading to a desire on the part of the Goths to have greater control over their own destiny. Led by Alaric, the Goths overran Greece and Illyricum, and engaged in a long period of hostility, which alternated between open warfare and uneasy truce. The aim of Alaric and his followers was not to establish an independent kingdom, but rather to secure a major military command within the Empire. For a period it appears that Alaric was formally granted the position of *magister militum per Illyricum* by Arcadius, who succeeded Theodosius as the eastern emperor in 395. Using this mandate he waged war against the western armies commanded by Stilicho, and led an abortive invasion of Italy. Later he reversed his loyalty and held Illyricum on behalf of the western emperor. In 409 the Goths invaded Italy a second time and sacked Rome in 410. Finally, eight years later, they formally established the Visigothic kingdom in southern France, later spreading into Spain.

A romanticised image of the meeting of Alaric, king of the Visigoths, and Emperor Honorius. (© Prisma/AAA Collection Ltd)

Gothic troops

The Goths were a whole people on the move, rather than an organised army. They fought with whatever weapons they were able to capture, and welcomed into their ranks men of any nationality who were willing to fight.

A warrior's appearance and status

The Gothic warrior often carried his wealth on his person. The warrior's status was measured by his success in war, and this could be visibly demonstrated by the quality of his equipment, which might be booty from a defeated enemy or the gift of a grateful chief. There was no such thing as a uniform in this disruptive period: each man equipped himself the best he could. The better, and therefore most successful, warriors might be fully equipped with brightly coloured and decorated clothes, horse, armour, helmet, sword, spear, axe and shield; poorer men, or those yet to establish a military reputation, would have no armour and be equipped only with a spear and shield. Poor Goths also often served as archers.

The basic clothing of the warrior was a tunic and trousers, over which a cloak was worn in inclement weather. Clothing was usually wool, but linen was also worn, as was a wool-linen mix. Belts were a universal item of military dress and served to indicate the wearer's status as a warrior. In the fourth century these belts could be extremely wide and were fitted with buckles and loops to attach equipment such as a sword, a purse and a firesteel. Some Goths, however, were quick to adopt Roman-style dress, and others adopted the looser fitting garments of the steppe peoples.

Training

We know very little of how warriors were trained, or even if any formal training was carried out. Most likely, young boys would imitate their fathers and be taught the warrior's skills by his family. A life based on subsistence agriculture and hunting would have kept

ALARIC, ROMAN OFFICER AND TRIBAL WARLORD

Alaric was born in about 370 into the Balthi, a leading family among the Gothic Tervingi. As a youth he probably participated in the Danube crossing of 376 and observed the subsequent encounters with imperial forces; at some stage he became an Arian Christian, the standard creed among the Goths. By the early 390s he had emerged as leader of a warband in the Balkans who opposed Emperor Theodosius, but in 394 he commanded tribal allies in Theodosius' expedition against the western usurper Eugenius. Disenchanted by inadequate recompense for his contribution to victory at the Frigidus river and the heavy casualties suffered by his followers, he proceeded to ravage the central and southern Balkans, taking advantage of tensions between Rome and Constantinople. By 399 he had secured one major wish, the senior Roman command of general of Illyricum, which provided him with salaries and provisions for his followers.

In 401 he invaded Italy and besieged the western emperor Honorius in Milan, but was defeated by the western generalissimo Stilicho; he was forced to withdraw to the Balkans as his men suffered from heat and poor food. He remained in the north-eastern Balkans, attempting to secure a permanent territory, until 407 when he was appointed general by Honorius as part of a western attempt to annex the Balkans. The planned campaign was cancelled, relations between Alaric and Honorius deteriorated, and Alaric invaded Italy again to secure payment for his contracted services. While negotiating with Honorius at Ravenna about territory, alliance and payments of gold and corn, Alaric besieged Rome. Honorius procrastinated, but in 409 the threat of starvation forced the Senate at Rome to agree terms; Alaric had the senator Attalus proclaimed emperor and Attalus appointed Alaric as a senior Roman general.

Tensions between Attalus and Alaric, plus further unsuccessful negotiations with Honorius, resulted in Alaric returning to Rome, which was easily captured on 24 August 410. Occupation of the city for three days may have relieved Alaric's frustrations, but did not satisfy his followers' needs for territory. Thereafter he led his forces south, with North Africa as his probable goal, but was thwarted while trying to cross to Sicily; as he withdrew northwards he became ill and died. His brother-in-law Athaulf took over the army, which he led into southern Gaul in 412 where the Visigothic kingdom was established in Aquitania.

most young men physically fit, and it is quite likely that their skills were honed by various sports and games. Games, together with hunting, would have taught the young warrior the basic individual weapons-handling skills he would need to survive.

There is no indication that any kind of unit or formation training was carried out by any of the Germans. A young warrior on his first campaign would probably accompany his relatives and stand in a rear rank where all he had to do was follow the actions of others.

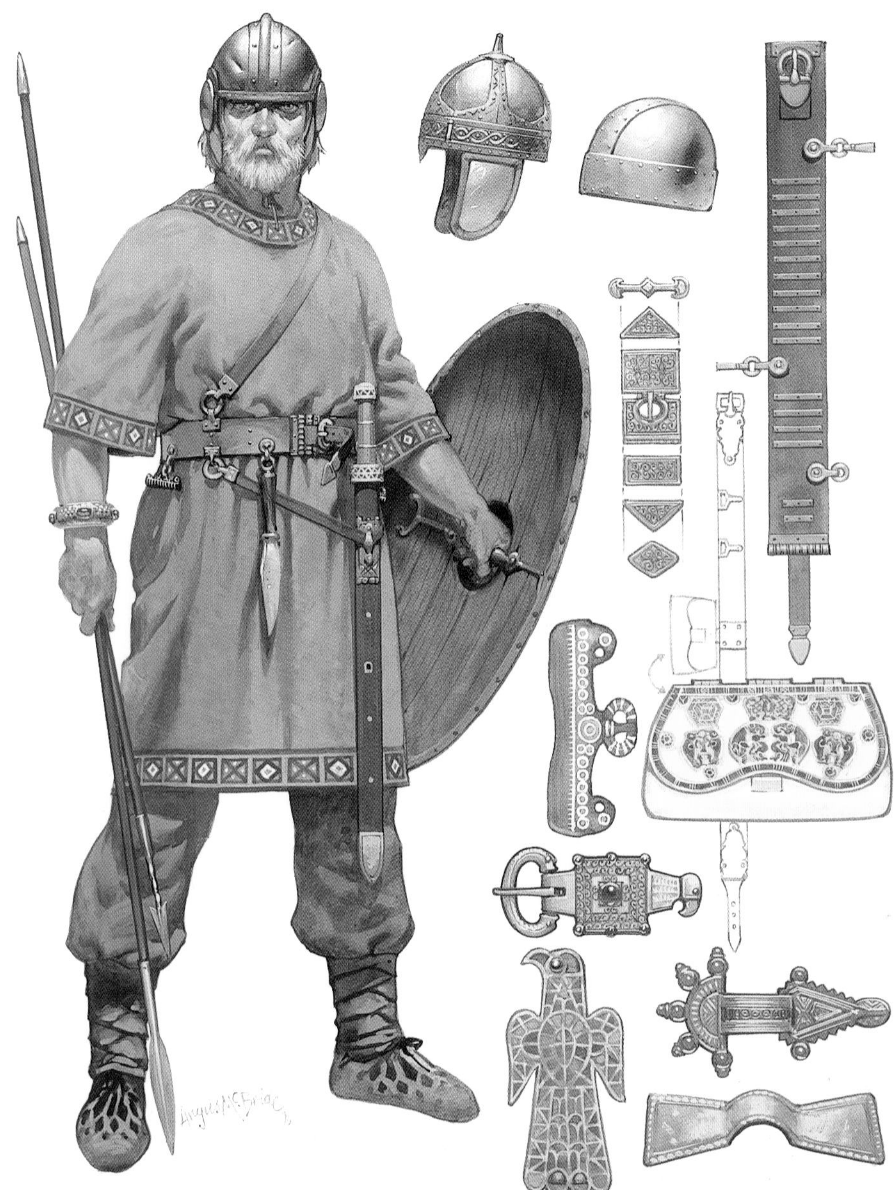

This Visigoth warrior, who may have crossed the Danube as a baby in 376, is one of the followers of Alaric, who sacked Rome in 410. He has lived all or most of his life within the Roman Empire, and he has fought both for and against Roman armies. Consequently most of his equipment is of Roman origin. (Painting by Angus McBride © Osprey Publishing Ltd)

Gradually, if he survived, he would acquire greater experience until he would be in a position to pass on his skills to younger men.

Arms, armour and equipment

The wars with Rome saw Gothic armies containing an ever-increasing number of well-equipped full-time warriors, and although plunder would greatly increase their arsenals, they were not

TERVINGI AND GREUTHUNGI

Most modern historians incorrectly call the Tervingi 'Visigoths' and the Greuthungi 'Ostrogoths', equating these fourth-century clans with the later fifth- to sixth-century kingdoms. The Visigoths, who established a kingdom in France in 418, were in fact descended from all of the people who followed Fritigern (including Tervingi, Greuthungi and non-Goths), augmented by the followers of Radagaisus who invaded Italy in 405. The Ostrogoths are mentioned by the poet Claudian in 399 as separate from the Greuthungi and may have been another clan who grew in power during the fifth century beyond the Roman frontier. Probably those people who formed the Ostrogothic kingdom in Italy at the end of the fifth century were a similar mixture of clans, no doubt including some Greuthungi, but not exclusively.

totally dependent on Rome for high-quality weapons. There were extensive, accessible iron deposits throughout Germania, and archaeologists have found evidence of sizeable workshops in production from the first century. Furthermore, the skills of Germanic smiths and other craftsmen were as good as, or better than those found inside the Roman Empire: the magnificent gold- and garnet-decorated equipment and pattern-welded blades are clear evidence of their abilities and certainly surpass the mass-produced weapons of the late Roman arms factories.

Once inside the Empire, much or all of the warrior's equipment could come from Roman sources. When the Tervingi crossed the Danube in 376 they were expected to give up their arms as a condition of entry into Roman territory. Although it is unclear how well they fulfilled this requirement, it is probable that they were not able to bring much military equipment over the Danube with them. Virtually all their weaponry post-376 therefore came from Roman sources. By the time of Adrianople, therefore, most of the Goths would have been completely equipped in Roman clothing and accoutrements and carrying Roman weapons.

Ammianus does not convey the impression that the Goths were ill equipped. His frequent descriptions of battles between Romans and Germanic peoples are usually presented as a contrast of equals when it comes to equipment. Using classic literary tradition, he portrays the Germanic warriors as wild and headstrong, contrasting this to the steady, cautious Romans, but when it comes to equipment, the two are portrayed as equal. He makes reference to Goths being weighed down by their arms, and during the battle of Adrianople he describes 'helmets and breast-plates' being split asunder on both sides.

Unlike many western Germanic peoples, the Goths apparently made a fairly wide use of missile weapons. Ammianus' battle descriptions continually refer to the use of missile weapons by the Goths, including javelins, slings and bows. It seems implicit in these accounts that warriors armed with missile weapons formed part of the main body of troops rather than being a distinct group of light infantry skirmishers. In fact, Ammianus' account of the battle of Ad Salices in 377 probably gives the best description of how the Goths normally fought:

> After an exchange of javelins and other missiles at long range, the opposing sides clashed and fought foot-to-foot with their shields locked.

Organisation and strategy

Typical of most Germanic warriors of this period, the Goths did not have clear divisions of cavalry and infantry. A warrior was a warrior, who might fight mounted or dismounted depending on the situation. It is unlikely that many horses could have been ferried across the Danube and any that did probably ended up as food in the early days. After conflict

The early Germans were noted by Tacitus for the practice of mixing light infantry with cavalry:

> Generally speaking, their strength lies in infantry rather than cavalry, so foot soldiers accompany the cavalry into action, their speed of foot being such that they can easily keep up with the charging horsemen. The best men are chosen from the whole body of the young warriors, and placed with the cavalry in front of the main battle-line.

(Painting by Angus McBride © Osprey Publishing Ltd)

broke out, horses would have been captured and as many men as possible would have been mounted, but primarily for strategic mobility rather than tactical advantage. As late as the sixth century, Ostrogoths were fighting on foot when in rough terrain or in defensive circumstances. It is probable, therefore, that those who had horses would have fought mounted when fighting in open terrain, or against small groups of disordered opponents, or to exploit a sudden advantage like the mounted charge by the Greuthungi at Adrianople. But on most occasions Goths seem to have preferred to fight on foot, particularly when on the defensive.

Fighting style

Protracted campaign may have exposed the weaknesses of the Gothic warrior, but battle brought out many of his strengths. As an individual fighter he was strong, brave and skilled in weapons handling. The *Strategikon*, a sixth-century Roman military manual, made the following observation (which might, of course, be tainted by Graeco-Roman stereotyping):

After driving off the Roman cavalry at Adrianople, the mounted warriors of the Greuthungi and Alans charged down onto the flank of the Roman infantry who were already engaged with Tervingi foot warriors to their front. The result was catastrophic. Confusion and disorder spread though the Roman ranks and men were pushed back into each other until they were so tightly pressed that they could not move. (Painting by Howard Gerrard © Osprey Publishing Ltd)

> The light-haired races place great value on freedom. They are bold and undaunted in battle. Daring and impetuous as they are, they consider any timidity and even a short retreat as a disgrace. They calmly despise death as they fight violently in hand-to-hand combat, either on horseback or on foot.

The tactics employed on the battlefield were not sophisticated. 'They are not interested in anything that is at all complicated,' says the *Strategikon*, their usual strategies being limited to either a straightforward charge or to standing to receive an enemy attack. Complicated tactics would have been difficult to achieve, since although the men in the ranks had achieved a certain degree of cohesion, they were not drilled and so would not have been able to carry out complex manoeuvres. Gothic tactics were not, however, entirely primitive, and key warriors were appointed to lead groups of men. Although their fighting style was probably loose and individualistic, the warriors could keep rank and obey orders, and the men who filled the ranks of a warlord's retinue, whether mounted or dismounted, retained a semblance of order and cohesion, even if this did not result in neat ranks and files marching in step as were seen in the armies of Rome.

The classic Germanic formation was the 'boar's head'. Adopted by the Romans and also known as the *cuneus*, it has been incorrectly translated in modern times as a 'wedge'. In fact, it would be better described as an attack column. The most realistic description of the boar's head comes from Tacitus, who describes the formation as 'closely compressed on all sides and secure in front, flank and rear'. The boar's head was an attack formation that could be used by mounted or unmounted troops. It would be formed around the leader, with the great man taking a prominent position in the front centre and his followers taking up positions beside and behind him, according to their rank and status. The prominent warriors would occupy the front ranks, with the lesser individuals falling in behind. Ammianus said of the Goths after the battle of Adrianople:

> The chiefs who filled the front ranks were on fire to lay hands on Valens' ill-gotten riches, and they were closely followed by the rest, eager to be seen to share the danger of their betters.

The son of Alaric I, the Visigothic Theodoric I (418–451) was variously an enemy and ally of the Romans, He was killed trying to drive Attila's Huns back from the Roman Empire. (© Prisma/AAA Collection Ltd)

THEODORIC, OSTROGOTHIC KING

Theodoric was born in the mid-fifth century into the Amal family which led one of the Gothic groups in the northern Balkans. In 461/62 he was sent as hostage to Constantinople, where he remained for ten years, receiving his education. After succeeding his father in 474, he spent 15 years attempting to establish a base for his people in the Balkans, either through negotiation with or intimidation of the eastern emperor Zeno. Theodoric's successes were marked by appointments as Roman general in 476/78 and again 483–87, when Zeno employed him against other tribesmen in the Balkans as well as Isaurian rebels in the east. Rebuffs resulted in the sacking of cities, such as Stobi in 479, or the ravaging of provinces, for example Macedonia and Thessaly in 482.

The death of his main Gothic rival, Theodoric Strabo, in 481, allowed Theodoric to unite most Balkan Goths under Amal leadership, but he was still unable to achieve his main goal of acquiring a secure and productive territory. In 488 Zeno agreed that Theodoric should move to Italy to attack Odoacer (who had ruled since deposing the last western emperor in 476): if successful, Theodoric could rule on behalf of Zeno. Theodoric forced Odoacer back into Ravenna; after three years of blockade the rival agreed to share power, but Theodoric soon accused Odoacer of treachery and had him killed. Zeno's death in 491 complicated Theodoric's position, but in 497 Emperor Anastasius recognised him as ruler of Italy; to his Gothic followers Theodoric was king, even sometimes Augstus (emperor), the status to which he clearly aspired, although he was careful to protest his subservience in dealings with Constantinople.

Theodoric's 33-year reign (493–526) came to be regarded as a golden age in Italy, especially in contrast to the fighting of the 540s, and his first two decades were highly successful. Martial diplomacy built links with the main tribal groups in the west, and from 507 brought the Visigothic kingdom in Spain under his control. The Senate and Pope at Rome were courted by special treatment and the carefully crafted Roman image of the new regime; religious divisions between Rome and Constantinople facilitated this rapprochement. For Goths Theodoric remained the war leader, but this was now only one facet of his complex public image. Theodoric's last decade was less rosy. The absence of a son and the early death of his son-in-law raised the issue of succession, while Anastasius' death in 518 brought religious reconciliation between Rome and Constantinople and so made Theodoric more suspicious of leading Romans. Theodoric's death in 526 rapidly brought to the surface the tensions within his kingdom.

The men in the formation were not drilled and would not have carried out manoeuvres to commands or signals. Rather they would have followed the movements of the leader, whose position would probably have been marked by a standard. Having a fairly narrow frontage, the boar's head would have been fairly manoeuvrable, and able to make changes of direction. The experienced men in the front would have known how to conform to the leader's movement, and the others only had to follow the men in front. On contact with the enemy, the formation would either have punched through or been halted. In the latter case, the boar's head would probably have flattened out as men from the rear ranks spread out to the flanks and the two lines would have become locked in combat. This would result in a situation like that described by Ammianus at the battle of Adrianople when:

> the opposing lines came into collision like ships of war and pushed each other to and fro, heaving under the reciprocal motion like the waves of the sea.

Chapter 16
THE HUNS

Hunnic campaigns against Rome

Background

The regions north of China were the fountainhead of a remarkable number of migrations out of Central Asia. One such migration was by the Hsiung-Nu, who are sometimes regarded as the mighty ancestors of the Huns. The Chinese described the Hsiung-Nu as having almost western features, while European chroniclers remark on the strong Asiatic appearance of the Huns. However, there were many differences in the cultural practises of these peoples. The Hsiung-Nu wore pigtails; the Huns did not, but may have scarred their

Attila the Hun is a perennial favourite for artists, having become almost the personification of evil after Roman and medieval propaganda. This detail is from the Raphael Avignon Tapestry. (© R. Sheridan/AAA Collection Ltd)

faces as warrior adornment. The Huns practised cranial deformation, making their skulls elongated, as did the Germans and Iranian Sarmatian nomads – but the Hsiung-Nu did not. The Huns, according to their foes, killed their own old folk, and lack of respect for the elderly characterised Indo-European peoples, but ran counter to east Asian tradition.

Whilst the origins of the Huns remains obscure, it is undisputed that the Huns had a devastating impact on the settled civilisations of the Middle East and Mediterranean.

The Huns who rode across the Russian steppes around 370, also known as 'Black Huns', seemed to have sprung from nowhere, yet they were not as unknown as Roman chroniclers claimed, Huns having lived north-east of the Black Sea before the second century. Nevertheless, a terrified Roman world invented fantastic legends to account for their sudden eruption. Some borrowed from ancient Greek myth to claim that the Huns followed a deer across the Cimmerian Straits, while others dug into Christian demonology to explain that the Huns were descended from fallen angels and witches. Whoever they were, these Huns overthrew the existing order. Germanic Goths who dominated areas west of the Dnepr river, Iranian-speaking Sarmatian and Alan nomads to the east, and the Greek-speaking Bosphoran kingdom around the Crimea all collapsed within a few years. Some remained under Hun rule, whilst others fled deeper into Europe. Indeed, during the murky years before Attila's reign, the Huns may have jostled the Goths, Vandals and other Germanics into the so-called Great Migrations, which in turn eventually destroyed half the Roman Empire.

The Huns began to arrive along the Danube in the early fifth century, but until 395 the epicentre had been further east as they had raided across the Caucasus. In 408/9 a Hunnic chief Uldin crossed the Lower Danube but his followers were seduced by Roman diplomacy. By the middle of the next decade the Huns were established on the Hungarian plains, and their approach should probably be connected with the construction of a massive new set of walls for Constantinople in 413.

Attila takes control

In the 420s Hunnic power expanded through subordination of neighbouring tribal groups, and consolidation of authority within a single ruling family, that of Rua, who was succeeded by his nephews, Attila and Bleda. Rua's advance into Roman territory had so scared the Emperor Theodosius that the Hunnic leader was able to extract annual peace payments from the eastern Empire, which were 700 pounds of gold in the 430s, increasing to 2,100 pounds in 447 (perhaps five per cent of total imperial revenue) at the height of Attila's power. Theodosius also ceded land south of the Danube to the Huns. In 434 the vast Hunnic realm was unified under a new leader – Attila. Around 455 Attila won the leadership of a confederacy of tribes and from then on the Huns grew from a barbarian nuisance into a deadly peril for the Romans. During the 440s, Attila ravaged the northern Balkans, sacking cities and driving off booty to fuel Hunnic prosperity, but in 450 he turned westwards.

The Roman payments had dried up after the accession of the Emperor Marcian, and Attila was determined to see them reinstated. At the same time, Attila became involved in

Theodosius II became sole ruler of the eastern empire in 408, aged only seven years. He was ably assisted in his early years by his sister, Pulcheria, who was made Augusta in July 414. (© R. Sheridan/AAA Collection Ltd)

a strange marriage arrangement with Honoria, sister of Emperor Valentinian III. Honoria had been involved in an affair with her steward, resulting in his execution and her probable pregnancy. In her isolation, Honoria looked to Attila to be her salvation, and managed to send a ring and a letter requesting support. Attila took this to be a marriage proposal, and added this to his reasons for leading a massive army across the Rhine to invade Gaul and Italy.

The Hunnic army invade Gaul

Attila amassed a large army of Huns, Alans, Goths and other Germans, and in 451 he led them into Gaul. Various historians have put the size of Attila's army at being between 300,000 and 700,000 – quite an astounding size for a fifth-century force. Attila's army swept along the Rhine and captured, and sacked, some of Europe's most powerful cities, including Metz, Rheims, Strasbourg and Cologne. The people of Gaul were in no doubt as to the ferocity of Attila's force, and fear became a useful weapon, as their reputation went before them. Attila reached as far as Orleans, which he attempted to siege. This plan failed, and Attila and his forces fell back to an area near Troyes and Châlons.

Here, on the Catalaunian Plains, Attila was met by a mixed army of Romans, Burgunduans, Salian Franks and Visigoths under the Roman commander Aetius. Aetius had learned the art of war from an early age, when he was sent as a hostage to Alaric the Goth, as well as to Rua, king of the Huns before Attila. Aetius had also commanded an army of 60,000 Huns under imperial pay, so he knew well what they were capable of. Bitter battle ensued, and some estimate the losses to be near 160,000. The battle was not conclusive, but the Huns were certainly checked by the Roman force, and were forced to withdraw back across the Rhine. This was a highly significant battle for the Roman army, revealing the strength of the warriors at the Empire's borders, and highlighting another fatal weakness in Rome's armour.

Attila's invasion of Italy

Attila may have been temporarily wounded, but he was not put off. The following year, he led his army over the Alps to invade Italy. The first city to fall under the Hunnic advance was Aquileia, and after a three-month siege, Attila's army reduced the regional capital, once described as 'the greatest of all the towns in the West', to a smouldering wasteland. Milan, Verona and Padua received similar treatment as Attila turned his attention to the Po Valley.

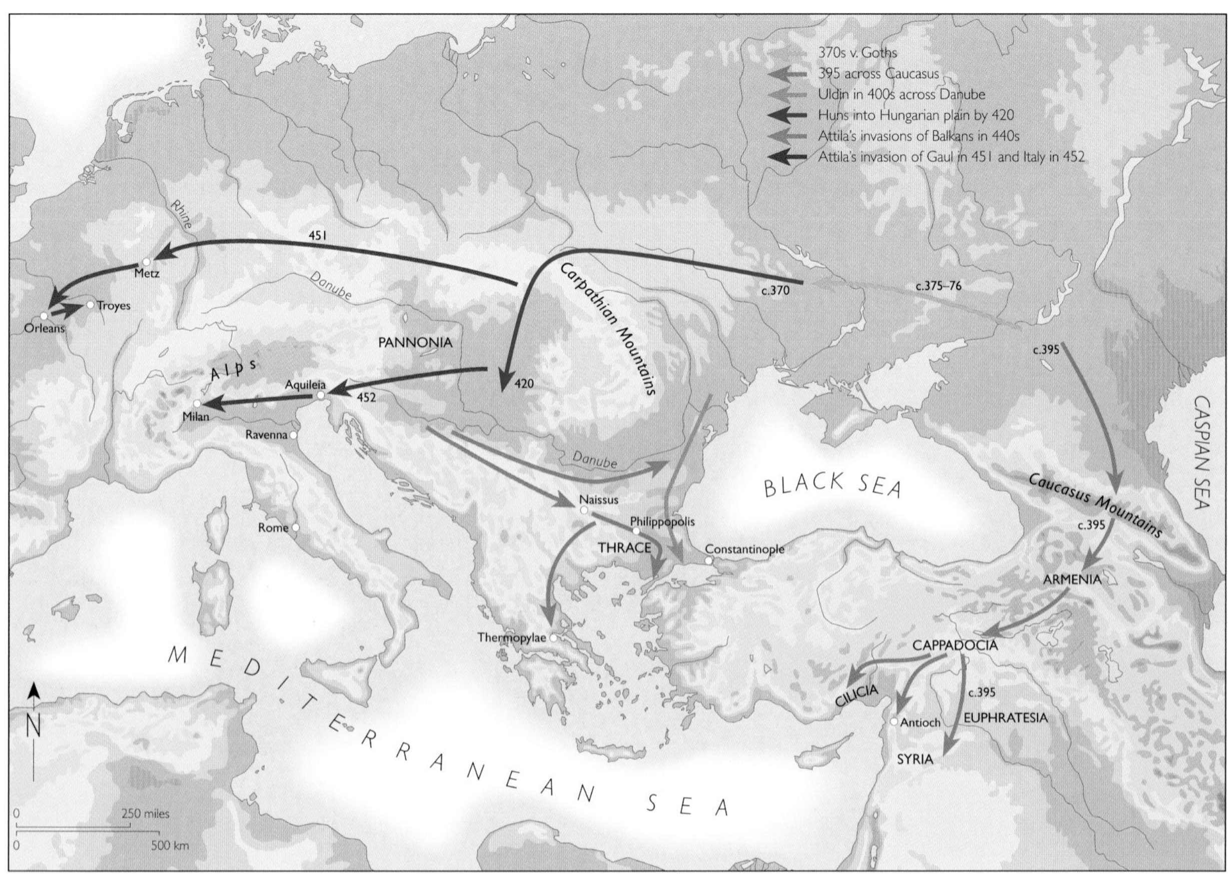

Hunnic raids and the disintegration of the western Empire.

IN THE COURT OF ATTILA

One of the best accounts of the world of Attila the Hun comes from Priscus of Panium. Priscus was part of a diplomatic mission sent by Emperor Theodosius II to the court of Attila in 449. Priscus witnessed much on this journey, which he wrote about in Greek. The following passage describes the opulent and civilised surroundings within which Attila lived:

> The next day I entered the enclosure of Attila's palace, bearing gifts to his wife...Within the enclosure were numerous buildings, some of carved boards beautifully fitted together, others of straight ones, fastened on round wooden blocks which rose to a moderate height from the ground. Attila's wife lived here, and, having been admitted by the barbarians at the door, I found her reclining on a soft couch. The floor of the room was covered with woollen mats for walking on. A number of servants stood round her, and maids sitting on the floor in front of her embroidered with colours linen cloths...

A romanticised portrait of the army of Attila the Hun, with Attila in front. (© Prisma/AAA Collection Ltd)

Meanwhile, the Emperor Valentinian III was holed up in Ravenna, no doubt very fearful of what Attila might do. Rome, too, was terrified of Attila's army advancing to their gates. What happened next has never been fully proven, but the story goes that Pope Leo I went to meet Attila in northern Italy, to try to persuade him to call off his invasion. How he may have done this is difficult to imagine, but according to the legend, Attila was overawed by the appearance of Saints Peter and Paul with the pontiff, and was persuaded to do the right thing and leave, to avoid the foretold death if he continued his advance. It is much more likely, however, that Attila's withdrawal from Italy was due to more earthly matters, like problems with logistics and supply, and disease. Attila never had the chance to conquer Rome, as in 453 he died, probably from an alcohol-related haemorrhage.

Attila's realm was divided among his sons, who promptly started a civil war. Their German subjects rose in rebellion and within a year the surviving Huns retreated back to the steppes of southern Russia. The chaos that they left is part of another story, but the Huns did not degenerate into a band of 'squalid brigands' as some historians claim. Under Attila's descendants many returned to nomadism but continued to raid the east Roman Empire. Others settled down inside Roman territory, garrisoning various areas as *foederati*, while yet others simply served as mercenaries in the last armies of the west Roman Empire.

In 454 the Gepids, and then the future Ostrogoths, Lombards, Heruls plus others emerged from the shadow of Hunnic control to confront the Romans along the Danube frontier. Attila's empire had collapsed, yet from this unpromising record arose legends that made Attila the Hun into one of the fiercest ogres of European history.

Valentinian III was not a strong ruler, and during his reign the decline of the western Empire accelerated. Valentinian murdered his senior general Aetius in 454, presumably in an attempt to make his rule autonomous. However, the Guard sought revenge and he was murdered by two members of his bodyguard the following year. (© R. Sheridan/AAA Collection Ltd)

The nature of Attila's rule

Hunnic power depended on the personal authority of their leader, his ability to dominate all members of his federation. This was achieved partly through the exercise of patronage and the disbursement of the rewards of military victory, but even more by the exercise of sheer terror: Attila repeatedly demonstrated that it was impossible to escape his grasp, and potential rivals were painfully killed. As a result the Romans could not operate their traditional diplomatic strategy of divide and subvert: they were required to hand back Huns, who were probably refugees from Attila's power, and so were denied the chance to cultivate alternative leaders to check the rise of Attila. Attila was also a skilled diplomat, with a wide knowledge of the international scene: he knew the invasion routes into Persia, timed his attacks on the Balkans to coincide with an eastern military expedition to Africa, and exploited tensions between Goths, Franks and Romans in the west; his reception of Roman envoys was a masterful demonstration of psychological pressure. As his federation expanded he came to control vast military resources, which it was in his interest to exploit. His armies, spearheaded by Hunnic cavalry, were capable of rapid movement to anticipate defences, while the masses of expendable subordinates could be thrown at Roman walls to supplement the Huns' considerable skill at siegecraft. The threat was such that Constantinople was provided with a further set of fortifications, the land walls, which stretched from the Sea of Marmara to the Black Sea.

Attila did use theatrical rages to inspire fear, while his campaigns show ruthlessness as well as strategic skill. Attila clung to the simple life of his ancestors, despite vast wealth. He frequently preferred political manoeuvre to open battle, and, despite the reports of Roman and Greek chroniclers, was no mere savage. Nor was he a 'divine ruler' to his own tribesmen, merely a great warrior-leader who, on his death, was buried with simple ceremony. The Huns had their own culture, which was neither barbarous nor any more

An anonymous medieval source details the meeting of Pope Leo and Attila the Hun as depicted in this tapestry, in the following way:

> Attila...came into Italy, inflamed with fury... He was utterly cruel in inflicting torture, greedy in plundering, insolent in abuse... Then Leo had compassion on the calamity of Italy and Rome, and with one of the consuls and a large part of the Roman senate he went to meet Attila. The old man of harmless simplicity, venerable in his gray hair and his majestic garb, ready of his own will to give himself entirely for the defense of his flock, went forth to meet the tyrant who was destroying all things...He spoke to the grim monarch, saying 'The senate and the people of Rome, once conquerors of the world, now indeed vanquished, come before thee as suppliants. We pray for mercy and deliverance. O Attila, thou king of kings, thou couldst have no greater glory than to see suppliant at thy feet this people before whom once all peoples and kings lay suppliant. Thou hast subdued, O Attila, the whole circle of the lands which it was granted to the Romans, victors over all peoples, to conquer. Now we pray that thou, who hast conquered others, shouldst conquer thyself. The people have felt thy scourge; now as suppliants they would feel thy mercy.'
> As Leo said these things Attila stood...silent, as if thinking deeply. And lo, suddenly there were seen the apostles Peter and Paul, clad like bishops, standing by Leo, the one on the right hand, the other on the left. They held swords stretched out over his head, and threatened Attila with death if he did not obey the Pope's command. Wherefore Attila was appeased, he who had raged as one mad.

(© R. Sheridan/AAA Collection Ltd)

cruel than that of the Roman Empire. Attila's greatest crime was to be different, in physical appearance, cultural background, and attitude towards urban civilisation. Even these differences seem to have been exaggerated, for by the time Attila built his empire the Huns were no longer simply steppe nomads.

It was Attila's foes who raised him to the status of an alien monster. Roman images portrayed the Huns as demonic human-headed serpents – the ancient symbol of those irrational giants who once fought Zeus. Other monuments to the defeat of the feared Hun might be a series of crude Roman carvings in eastern France. Yet the greatest memorial must be Attila's role as the wicked Etzel in the medieval German epic poem, *The Nibelungenlied*, which inspired Wagner's operatic cycle *The Ring*.

Attila's army

Transition from a steppe force to a Germanic army

While in southern Russia, the Hun army seems to have been a typical steppe nomadic force. They used lassoes, as did most nomads whether of Turkish or Iranian origin, and they

FEASTING WITH THE KING OF THE HUNS

Priscus wrote this about sharing dinner with Attila:

> When we returned to our tent...*[we were given]* an invitation from Attila to a banquet at three o'clock. When the hour arrived we went to the palace...and stood on the threshold of the hall in the presence of Attila. The cup-bearers gave us a cup, according to the national custom, that we might pray before we sat down. Having tasted the cup, we proceeded to take our seats; all the chairs were ranged along the walls of the room on either side. Attila sat in the middle on a couch...When all were arranged, a cup-bearer came and handed Attila a wooden cup of wine. He took it, and saluted the first in precedence...All the guests then honoured Attila in the same way, saluting him, and then tasting the cups; but he did not stand up...When this ceremony was over the cup-bearers retired, and tables, large enough for three or four, or even more, to sit at, were placed next to the table of Attila, so that each could take of the food on the dishes without leaving his seat. The attendant of Attila first entered with a dish full of meat, and behind him came the other attendants with bread and viands, which they laid on the tables. A luxurious meal, served on silver plate, had been made ready for us and the barbarian guests, but Attila ate nothing but meat on a wooden trencher. In everything else, too, he showed himself to be temperate; his cup was of wood, while to the guests were given goblets of gold and silver. His dress, too, was quite simple, affecting only to be clean. The sword he carried at his side, his shoes, the bridle of his horse were not adorned...with gold or gems or anything costly. When evening fell torches were lit and two barbarians coming forward in front of Attila sang songs they had composed, celebrating his victories and deeds of valour in war.

adopted many fashions from those Alans whom they now ruled. Cavalry, archery and speed of manoeuvre rather than numbers made the steppe nomad virtually invincible within his own terrain, at least until the spread of firearms. The Huns were also able to feed and supply to an army huge numbers of horses when needed. But almost everything seems to have changed once the Huns moved out of the steppes into the Hungarian plain. They lost their nomad logistical base, and their success in raiding Roman territory probably owed more to a lack of effective opposition than to a continued use of Central Asian military styles. Only a minority of Huns would have worn armour, but those who later served as mercenaries in Rome and Byzantium were expected to arm themselves. Like their predecessors they probably captured or purchased Roman-Byzantine or Goth equipment. Nevertheless, iron cuirasses and a few gilded helmets are mentioned during Attila's time. Even Attila's campaigns were more Germanic than nomad in character, particularly those undertaken in summer, which would have been almost unthinkable for a steppe army.

Roman sources no longer emphasised massed Hun cavalry, and by the late fourth century Hun horses are rarely mentioned at all. Of course, Hun cavalry did exist, and its armoured elite fought with long spears as well as bows. Huns are also described as dismounting to fight, as serving as infantry archers, and as carrying shields large enough to lean upon. When worsted the Hun army now tended to retreat into its camp rather than dispersing at high speed as was normal for nomad cavalry. Other sources make it quite clear that the Huns increasingly relied upon infantry in Europe and that they fielded a siege train which might have been operated by Roman renegades. In fact a major part of Attila's army was clearly of German or Alan origin, and the name Hun, in Roman chronicles, must refer to political rather than ethnic origin.

The Huns in Europe now lived by predation, in other words raiding, rather than nomadism. Society was still tribal, with each tribe apparently sub-divided into clans or families under its own aristocratic leadership. Prisoners were generally ransomed, as the Huns, unlike the Romans, had little need for slaves, while those who remained in their hands could even rise to prominence. There is unlikely to have been a large social gap between a free warrior and his chief but there were degrees of status at Attila's court. Roman commentators referred to Attila's *logades*, 'friends' or 'companions', many of whom had German names. Their role is unclear but they were probably prominent men rather than a military aristocracy. Other Germanic leaders in Attila's army may have led mercenary bands. Such a state was more Germanic than Turco-Mongol, and had little in common with the empires of the steppes. The Huns also appear to have been on the verge of converting to Christianity when their empire suddenly collapsed.

Appearance and status

The best description we have of the Huns comes from Roman historian Ammianus Marcellinus, though his colourful prose must be taken with the necessary pinch of salt. It must also be remembered that Ammianus is describing a Hun from his day, in the late fourth century AD, and not from the time of Attila:

> The nation of the Huns ... surpasses all other Barbarians in wildness of life ... At birth the cheeks of the infants are deeply marked by an iron, in order that the usual vigour of their hair, instead of growing at the proper age, will be withered by the scars; so they grow up without beards and therefore without beauty, like eunuchs, though they all have strong limbs, and plump necks; they are of great size, and low legged, so that you might fancy them two-legged beasts, or the fat figures that are carved in a rude manner with an axe on the posts at the end of bridges. And though they do just bear the likeness of men (of a very ugly pattern), they are so little advanced in civilisation that they make no use of fire, nor any kind of relish, in the preparation of their food, but feed upon the roots which they find in the fields, and the half-raw flesh of any sort of animal. I say half-raw, because

This scene shows a shieldwall of Visigoths serving in the army of Aetius standing firm in the face of an attack from mounted Ostrogoths serving Attila. (Painting by Angus McBride © Osprey Publishing Ltd)

> they give it a kind of cooking by placing it between their own thighs and the backs of their horses....
>
> They wear linen clothes, or clothes made from the skins of field mice; they do not wear a different dress outside from that which they wear inside; but after a tunic is put on, however it becomes worn, it is never taken off or changed until it actually becomes so ragged that it falls to pieces. They cover their heads with round caps and their legs with goatskins; their shoes are...so unshapely as to prevent them from walking properly. It is for this reason they are not well suited to infantry battles, but are nearly always on horseback...

The warrior and his horse

The Turkish pony was a hardy beast, though small and ugly to the eyes of Westerners. Unlike the stall-fed horses of Europe it was able to survive harsh climates and live on grass alone. In general it was also better at climbing, jumping and swimming than medieval European horses. Steppe herds often interbred with wild horses and thus retained their vigour, nor was there only one type of steppe pony. Various peoples bred horses for travel, hunting or war, while others specialised in breeding for export.

The main characteristics looked for were a flat back for ease of riding, and the long neck of a good jumper. The colour of an animal's hair also had great significance, the lightest colours being reserved for people of rank. Hun practice was to nick the ears of the animals, or brand them, to mark out ownership. The Huns probably used a wood-framed saddle, which was more comfortable to ride and much less wearing to a horse. There is no evidence, however, that stirrups were used. For transport, Huns used heavy wagons to carry their homes, families and military supplies. Some wagons were very heavy and had iron tyres.

Weapons

The bow

Of all the weapons of the nomads, the bow remained paramount. The typical type was of composite wood, horn and sinew construction, often with bone stiffeners. It was usually asymmetrical with a characteristic thick bow-string permanently tied to the longer arm. Composite bows gave a much greater power-to-weight ratio than the 'self' bow, of which the longbow was the most famous version, with about twice the range. The compound curve or reflex shape reduced the actual height of the bow but permitted a very long draw. The bow's character also depended, of course, on the type or weight of the arrow used, the bowstring, the use or otherwise of thumbrings and various other factors. Arrows wholly or partly of reed would quickly absorb the vibration of being loosed and thus straightened out more quickly than wooden arrows.

Given the importance of archery among the Huns, it is not surprising to find bows covered in gold being symbols of princely rank. What is more surprising is that such impractical gilded weapons were not found among other peoples, not even among the Hsiung-Nu, who are sometimes regarded as the Huns' forebears.

Swords

Although the curved sabre was known as the *gladius hunniscus* in Central Europe from the eighth century, there is no evidence that the Huns actually used single-edged sabres. Their swords were of the long double-edged Sassanian type suitable for cavalry warfare, also adopted by some Goths. The Huns also used a second short sword or large dagger, possibly descended from an ancient Iranian or Scythian short sword. Gilded sword and dagger grips were characteristic of the Huns.

Organisation and tactics

The homeland of the Huns, the steppe, was an arid area, no good for cultivation, which is why the Huns were nomadic – following the herds from place to place to find food. This sort of lifestyle had hunting at its core, as food had to be found on the move. Huns were born hunters, and the skills they developed for this necessity of survival were also to prove invaluable in war. The Huns were therefore superb horsemen and archers, with a devastatingly accurate aim.

It is not known whether or not the Huns continued to dress in Central Asian style after settling in Europe. Nevertheless, Attila has here been given the kind of fur-lined hat, long coat, baggy trousers and soft boots worn by Huns and other nomads further east. Attila also carries a symbolic gold-covered bow. (Painting by Angus McBride © Osprey Publishing Ltd)

Attila had amassed a large number of infantry from many barbarian tribes, but it is no surprise that the core of his army was still the mounted cavalry. Their excellence on horseback made the Huns skilled in a blitzkrieg style of warfare, able to arrive on the battlefield at great speed, seemingly out of nowhere. The main tactics of the Hunnic army were to deploy the horse-archers first, to let loose the first volleys of arrows from a safe distance. Some of these arrows had whistles attached to them, which made an eery shrieking noise as the arrows flew through the air, no doubt adding to the terror being

This is a 19th-century fictionalised portrayal of a battle of Huns and Franks, from Neuschwanstein. (© R. Sheridan/AAA Collection Ltd)

experienced by the enemy. They would then advance on horseback at great speed, and fight at close quarters with swords and lassoes, made from plaited strips of cloth, used by Huns to immobilise their foe before capturing, or killing him.

Ammianus says that the Huns were able to fight in single combat, but were more likely to band together and fight in formation. This formation might then be rapidly disbanded, and the individual horsemen disperse to different areas of the field, only to reunite and return. This tactic must have caused great confusion to the Romans, and made the Huns a much more difficult enemy to defeat piecemeal.

> When attacked, they will sometimes engage in regular battle. Then, going into the fight in order of columns, they fill the air with varied and discordant cries. More often, however, they fight in no regular order of battle, but by being extremely swift and sudden in their movements, they disperse, and then rapidly come together again in loose array, spread havoc over vast plains, and flying over the rampart, they pillage the camp of their enemy almost before he has become aware of their approach. It must be owned that they are the most terrible of warriors because they fight at a distance with missile weapons having sharpened bones admirably fastened to the shaft. When in close combat with swords, they fight without regard to their own safety, and while their enemy is intent upon parrying the thrust of the swords, they throw a net over him and so entangle his limbs that he loses all power of walking or riding. (Ammianus Marcellinus)

Siege warfare

The Huns were also skilled in siege warfare, which set them apart from many other barbarian warriors. At Naissus, during Attila's campaigns of 441, the Roman army refused to leave the city and fight Attila and his army. The Huns erected platforms consisting of wooden beams on wheels, which allowed the Hun archers greater height to fire over the city battlements. They also used siege engines of the battering type, with massive metal-tipped beams that were swung back on chains, and released to smash into the city walls. Eventually the walls crumbled and the Huns swarmed into the city. Priscus, a Roman who witnessed some of Attila's campaigns whilst on a diplomatic mission from Emperor Theodosius II, has this to say about the fate the city suffered:

> When we arrived at Naissus we found the city deserted, as though it had been sacked; only a few sick persons lay in the churches. We halted at a short distance from the river, in an open space, for all the ground adjacent to the bank was full of the bones of men slain in war.

Despite attempts to restore Naissus to its former glory, the city never again fully recovered after this devastation at the hands of the Huns.

FURTHER READING

Campaign 36	*Cannae 216BC – Hannibal smashes Rome's Army*
Campaign 84	*Adrianople AD378 – The Goths Crush Rome's Legions*
Essential Histories 16	*The Punic Wars 264–146BC*
Essential Histories 21	*Rome at War AD293–696*
Essential Histories 42	*Caesar's Civil War 49–44BC*
Essential Histories 43	*Caesar's Gallic Wars 58–50BC*
Elite 50	*The Praetorian Guard*
Elite 110	*Sassanian Elite Cavalry AD226–642*
Elite 120	*Mounted Archers of the Steppe 600BC–AD1300*
Elite 121	*Ancient Siege Warfare: Persians, Greeks, Carthaginians and Romans 546–146BC*
Elite 126	*Siege Warfare in the Roman World 146BC–AD378*
Men-at-Arms 46	*The Roman Army from Caesar to Trajan*
Men-at-Arms 93	*The Roman Army from Hadrian to Constantine*
Men-at-Arms 121	*Armies of the Carthaginian Wars 265–146BC*
Men-at-Arms 129	*Rome's Enemies (1) Germanics and Dacians*
Men-at-Arms 137	*The Scythians 700–300BC*
Men-at-Arms 158	*Rome's Enemies (2) Gallic and British Celts*
Men-at-Arms 175	*Rome's Enemies (3) Parthians and Sassanid Persians*
Men-at-Arms 180	*Rome's Enemies (4) Spanish Armies*
Men-at-Arms 243	*Rome's Enemies (5) The Desert Frontier*
Men-at-Arms 283	*Early Roman Armies*
Men-at-Arms 291	*Republican Roman Army 200–104BC*
Men-at-Arms 360	*The Thracians 700BC–AD46*
Men-at-Arms 373	*The Sarmatians 600BC–AD450*
Men-at-Arms 374	*Roman Military Clothing (1) 100BC–AD200*
Men-at-Arms 390	*Roman Military Clothing (2) AD200–400*
Warrior 9	*Late Roman Infantryman AD236–565*
Warrior 15	*Late Roman Cavalryman AD236–565*
Warrior 17	*Germanic Warrior AD236–568*
Warrior 30	*Celtic Warrior 300BC–AD100*
Warrior 39	*Gladiators 100BC–AD200*
Warrior 50	*Pictish Warrior AD297–841*
Warrior 71	*Roman Legionary 58BC–AD69*
Warrior 72	*Imperial Roman Legionary AD161–284*
Fortress 2	*Hadrian's Wall AD122–410*
New Vanguard 78	*Greek and Roman Siege Machinery 399BC–AD363*
New Vanguard 89	*Greek and Roman Artillery 399BC–AD363*

INDEX

Figures in **bold** refer to illustrations